Bloom's Shakespeare Through the Ages

Bloom's Shakespeare Through the Ages

AS YOU LIKE IT

Edited and with an introduction by
Harold Bloom
Sterling Professor of the Humanities
Yale University

Volume Editor
Pamela Loos

BLOOM'S
LITERARY CRITICISM
An imprint of Infobase Publishing

Bloom's Shakespeare Through the Ages: As You Like It

Copyright ©2008 by Infobase Publishing

Introduction ©2008 by Harold Bloom

Bloom's Literary Criticism
An imprint of Infobase Publishing
132 West 31st Street
New York NY 10001

Library of Congress Cataloging-in-Publication Data
As you like it / edited and with an introduction by Harold Bloom ;
volume editor, Pamela Loos.
        p. cm. — (Bloom's Shakespeare through the ages)
   Includes bibliographical references and index.
   ISBN-13: 978-0-7910-9591-1 (acid-free paper)
   ISBN-10: 0-7910-9591-6 (acid-free paper) 1. Shakespeare, William, 1564–1616.
As you like it. I. Bloom, Harold. II. Loos, Pamela. III. Shakespeare, William, 1564–1616.
As you like it.
   PR2803.A2B66 2007
   822.3'3—dc22   2007026810

You can find Bloom's Literary Criticism on the World Wide Web at
http://www.chelseahouse.com

Series design by Erika K. Arroyo
Cover design by Ben Peterson
Cover photo © The Granger Collection, New York

Printed in the United States of America

Bang EJB 10 9 8 7 6 5 4 3 2 1

This book is printed on acid-free paper.

CONTENTS

❖ *As You Like It* in the Twentieth Century **105**

SERIES INTRODUCTION
❧

Shakespeare Through the Ages presents not the most current of Shakespeare criticism, but the best of Shakespeare criticism, from the seventeenth century to today. In the process, each volume also charts the flow over time of critical discussion of a particular play. Other useful and fascinating collections of historical Shakespearean criticism exist, but no collection that we know of contains such a range of commentary on each of Shakespeare's greatest plays and at the same time emphasizes the greatest critics in our literary tradition: from John Dryden in the seventeenth century, to Samuel Johnson in the eighteenth century, to William Hazlitt and Samuel Coleridge in the nineteenth century, to A.C. Bradley and William Empson in the twentieth century, to the most perceptive critics of our own day. This canon of Shakespearean criticism emphasizes aesthetic rather than political or social analysis.

Some of the pieces included here are full-length essays; others are excerpts designed to present a key point. Much (but not all) of the earliest criticism consists only of brief mentions of specific plays. In addition to the classics of criticism, some pieces of mainly historical importance have been included, often to provide background for important reactions from future critics.

These volumes are intended for students, particularly those just beginning their explorations of Shakespeare. We have therefore also included basic materials designed to provide a solid grounding in each play: a biography of Shakespeare, a synopsis of the play, a list of characters, and an explication of key passages. In addition, each selection of the criticism of a particular century begins with an introductory essay discussing the general nature of that century's commentary and the particular issues and controversies addressed by critics presented in the volume.

Shakespeare was "not of an age, but for all time," but much Shakespeare criticism is decidedly for its own age, of lasting importance only to the scholar who wrote it. Students today read the criticism most readily available to them, which means essays printed in recent books and journals, especially those journals made available on the Internet. Older criticism is too often buried in out-of-print books on forgotten shelves of libraries or in defunct periodicals. Therefore, many students, particularly younger students, have no way of knowing that some of the most profound criticism of Shakespeare's plays was written decades or centuries ago. We hope this series remedies that problem, and, more importantly, we hope it infuses students with the enthusiasm of the critics in these volumes for the beauty and power of Shakespeare's plays.

INTRODUCTION BY
HAROLD BLOOM

As You Like It is Shakespeare's happiest play. I suspect Shakespeare himself knew that, and almost the entire critical tradition also has rejoiced in Rosalind. My hero, Dr. Samuel Johnson, termed the comedy "wild and pleasing," while my next favorite English critic, William Hazlitt, charmingly remarked of Rosalind: "She talks herself out of breath, only to get deeper in love."

My favorite American exegete of Shakespeare, Harold C. Goddard, beautifully said that "Rosalind is wit with love, which is humor, humor being what wit turns into when it falls in love." Another superb American critic, my lamented friend C.L. Barber, died too young about 30 years ago. He haunts me whenever I teach *As You Like It*, and I go into the classroom frequently remembering a radiant sentence of his:

> In dramatizing love's intensity as the release of a festive moment, Shakespeare keeps that part of the romantic tradition which makes love an experience of the whole personality, even though he ridicules the wishful absolutes of doctrinaire romantic love.

Watching Rosalind Hall play Rosalind, in a fairly recent production directed by her father, Peter, I had the illusion that Shakespeare's heroine was playing herself. But is that not true within the play, just as Falstaff, Hamlet, Iago, and Cleopatra seem to know that they are playing themselves? Shakespeare, himself higher in concept than any high-concept director, goes on anticipating anything valuable that we do with him. He is hardly responsible for our travesties of him; as I write there is an aquatic *Romeo and Juliet* in New York City, and a buck-naked *Macbeth* is also playing at this moment, though fortunately I forget where.

The Forest of Arden is Shakespeare's Arcadia and *may* be named for the Bard's mother, Mary Arden, or for a French region. Shakespeare's cheerful carelessness as to geography is manifested by the odd mix of English names (Rosalind, Celia, and others) with French (Jaques, pronounced "Jakes" by the English audience, and so a privy or outhouse). Other names are ironic: Touchstone, Orlando, Duke

Senior. And yet, *As You Like It* is anything but a grab-bag or hodge-podge, as are *Two Gentlemen of Verona* and *The Merry Wives of Windsor*.

Together with *Twelfth Night*, Rosalind's drama is the triumph of Shakespearean romantic comedy. Perhaps *Twelfth Night* is an advance upon *As You Like It*, since Malvolio transcends Jaques as a superb caricature of Shakespeare's friend and rival Ben Jonson. And yet Viola, charmingly zany as she is, is not of Rosalind's splendor. Of all Shakespeare's personages, only Falstaff and Hamlet rival Rosalind in wit.

These are three very different modes of wit. Rosalind's is free of the will to power, whether in self-interpretation, or over others, including her lover, Orlando. Delightfully she transforms him by educating her future husband until he wonderfully, yet rather lightly, protests: "I can live no longer by thinking." Marriage rapidly ensues, as centerpiece in a carnival of weddings, presided over by Rosalind as the very genius of nuptials.

The secret of Shakespeare's most radiant heroine first was discerned (to the best of my memory) by C.L. Barber, whom I quoted earlier. Rosalind is so perceptive a character that she is not subject to dramatic irony: We cannot achieve a perspective upon her that she does not anticipate. Of no one else in Shakespeare could that be said. Jaques and Touchstone, both decapitated by her wit, do not know everything about themselves. Where it matters, we do come to a complete apprehension of Rosalind.

My favorite among all her observations in the play is universally esteemed. When Orlando, playing the game by rules she has set, responds to "I will not have you" with the equally insouciant "I die," she delights me with her marvelous: "men have died from time to time, and worms have eaten them, but not for love." I go about constantly murmuring that, moved both by her wisdom and her benign realism.

BIOGRAPHY OF
WILLIAM SHAKESPEARE
※⁓

WILLIAM SHAKESPEARE was born in Stratford-on-Avon in April 1564 into a family of some prominence. His father, John Shakespeare, was a glover and merchant of leather goods who earned enough to marry Mary Arden, the daughter of his father's landlord, in 1557. John Shakespeare was a prominent citizen in Stratford, and at one point, he served as an alderman and bailiff.

Shakespeare presumably attended the Stratford grammar school, where he would have received an education in Latin, but he did not go on to either Oxford or Cambridge universities. Little is recorded about Shakespeare's early life; indeed, the first record of his life after his christening is of his marriage to Anne Hathaway in 1582 in the church at Temple Grafton, near Stratford. He would have been required to obtain a special license from the bishop as security that there was no impediment to the marriage. Peter Alexander states in his book *Shakespeare's Life and Art* that marriage at this time in England required neither a church nor a priest or, for that matter, even a document—only a declaration of the contracting parties in the presence of witnesses. Thus, it was customary, though not mandatory, to follow the marriage with a church ceremony.

Little is known about William and Anne Shakespeare's marriage. Their first child, Susanna, was born in May 1583 and twins, Hamnet and Judith, in 1585. Later on, Susanna married Dr. John Hall, but the younger daughter, Judith, remained unmarried. When Hamnet died in Stratford in 1596, the boy was only 11 years old.

We have no record of Shakespeare's activities for the seven years after the birth of his twins, but by 1592 he was in London working as an actor. He was also apparently well known as a playwright, for reference is made of him by his contemporary Robert Greene in *A Groatsworth of Wit*, as "an upstart crow."

Several companies of actors were in London at this time. Shakespeare may have had connection with one or more of them before 1592, but we have no record that tells us definitely. However, we do know of his long association with the most famous and successful troupe, the Lord Chamberlain's Men. (When James I came to the throne in 1603, after Elizabeth's death, the troupe's name changed to the King's Men.) In 1599 the Lord Chamberlain's Men provided the financial backing for the construction of their own theater, the Globe.

The Globe was begun by a carpenter named James Burbage and finished by his two sons, Cuthbert and Robert. To escape the jurisdiction of the Corporation of London, which was composed of conservative Puritans who opposed the theater's "licentiousness," James Burbage built the Globe just outside London, in the Liberty of Holywell, beside Finsbury Fields. This also meant that the Globe was safer from the threats that lurked in London's crowded streets, like plague and other diseases, as well as rioting mobs. When James Burbage died in 1597, his sons completed the Globe's construction. Shakespeare played a vital role, financially and otherwise, in the construction of the theater, which was finally occupied sometime before May 16, 1599.

Shakespeare not only acted with the Globe's company of actors; he was also a shareholder and eventually became the troupe's most important playwright. The company included London's most famous actors, who inspired the creation of some of Shakespeare's best-known characters, such as Hamlet and Lear, as well as his clowns and fools.

In his early years, however, Shakespeare did not confine himself to the theater. He also composed some mythological-erotic poetry, such as *Venus and Adonis* and *The Rape of Lucrece*, both of which were dedicated to the earl of Southampton. Shakespeare was successful enough that in 1597 he was able to purchase his own home in Stratford, which he called New Place. He could even call himself a gentleman, for his father had been granted a coat of arms.

By 1598 Shakespeare had written some of his most famous works, *Romeo and Juliet, The Comedy of Errors, A Midsummer Night's Dream, The Merchant of Venice, Two Gentlemen of Verona,* and *Love's Labour's Lost*, as well as his historical plays *Richard II, Richard III, Henry IV,* and *King John*. Somewhere around the turn of the century, Shakespeare wrote his romantic comedies *As You Like It, Twelfth Night,* and *Much Ado About Nothing*, as well as *Henry V,* the last of his history plays in the Prince Hal series. During the next 10 years he wrote his great tragedies, *Hamlet, Macbeth, Othello, King Lear,* and *Antony and Cleopatra*.

At this time, the theater was burgeoning in London; the public took an avid interest in drama, the audiences were large, the plays demonstrated an enormous range of subjects, and playwrights competed for approval. By 1613, however, the rising tide of Puritanism had changed the theater. With the desertion of the theaters by the middle classes, the acting companies were compelled to depend more on the aristocracy, which also meant that they now had to cater to a more sophisticated audience.

Perhaps this change in London's artistic atmosphere contributed to Shakespeare's reasons for leaving London after 1612. His retirement from the theater is sometimes thought to be evidence that his artistic skills were waning. During this time, however, he wrote *The Tempest* and *Henry VIII*. He also wrote the "tragicomedies," *Pericles, Cymbeline,* and *The Winter's Tale.* These were thought to be inspired by Shakespeare's personal problems and have sometimes been considered proof of his greatly diminished abilities.

However, so far as biographical facts indicate, the circumstances of his life at this time do not imply any personal problems. He was in good health and financially secure, and he enjoyed an excellent reputation. Indeed, although he was settled in Stratford at this time, he made frequent visits to London, enjoying and participating in events at the royal court, directing rehearsals, and attending to other business matters.

In addition to his brilliant and enormous contributions to the theater, Shakespeare remained a poetic genius throughout the years, publishing a renowned and critically acclaimed sonnet cycle in 1609 (most of the sonnets were written many years earlier). Shakespeare's contribution to this popular poetic genre are all the more amazing in his break with contemporary notions of subject matter. Shakespeare idealized the beauty of man as an object of praise and devotion (rather than the Petrarchan tradition of the idealized, unattainable woman). In the same spirit of breaking with tradition, Shakespeare also treated themes previously considered off limits—the dark, sexual side of a woman as opposed to the Petrarchan ideal of a chaste and remote love object. He also expanded the sonnet's emotional range, including such emotions as delight, pride, shame, disgust, sadness, and fear.

When Shakespeare died in 1616, no collected edition of his works had ever been published, although some of his plays had been printed in separate unauthorized editions. (Some of these were taken from his manuscripts, some from the actors' prompt books, and others were reconstructed from memory by actors or spectators.) In 1623 two members of the King's Men, John Hemings and Henry Condell, published a collection of all the plays they considered to be authentic, the First Folio.

Included in the First Folio is a poem by Shakespeare's contemporary Ben Jonson, an outstanding playwright and critic in his own right. Jonson paid tribute to Shakespeare's genius, proclaiming his superiority to what previously had been held as the models for literary excellence—the Greek and Latin writers. "Triumph, my Britain, thou hast one to show / To whom all scenes of Europe homage owe. / He was not of an age, but for all time!"

Jonson was the first to state what has been said so many times since. Having captured what is permanent and universal to all human beings at all times, Shakespeare's genius continues to inspire us—and the critical debate about his works never ceases.

SUMMARY OF
AS YOU LIKE IT
✌︎

Act I

Scene 1 takes place in the orchard of Oliver de Boy's house and provides a view of some of the main characters of the play as well as the tensions among them. It opens with Orlando, Oliver's youngest brother, speaking to Adam, a servant of the family for many years. We sympathize with Orlando, who is distressed and weary of the poor treatment he receives from Oliver. As the oldest brother, Oliver is responsible for Orlando and Jaques, the middle brother, now that their father is dead. While Oliver gives Jaques what he needs to be properly schooled as a gentleman should, Orlando is left with nothing. Orlando says he will not put up with this treatment any longer, although he is not sure what steps he should take.

Adam warns that Oliver is approaching, and Orlando tells Adam he will now see how poorly Oliver treats him. Oliver asks why Orlando is here; Orlando twists his question as if he had asked what he is accomplishing here, so he can smartly answer that he is not accomplishing anything since he has not been properly educated. The questions and answers between the two continue in this way, and the antagonism builds. Oliver slaps his brother and Orlando grabs Oliver, saying he will not let go until his brother promises to provide for him to become a gentleman.

Since Oliver is unable to free himself, he agrees to his brother's demand. Orlando lets go. Oliver tells Orlando—as well as Adam, whom he refers to as an "old dog"—to leave. Adam is insulted because he has worked for the family for years and says the men's father would never have referred to him in such a disparaging way.

As soon as the two men are gone, Oliver reveals that, contrary to what he has just promised, he will give Orlando nothing. He meets with a wrestler, Charles, and asks for news on the court. We find that nothing is different but that the old duke remains banished; his daughter stays with the new duke, since she and the new duke's daughter, her cousin, are such close friends. Charles also warns Oliver that Orlando plans to wrestle Charles but will probably be severely hurt in the process. Oliver manipulates the situation to his advantage, telling Charles

5

that Orlando is wicked and deserves to be hurt. Actually, he says, if Charles does not seriously hurt him, Orlando will only come after him post-match and not be happy until Charles is dead. When Charles leaves, we learn that Oliver hates Orlando. He says he does not know why but then goes on to explain his jealousy, stating that Orlando is gentlemanly without having been schooled and that the people love him.

Scene 2 takes place at the palace. Celia, Duke Frederick's only daughter, tries to cheer up her cousin Rosalind, who is distressed over the banishment of her father, Duke Senior, Frederick's older brother. Celia explains that if she and Rosalind were to switch places, Celia, since she loves Rosalind so much, would see Rosalind's father as her own. She goes on to declare how great her love is for Rosalind by saying that once her father is dead, she will return to Rosalind all that Duke Frederick took from Duke Senior.

With this, Rosalind says she will be more cheerful. She asks what they should do to head her on the right track. Perhaps they should play at falling in love, she says, which Celia opposes. These lines foreshadow what is yet to come, when Rosalind will fall in love and Celia will be against it. Next the two consider mocking Fortune for the inequality she makes in the world. These comments serve to point out the role of Fortune in the play overall; already we have seen that Orlando, while seemingly a good person, has the ill fortune of a brother who despises him and that Rosalind, also seemingly a good person, has the ill fortune of seeing her father banished and stripped of his role of duke.

We also see the wit and intelligence of Celia and Rosalind as they play with words; this continues when Touchstone, the court clown, enters. He, too, is quick-witted—not the traditional fool who seems to know almost nothing and therefore provokes laughs. Touchstone, in contrast, makes fun of others in a keen way. Here he says it is not so hard to sound quite sincere in making a promise, but that promise can easily be only disguised as a promise and not one to be believed after all. In a play in which we still do not know why the duke has been banished, it seems fitting that fake promises would be spoken of. Similarly, in such a world it is not surprising, as Touchstone comments, that fools are not allowed to make wise comments about the foolishness of supposed wise men.

Le Beau, a courtier, enters, and as he tries to give the group news, they continue to show their wit through wordplay. Le Beau, unlike Touchstone, doesn't have the wherewithal to join in and even admits his confusion while listening to the threesome. The joking finally stops as Le Beau gets to the substance of his news, namely that the wrestler Charles has already brutalized three of his opponents and is on his way to the court now to take on another challenger, who undoubtedly will be equally destroyed. The question of gender roles comes into play here, for, as the group remarks, usually women are not spectators at wrestling matches or to bones breaking, and yet these women want to see what will happen.

Duke Frederick arrives ready to watch the match and, in a momentary showing of goodness, asks the women to try to dissuade the challenger from participating against Charles, since the challenger stands such a poor chance. The women then take on the traditional role of fearing for the safety of men and trying to discourage their risky behavior. Here, as in so many other such situations, the man refuses to be dissuaded. Fearing for the underdog, the women root for him and he wins. He says he has not even warmed up, yet he has rendered Charles helpless and unable to speak. Only at this point does the duke ask the challenger who he is. He says he is Orlando, son of Sir Rowland de Boys. At this the duke is unhappy; though the world found Sir Rowland honorable, to the duke he was always an enemy. We see here, then, part of the same explanation Oliver gave earlier about why he is against his brother: Jealousy appears to be a strong force.

The duke leaves, and Celia questions his negative comments about Orlando. Orlando says he is still proud of his father, and Rosalind adds that her father, with whom all the people agreed, loved Sir Rowland. The women congratulate Orlando on his great defeat of the champion, and Rosalind even gives him a chain, which she says he should wear for her, "one out of suits with fortune." Indeed, Fortune came to his aid, seemingly since he deserved it. Orlando is left speechless. The women leave, and Orlando wonders why he was not able to respond. His good fortune takes a turn for the worse when he hears from Le Beau that the duke is disturbed over Orlando's victory and that Orlando should leave quickly. Le Beau gives other bad news when Orlando inquires about the two women who just left, for he reveals that the duke is very much against Rosalind as well, since the people like her and feel sorry for her without her father in his rightful role as duke.

Rosalind and Celia are together in the castle in scene 3. Rosalind admits that she is smitten with Orlando. When Celia asks how this could have happened so suddenly, Rosalind responds that her father loved Orlando's father, but Celia pokes holes in this logic. Duke Frederick enters and announces that Rosalind must leave as quickly as she can and be beyond 20 miles of the court within 10 days or she will be killed. The women are stunned; Rosalind asks why this must be. Frederick says she must go because she is a traitor, he doesn't trust her, and she is daughter to Duke Senior. Curiously, Rosalind has just used the argument that she is like her father when she explained her love for Orlando to Celia, yet now she argues against the logic of Frederick, which connects her to her father. Rosalind also points out that her father was no traitor.

Celia steps in to try to talk her father out of his decision. He responds that he had only allowed Rosalind to stay because Celia wanted her to. Yet Celia argues against this, saying the decision had been his because he had pitied Rosalind.

She adds that since Rosalind has been with Celia, they have been so inseparable that if Rosalind is a traitor, then so is Celia. Frederick responds that Rosalind is too crafty and that the people pity her, taking the rightful attention away from Celia. He will not change his mind about his decision, and Celia says that his decision, then, is also against her, since she cannot live without Rosalind. Frederick reiterates his decision and says that if Rosalind does not follow it, she will die. He then exits.

Celia says that her father has banished her as well since she so loves Rosalind and cannot be separated from her. Celia states that they must go to the forest and seek out Rosalind's father. To ward off any potential danger, the two decide to disguise themselves. Celia will make herself appear poor and call herself Aliena; Rosalind will dress as a man, named Ganymede. Additionally, Rosalind suggests that they bring Touchstone along for comfort, and Celia says she will persuade him to come.

Love will be a major topic in the play, and already in this act we see at least two types: that between the intensely close cousins Celia and Rosalind and that between Rosalind and Orlando, two people who fall in love suddenly. Life in court will also be contrasted with life outside of court, and pastoral stereotypes will be explored. So far, we have had a taste of the dangers of court life and have only heard about the forest. It is a place of banishment, yet here in this last scene Celia describes it as a place of liberty. Gender roles will also be examined. Thus far we've seen that Celia and Rosalind are not the stereotypical weak females, and we realize that because Rosalind will disguise herself as a man, life might be quite different for her than would be otherwise expected.

Act II

The second act opens in the Forest of Arden, which was mentioned in Act I. The first character to speak is Duke Senior, about whom we've heard several favorable comments in Act I as well. Here he speaks to his lords about living in this forest. From his perspective, while there are difficulties to life here, they are not as bad as those difficulties encountered in court. He also points out a certain duality; for instance, even the ugly toad has some beauty, and the other natural things surrounding them provide the lessons and knowledge that they had once garnered from books and other man-made items.

Amiens, one of the lords attending to the duke, says he appreciates the duke's positive perspective. When the duke mentions that they should find some venison, even though he feels bad about killing deer, the comment reminds the lords of their coming upon Jaques, another lord of the duke's. The lords explain how they saw a wounded deer and heard Jaques philosophizing about it and the harsh realities of its world; they mention how Jaques views them, not just the duke now in court, as usurpers as well, because they kill animals in the forest.

In scenes 2 and 3, we return very briefly to the evil outside the forest. Scene 2 takes place in the palace, where Duke Frederick is disturbed that his daughter is gone. One of his servants says that it's thought she is with her cousin and Orlando. With this, the duke orders them to find Orlando or, at least, his brother, as well as the duke's daughter.

Scene 3 brings us to Orlando's home. His servant, Adam, tells him he is in grave danger. So far, though, the two do not know that the duke is after Orlando. Instead Adam tells Orlando that his brother is intent on burning down Orlando's house with him in it, because he is so disturbed that Orlando did well in the wrestling match. Orlando does not want to leave, but Adam says he will give him all the money he's saved and leave with him and be his servant, that even though he is old he is strong and can provide the same service a younger servant could. Orlando is struck by the man's kindness and generosity, which are motivated purely by a desire to help; these are qualities that people had in earlier times, Orlando says. Adam says that even when their money runs out, he will stay with Orlando, and so we see yet another type of love in this play.

Scene 4 returns to the forest, but it appears to be a very different forest from the one Duke Senior cast in such a positive light in the opening scene of Act II. Rather than a welcoming forest, this forest is one that has worn people out. Rosalind, Touchstone, and Celia enter, exhausted. Touchstone goes so far as to say that he was better off when he was in court, a direct contrast to Duke Senior's earlier perspective. Corin and Silvius, two shepherds, enter. Silvius explains how he is madly in love, while Corin tries to give him some pragmatic advice. Silvius, though, is completely lovestruck and does not believe Corin can truly imagine how he feels. Corin, however, says he has been in love but has forgotten the foolish things he did during that time. Silvius runs off crying out for his beloved Phebe.

Rosalind is reminded of her own lovesick heart, yet before she can say much, Touchstone chimes in with memories of his own experience of being in love. His description shows the extremely foolish side of love, but Rosalind, like Silvius previously, can only think of her own intense feelings and is blind to the point Corin and Touchstone are making about how nonsensical love can be. Celia interrupts and says one of them must ask Corin if he can sell them some food, for she is ready to faint. Touchstone calls to the shepherd as if he were an underling, and Rosalind addresses him, too, for the first time having to act the part of the man she is dressed as.

Corin responds that he would like to help but is only a poor man himself, working for a man who is miserly but looking to sell his cottage, sheep, and pastures. The master is not home, but Corin says they can come and have what little food might be there. Rosalind asks if they can buy the cottage, sheep, and pastures, and Celia (as Aliena) tells Corin he can work for them and at a better wage. In this scene, pastoral life is not so blissful as Duke

Senior had described—masters are unfeeling and shepherds are poor. Yet both the shepherd's life and the three newcomers' lives improve because of their very practical plan; money is important, then, even in this natural, seemingly noncommercial world.

Scene 5 opens in another part of the forest, with Amiens singing a song that reiterates some of Duke Senior's earlier comments. The duke is not present, but Jaques, whom we so far have only heard others speak of, is here. He turns out to be just as the others described, a melancholy man who wants to remain melancholy. He speaks negatively of Duke Senior; his words stand out since others have spoken well of the duke and since we know the people support him. The other lords that are present prepare for the duke's arrival; certain aspects of courtly life remain with these men in the forest, for they set up a table and some men retain subservient roles.

Scene 6 takes place in another part of the forest. It reminds us of scene 4, in which Rosalind, Touchstone, and Celia entered exhausted, but here the situation is even more dire. In this scene Adam and Orlando are alone, having been traveling in the woods, and Adam says he can go no farther; he needs food or will die. Orlando promises to find him some. Here we have not just exhaustion but severe hunger plaguing an old man. The forest is again shown as a place of difficulty, although in light of the assistance Rosalind and her counterparts found earlier, we are hopeful that Orlando and Adam will also quickly find help.

In scene 7 we are still in the forest, this time with Duke Senior and his men. The duke has been looking for Jaques. When one lord tells the duke he saw Jaques, seemingly happy, the duke is most surprised. With this, Jaques enters and the duke says he does, in fact, look happy. Jaques is almost giddy with pleasure, explaining that he has met someone, a fool, in the forest. His exclamation, "A fool, a fool! I met a fool i' th' forest" almost reminds us of the extreme emotion of Silvius for Phebe as he called out for her. Just as Silvius cannot be steered away from his love for Phebe, Jaques, too, is intent on his attraction to Touchstone (although not romantic or sexual in nature). Indeed, after meeting Touchstone, Jaques wants to change his own life, to take on the life of a motley fool himself. Just as Corin tried to dissuade Silvius in his pursuit of Phebe, so here the duke says that Jaques is not suited to becoming a motley fool and transforming the world.

Orlando enters with his sword drawn, an indication of his vision of what country people are like. Apparently he believes they are people whom one must use force with; he tells them he expected them to be "savage." Of course, the duke and his men are not true people of the forest, although Orlando assumes they are. Orlando is desperate for food and tells them he must have it. The duke sees that Orlando must be in great distress to act in such a way, and he kindly tells Orlando he can have what he needs. Orlando goes back to get Adam, since he is the one most in need of food. While he is gone, the duke remarks that Orlando is in worse shape than they are. With this, Jaques launches into the famous "All the world's a stage" speech, wherein he describes the various stages that men live through, all of them miserable.

When Jaques finishes, Orlando enters with Adam on his back, reminding the audience that Jaques's speech about the horrors of living leaves out any mention of the joy and wonder of a close relationship. The power of a positive relationship is again brought to the forefront when Orlando tells the duke who he is. The duke replies that he loved Orlando's father and he therefore welcomes Adam and Orlando even more warmly; he wants to hear how they ended up in this forest in such a state.

Act III

This act opens with a short scene in the palace, the last scene in the play to take place there. Duke Frederick is angry that Orlando still has not been found. He tells Oliver that he must bring Orlando to him. In the meantime, all of Oliver's land and other possessions will be seized.

Scene 2 is quite long, pulling together a number of characters and, finally, Orlando and Rosalind for the first time since they saw each other and fell in love at the wrestling match. The scene opens with Orlando hanging love poems to Rosalind in the forest. After he leaves, Touchstone and Corin appear and talk about life. Touchstone sounds poetic but comments first one way and then in the converse way about each item he considers. Corin attempts to sound as poetic and philosophical.

When Touchstone finds out that Corin has never been to court, he admonishes Corin and says that he must therefore have no good manners and ultimately will be condemned to hell. While Touchstone remains condescending throughout the scene, Corin does not allow himself to be so readily taken advantage of. He gives numerous logical reasons for why manners learned in court do not apply in the forest. Touchstone dismisses each reason with some excuse. Corin finally stops the argument, ending it with his own fine commentary on why he is content with his life; the speech is pragmatic and indicates a man at peace with the world.

Rosalind enters dressed as Ganymede and reading a paper containing a love poem about Rosalind. Touchstone makes fun of it, creating his own strongly rhyming and sexual poem about Rosalind. Despite the protests of Rosalind (as Ganymede), Touchstone continues to make fun, and then Celia (as Aliena) enters, reading poetry similar to what Rosalind has found. In this poem, the poet also brings up some themes mentioned earlier in the play—the brevity of life and the inability to trust others, for example.

Celia urges Touchstone and Corin to leave and then asks Rosalind if she knows who the poet is. Rosalind says she doesn't, although perhaps she is only saying that to have some fun in a guessing game with Celia. As soon as Celia reveals that Orlando has left the poetry, Rosalind bombards her with many questions about him. Celia tells her where she saw him, and Rosalind interrupts with numerous loving comments about him after each piece of information that Celia reveals.

As they speak of Orlando, he enters with Jaques, and the women hide and listen to the two men. Immediately it is clear that the men find each other antagonizing. Jaques realizes, though, that Orlando has a "nimble wit" and is intrigued enough to ask Orlando if he would like to complain together about the world. Orlando says that he should criticize only himself, indicating his perspective that everyone has faults and should be concerned with only his own. Jaques resumes being annoyed and the two men separate, Jaques seeing Orlando as foolish for being so in love and Orlando seeing Jaques as overly depressed.

Jaques goes offstage, but before Orlando leaves, Rosalind (as Ganymede) stops him and asks for the time. When Orlando replies that there are no clocks in the forest, Rosalind remarks that there must be no true lovers in the forest. Orlando asks her to explain her reasoning and Rosalind does so, also describing how time moves at different paces depending on one's circumstance. With each example, Orlando listens closely. After Rosalind gives the last one, Orlando asks her where she lives and if this is where she is originally from, because her accent does not sound like that of the others in the forest. Rosalind has a quick answer, but the audience may wonder if Orlando believes what she says or if he might realize she is in disguise.

Rosalind's explanation is that she was taught to speak by an uncle who lived in a city when he was young. She adds that he had fallen in love and spoke against it many times. She states that women have many faults; Orlando asks her for the principal ones. She says, however, that she will not enumerate them except to those who will benefit from her doing so—such as the man leaving poetry in the woods. Orlando admits that he is that man. Rosalind says she is not convinced, however, since he shows none of the signs of a person in love. Still, Orlando repeatedly insists that he is the poet and that he is very much in love.

Love is madness, Rosalind then tells him, but she says she's cured one man of it. She had him woo her every day and she responded as a woman would, in the most mad manner, until the man was no longer madly in love but mad himself. Rosalind then offers to cure Orlando in this way. Orlando says it will not work on him, but when Rosalind urges him to come and woo her every day to see, he agrees. Again we wonder if he might realize who she is, for while someone in love might want to be out of love, would that person want to be driven mad, as Ganymede supposedly had done to the earlier subject?

In scene 3 Touchstone and Audrey, a country wench, are together. Jaques is hidden and listening. Audrey does not understand what Touchstone says; he says he wishes she did, but he makes no effort to speak in a less complex manner. He compares himself to the poet Ovid, but goes on to say that poetry is full of pretense and, since lovers speak poetry to each other, they are not being honest with each other. His perspective stands in contrast to Rosalind's in the preceding scene; while she pokes fun at the poetry Orlando has left, she never questions its truthfulness or sincerity.

Despite their differences and Touchstone's belief that all women cheat on their husbands, Touchstone has decided to marry Audrey and has arranged for Oliver Martext, a vicar from the next village, to meet them and marry them. Jaques comes out and Touchstone explains to him that he wants to get married because of his desires. Still, Jaques talks Touchstone out of getting married by this vicar, saying it is not appropriate that a man of his standing be married here; he advises Touchstone to speak to a "good priest" about marriage. Touchstone tells him he wanted this vicar to perform the ceremony because the marriage would then seem less like a real one—and he could more easily get out of it—he still goes along with Jaques's request that the marriage not take place here.

In scene 4 Rosalind (dressed as Ganymede) and Celia (as Aliena) wait for Orlando to arrive for his first session of being talked out of love. While they wait, Rosalind praises him but wonders where he is; Celia says she believes him untrue and not really in love at all. Corin arrives and tells them Silvius and Phebe are nearby, and they all go to see what's happening with this frustrated couple.

Silvius and Phebe enter scene 5 together, Silvius begging Phebe not to be scornful toward him. Rosalind (as Ganymede), Celia (as Aliena), and Corin then enter. Phebe is responding to Silvius, saying that her eyes alone cannot cause the pain that Silvius seems to believe they can. Phebe says Silvius should not come near her, and Rosalind interrupts; she chastises Phebe for being so cold and asks her how she thinks this is fair since Phebe herself is no special person. Rosalind rails at Silvius as well for making Phebe believe she is better than she is. Rosalind reminds the woman that she doesn't have much to offer and therefore should be grateful for a good man like Silvius.

The plot becomes more complex as Phebe falls in love with Ganymede (the disguised Rosalind). Rosalind sees this and does what she can to stop it. As Ganymede, she blatantly tells Phebe that Ganymede does not like her and is also a liar. Rosalind leaves abruptly with Celia and Corin.

Phebe tells Silvius that she does pity him for loving her and that, while she had hated him, she will put up with him now. Silvius is grateful for whatever smattering of positive feeling she will bestow upon him. Phebe then thinks about Ganymede; she enumerates his many traits, considering the merits of each, and remarks that some women would love him, but she should be angry because he chided her so. She's decided, she says, to write him a curt letter because of the way he treated her. When she asks Silvius to deliver it, he is ready to do so with all his heart.

Act IV

Rosalind (as Ganymede), Celia (as Aliena), and Jaques are together in the forest. This is the first meeting of two strong characters, Rosalind and Jaques. Because Rosalind's father enjoys Jaques's company and Orlando does not like it at all, it might be difficult for the audience to predict how Rosalind and Jaques will get along. Jaques says he's wanted to meet Ganymede, but Rosalind as Ganymede responds coolly that Jaques is known to be melancholy. Jaques gives his explanation of what makes his melancholy good as well as unique, but Rosalind is not only unimpressed—she also scorns Jaques. He is a traveler who does not appreciate his home country, she says, and who puts on an accent and wears foreign clothes. As Rosalind berates him, Orlando arrives, and Jaques starts to leave, remembering his last negative interaction with Orlando.

Rosalind's attention turns to Orlando. Dressed as Ganymede, she acts as his lover Rosalind, who is distressed that he is late. She also explains how husbands are destined to be cheated on by their wives. Orlando says he knows this won't be the case with his Rosalind, however. Rosalind encourages him to woo her, and when he says he would start by kissing her, she tells him why this would be a mistake. Throughout the scene Rosalind is witty and punning; Orlando tries to keep up. He remains committed to standing up for Rosalind and true love, despite all the negativity she conjures to scare and deter him. Though he gets in few words, the few he does manage she often dismisses. For instance, when he says, as the stereotypical lover would, that he would die if Rosalind said she didn't want him, Rosalind says no one ever dies because of love, and she launches into a list of famous lovers and describes their deaths. When he starts to woo her again and asks her to love him, she responds that she will love him and several others as well.

Still, Orlando remains undeterred. He agrees to go through the pretend marriage ceremony, with Celia presiding. When afterward he declares he will love Rosalind "For ever and a day," Rosalind tears that apart as well, saying that it would be more realistic for him to promise to love for just a day, since women do incredible things that drive men mad. Women make no sense and do just the opposite of what men desire at a particular moment, Rosalind says. Again, too, she explains how women are often found in their neighbors' beds, although they manage to blame this on their husbands. Orlando says he must leave for two hours, and Rosalind cries out that she knew he was the deserting type. Rosalind is left with Celia and again proclaims how thoroughly in love she is, yet Celia does not believe it.

Scene 2 moves to another part of the forest, with Jaques and the lords. Jaques says that they should take the man who killed the deer and present him, as if a great victor and with the deer's horns on his head, to the duke. In light of the earlier scene in which Jaques spoke poorly of hunting, we doubt that Jaques sees the hunter favorably. The men sing a song that reinforces this, a song that talks about how all men end up with horns, indicating their wives have cheated on them; men are not so powerful after all. The scene bolsters Rosalind's comments in the previous scene, but Rosalind was making such statements to see how Orlando would respond, whereas Jaques and these men seem to have accepted cheating as an inevitable part of life.

Rosalind (as Ganymede) and Celia (as Aliena) are together in another part of the forest in scene 3, waiting for Orlando to return after the two hours are up. Silvius enters with the letter from Phebe for Ganymede. He apologizes, believing the letter is full of anger, as Phebe had told him it would be. Rosalind acts riled by the letter, which she says is quite accusatory—so much so that she says it must have actually been written by Silvius, since this is something a man would write. Silvius assures her he didn't write it, and when Rosalind asks if he would like to hear it, he responds that he would, even though he says he has heard Phebe's cruelty often.

As Rosalind reads the letter, it is apparent that it is a love letter rather than an angry letter. Rosalind reads pieces and initially tries to pretend that it is angry, but even Silvius realizes it is just the opposite. Phebe proclaims her love and asks that Ganymede write back and tell whether he wants her. Celia is sympathetic, realizing how upsetting it is for Silvius to hear the letter, but Rosalind says he should not be pitied, since he has chosen to love Phebe. Apparently, though, Rosalind does feel pity as well, for she tells Silvius to give her response to Phebe, which is that Phebe must love Silvius. The difficulties of Phebe and Silvius point to the pain of unrequited love but also to the importance of making a wise choice when picking a partner.

Silvius leaves and another man enters, saying he is looking for two people, Rosalind (as Ganymede) and Celia (as Aliena). He says he has been sent by Orlando and with a bloody handkerchief. He explains why Orlando has not returned to them. While Orlando was in the forest, he came upon a man asleep in the forest with a snake around his neck, but when the snake saw Orlando, it slinked away, causing no harm. As the snake slipped under a bush, Orlando noticed a lion ready to pounce on the sleeping man. Orlando moved closer to the man and realized it was his own wicked brother, Oliver. While Orlando could have turned away, instead he chose to fight off the lion, the storyteller explains. Then he admits that he is that brother Orlando saved, but Oliver says he is a very different man than he had once been.

He goes on to tell how Orlando brought him to Duke Senior, who treated him most hospitably, and only later did they realize that Orlando had been wounded by the lion, wounded enough to cause him to faint. When he regained consciousness, he asked Oliver to go to Rosalind, explain what happened, and ask her to excuse him for not arriving on time. With this, Rosalind herself feels weak and faints. Oliver helps Celia bring Rosalind inside, and he says he is surprised to see a man faint. Rosalind, ever ready with a reply, says she did it because she is playing the role of the woman Rosalind and is quite good at doing so.

Act V

In the first scene of this last act, Audrey is disappointed that Touchstone stopped Martext from marrying them. Touchstone, however, says they will be married soon. He asks her about another man who loves her. She says the man has no interest in her. Just then the man appears—precisely as in other parts of the play when the person under discussion suddenly appears. That this happens a few times in the play suggests these occurrences are not just coincidences, but rather there is an aura of enchantment surrounding the events. In this case the man who appears is William, a shepherd. Touchstone says that he is a good target to be mocked, yet Touchstone starts by speaking to the man in a courteous way, asking him about himself. When he asks William if he is wise and then if he is learned, he begins his mockery. Finally he tells William, in a degrading way, to stay away from Audrey or be killed. William still politely wishes Touchstone well but then departs. Corin enters and calls Touchstone to come to Ganymede and Aliena.

Scene 2, however, does not show Touchstone, Audrey, Ganymede, and Aliena together; we must wait for that. In this scene it is Oliver and Orlando who are together. Orlando is amazed to hear that when Oliver found Aliena and Ganymede and relayed the circumstances of Orlando's confrontation with the lion, Oliver fell in love with Aliena at first sight. Oliver wants Orlando's approval to marry Aliena the next day; he says, too, that he will give Orlando their father's house and money, since Oliver plans to stay in the forest and live as a shepherd with Aliena.

Rosalind (as Ganymede) enters as Orlando gives his consent and says he will invite the duke and his followers to the wedding. Rosalind says she is disturbed to see Orlando's arm in a sling as a result of his injuries from the lion. Orlando, though, is still thinking about Oliver proclaiming his love for Aliena, and Rosalind agrees that it has happened quickly but that it cannot be denied. Orlando says he will be even more unhappy at the wedding, since Oliver will be happily married while Orlando still remains without the woman he loves. Rosalind asks if he will not see her for their pretend wooing, but Orlando says he cannot do it any longer.

With this, Rosalind realizes the playing must stop. She tells Orlando that she has good magical powers and will produce Rosalind for him the next day so he can marry her, just as his brother will marry Aliena. Rosalind bids him to prepare, but before they can depart, Silvius and Phebe enter. Phebe chastises Rosalind (as Ganymede) for revealing to Silvius the contents of the love letter she had written. Rosalind says she is not sorry, however, and that Phebe should love Silvius, the man who truly worships her.

Phebe asks Silvius to tell Ganymede what love is all about. He says it is "all made of sighs and tears" and that this is what he feels because of his love for Phebe. Phebe says she feels this because of Ganymede, Orlando says he feels this because of Rosalind, and Rosalind says she feels this for no woman. Each person's response follows the same form, as if this were some formal oath they are repeating. Here it becomes quite clear how mixed up the situation is, with all present feeling dissatisfied with love. Silvius makes another comment about love and they all respond in agreement, again phrasing their responses in the same manner. After this happens yet again, Rosalind puts a stop to it by saying she will fix everything. She will find Rosalind so Orlando will be happy; she will marry Phebe if she could ever marry a woman, but if she can't Phebe must promise to marry Silvius; and Silvius, in that case, must promise to marry Phebe. All agree.

Scene 3 returns to Touchstone and Audrey, excited to be married the next day yet not needing to be untangled from complications like the couples in the previous scene. The duke's pages enter and Touchstone asks them to sing a song. They agree and sing a happy song about lovers in spring, the time when most get married. The song says that life is like a flower in spring and hence we must get all we can out of each day. Touchstone is annoyed at the song, though, calling it foolish, and he tells Audrey they must leave. Touchstone's reaction reminds us of a response we would see from the negative Jaques. Perhaps Touchstone does not want to admit that life really is as fleeting as the song says.

Duke Senior speaks to Orlando in scene 4, asking him if he believes Ganymede can fix everything as he has claimed. With them are Amiens, Jaques, Oliver, and Celia (as Aliena). Rosalind (as Ganymede) enters with Silvius and Phebe and asks them all, as well as the duke, if they are in agreement with the events she plans—that the duke will allow Orlando to marry Rosalind; that if Ganymede cannot marry a woman, then Phebe will marry Silvius; and that Silvius will agree to this. All promise and Rosalind and Celia leave. The duke and Orlando remark on how Ganymede reminds them of Rosalind, but Orlando seems convinced that Ganymede is who he says he is.

Touchstone and Audrey enter. Jaques is very pleased to see Touchstone, the fool he admires so much. Touchstone explains that he indeed was a courtier. After the explanation Jaques asks if the duke, too, likes Touchstone, and he says he does. Touchstone says that he also admires the duke and explains that Audrey is the woman he plans to marry, someone who has a poor exterior but is virtuous.

Jaques encourages Touchstone to finish his story about being in courtly quarrels. Touchstone explains that just as there is a book of manners, so is there a proper way of fighting. He enumerates the list of steps and explains that when he criticized how a courtier's beard was cut, he carefully followed all the prescribed steps of fighting but never ventured too far, so the fight could be halted. Indeed, he satirizes the court's rules. By applying rules even to a comment about something as trivial as the cut of someone's beard, he mocks the seemingly excessive and nonsensical structure of rules. Jaques continues to be enthralled by Touchstone's clever commentary and keeps asking the duke if he is similarly impressed.

This interlude has given Rosalind and Celia time to dress themselves; for the first time they now appear as themselves in the forest rather than as Ganymede and Aliena. They enter with Hymen, the god of marriage. He calls on the duke to receive his daughter so the marriages may take place. Both the duke and Orlando are delighted to see Rosalind, and they and the others realize there never was a real male Ganymede or a poor Aliena. Phebe, seeing that there is no Ganymede to marry, sticks to her promise of being ready to marry Silvius. Hymen has all four couples come together and joins them—Rosalind and Orlando, Celia and Oliver, Phebe and Silvius, and Audrey and Touchstone. They sing a wedding song, and the duke welcomes Celia as if she were a daughter.

A man appears and says he is Jaques de Boys, the second son of Sir Rowland, making him the brother of Orlando and Oliver. He says he has news for them of how Duke Frederick amassed men to come to the forest to attack Duke Senior but that as he reached the forest rim he met an old religious man who transformed him. As a result of the transformation, Frederick halted his plot against his brother and decided to give him back the dukedom. He also declared he would return the property he had seized from those who followed the duke into the forest. Additionally Frederick decided to give up life as he knew it and live in the forest himself, away from the rest of the world.

Duke Senior welcomes the young man and says he is delighted to hear the news. He says they should return to their rustic celebration. However, rather than celebrating or planning to return to society, Jaques says he will keep living in the woods and will go off to find Frederick, since there will be much to learn from a man who has undergone such a conversion. He bids good wishes to Duke Senior and each married couple, although he tells Touchstone he predicts his marriage will last only for two months. Duke Senior wants him to stay, but Jaques is not one for revelry. He leaves, and the duke encourages all of the others to celebrate.

Epilogue

Rosalind, now alone on stage, speaks the final words of the play. She points out that, although women usually do not give epilogues, this play has questioned male and female roles and has also given a most prominent role to a female character (although for most of the play she has pretended to be a male). She says that good plays appear better if they have a good epilogue, but since she is not a beggar she must use her conjuring abilities to convince the audience that this indeed was a good play. Referring to the love theme, she charges the women, in the name of the love they have for men, to delight in the play. She charges the men with the same but goes a step further. She says what she would do to them if she were a woman, clearly reminding them that while she played Rosalind on stage, she is actually a male actor. This male, then, tells them if he were female he would kiss as many of them that appealed to him as he could and that, because of this pledge, he knows they will applaud.

Key Passages in
As You Like It
❧

Act II, i, 1–24

Duke Senior: Now, my co-mates and brothers in exile,
Hath not old custom made this life more sweet
Than that of painted pomp? Are not these woods
More free from peril than the envious court?
Here feel we not the penalty of Adam;
The seasons' difference, as the icy fang
And churlish chiding of the winter's wind,
Which, when it bites and blows upon my body
Even till I shrink with cold, I smile and say
"This is no flattery; these are counselors
That feelingly persuade me what I am."
Sweet are the uses of adversity,
Which, like the toad, ugly and venomous,
Wears yet a precious jewel in his head;
And this our life, exempt from public haunt,
Finds tongues in trees, books in the running brooks,
Sermons in stones, and good in everything.

Amiens: I would not change it; happy is your Grace
That can translate the stubbornness of fortune
Into so quiet and so sweet a style.

Duke Senior: Come, shall we go and kill us venison?
And yet it irks me the poor dappled fools,
Being native burghers of this desert city,
Should, in their own confines, with forkèd heads
Have their round haunches gored.

In this passage Duke Senior speaks to the men who have come with him into
the woods. While he has lost his dukedom, his life in the castle, and even the

opportunity to spend time with his own daughter, the duke says his new life in the forest is better. Here, he says, is a life that relies on old customs, that reminds him of the good old days, that does not have the false ceremony of the court nor its dangers.

While Adam was the first man to live an idyllic life with nature, the duke says, he also brought a curse on all men—yet the duke does not feel this curse. He admits, though, that he feels the harshness of winter, and in his speech he makes winter into a being that has fangs, bites, and blows. Still, even though he suffers from this winter beast, there is no falseness to it as there was in court. Here winter is winter; how the duke responds to it shows who he truly is. This is quite contrary to what happens in court, where so many false words are bandied about that one may actually believe the flatterers and lose sight of one's self. The suffering brought by winter is good, the duke says, and he reminds his listeners that even an ugly and poisonous toad has positive attributes, indicating there is goodness even in nature's harshness.

The duke admits that he may miss the learning that takes place in society, but learning can be accomplished in the woods as well: The trees, brooks, and stones also provide knowledge. After Duke Senior's long commentary, Amiens, one of the duke's lords, says he, too, is happy in this place. But he adds that the duke should be happy here, since his disposition makes him see what is good even in a negative experience like banishment. We have also heard others speak highly of the duke, so it is not surprising that Amiens is so complimentary here.

The duke then says that they should go and kill some venison. He seems to be involved in the hunt for food just as anyone else in the forest would be, even though he held such a high position in court. He voices his discomfort in killing the deer, since this forest is their place. Still, the killing only "irks" him and does not disturb him to such a degree that he tries to come up with other options for sustenance. The killing of animals, of course, is also what men who are forest natives do, so if the duke truly is embracing the life here, it seems he should accept this practice, as he does for the most part. His comment about killing the deer reveals his compassion and shows that he is a thinking man.

Act II, i, 45–63

O, yes, into a thousand similes.
First, for his weeping into the needless stream:
"Poor deer," quoth he, "thou mak'st a testament
As worldlings do, giving thy sum of more

To that which had too much." Then, being there alone,
Left and abandoned of his velvet friend:
"'Tis right," quoth he, "thus misery doth part
The flux of company." Anon a careless herd,
Full of the pasture, jumps along by him
And never stays to greet him: "Ay," quoth Jaques,
"Sweep on, you fat and greasy citizens,
'Tis just the fashion: wherefore do you look
Upon that poor and broken bankrupt there?"
Thus most invectively he pierceth through
The body of the country, city, court,
Yea, and of this our life, swearing that we
Are mere usurpers, tyrants, and what's worse,
To fright the animals and to kill them up
In their assigned and native dwelling place.

In this speech a lord tells Duke Senior what he saw Jaques do and say in another part of the forest. The telling gives us a taste of who Jaques is before he appears onstage. We already know something of Duke Senior, who finds Jaques interesting company, but we do not understand why. Curiously, the story that the lord tells involves a deer, and it comes shortly after Duke Senior has said he feels bad for the deer in the forest since he and his men kill them for food.

Here the lord tells us that Jaques saw an injured deer in the forest. The deer let his tears drop into a nearby stream. Jaques says that, just as people's grievances fall on deaf ears (for they complain to others who are already full of the world's complaints), this deer drops his tears into a stream that is already filled. In both cases the act is pointless, according to Jaques, for there is no sympathy to be had.

Jaques is also not surprised that the deer has been abandoned, since, he believes, misery chases others away. Jaques personifies the deer and in the process makes a point not just about nature but about people as well. When he sees a group of deer pass the injured one, Jaques again sees the behavior as comparable to that of humans, who would easily go by and remain unconcerned about a fellow being in trouble. He calls those that go by "fat and greasy citizens," making their ugly physicality a direct reflection of their internal immorality.

From the perspective of the lord who is narrating the story, Jaques criticizes everyone—whether from country, city, or court. Whereas at other points in the play it seems that such distinctions matter, here, in Jaques's view, all distinctions are lost, since man, at his core, is the same ugly beast no matter his background. The lord says that Jaques even railed against Duke Senior and his accompanying lords, placing them in the same category as Duke Frederick, for example—a tyrant who simply takes what he wants. Jaques sees Duke Senior and his men in this light because they have come into the forest and wreaked havoc with the natural world. They believe it is acceptable to kill deer for food, even though the forest rightfully belongs to its natural inhabitants, the deer being just one such group.

Jaques's perspective is not dissimilar to the comment the duke made earlier about killing deer, although Jaques sees the situation in a more extreme way and is unable to shrug it off quite so easily. We see, then, why the duke might appreciate having Jaques around, for Jaques says what he thinks and thinks, in some ways at least, like the duke himself. In this case, he appears more idealistic than the duke, who perhaps realizes the importance of keeping such a perspective in mind. Ultimately, though, Duke Senior is the one admired by the people, and Jaques, except in his dealings with Touchstone and the duke, is seen as grating and overly melancholy.

Act II, vii, 139–166

All the world's a stage,
And all the men and women merely players;
They have their exits and their entrances,
And one man in his time plays many parts,
His acts being seven ages. At first, the infant,
Mewling and puking in the nurse's arms.
Then the whining schoolboy, with his satchel
And shining morning face, creeping like snail
Unwillingly to school. And then the lover,
Sighing like furnace, with a woeful ballad
Made to his mistress' eyebrow. Then a soldier,
Full of strange oaths and bearded like the pard,
Jealous in honor, sudden and quick in quarrel,
Seeking the bubble reputation
Even in the cannon's mouth. And then the justice,
In fair round belly with good capon lined,
With eyes severe and beard of formal cut,
Full of wise saws and modern instances;
And so he plays his part. The sixth age shifts
Into the lean and slippered pantaloon,
With spectacles on nose and pouch on side;
His youthful hose, well saved, a world too wide
For his shrunk shank, and his big manly voice,

Turning again toward childish treble, pipes
And whistles in his sound. Last scene of all,
That ends this strange eventful history,
Is second childishness and mere oblivion,
Sans teeth, sans eyes, sans taste, sans everything.

This is one of Shakespeare's most famous passages, spoken by the cynical and unhappy Jaques, whose characteristics clearly color the speech. In it Jaques envisions man as a pawn in a drama over which he has no control. Man enters (is born) and exits (dies) at his appointed times and in between plays several horrid parts as he ages and progresses through his life span.

Initially, he is a baby who must be taken care of, weak and ill in a nurse's arms. Then he is an unhappy child, moving along at a snail's pace on his way to school each day because of his great distaste for it. He eventually becomes a lover, which one might think a fortunate turn of events, yet here Jaques speaks of the lover's sad and foolish love song, with no mention of that love being returned. Next man becomes a soldier, jealous of others, quick to fight, and intent on gaining the reputation of a hero. He puts himself in great peril for a reputation that is highly vulnerable and fleeting. Afterward, he advances to become a justice, again a position that one might think would be favorable but that Jaques sees as seriously flawed. In his view, while a judge is supposed to administer justice, in actuality the man in this role makes judgments based not on what is right but on the bribes he receives (judges at the time were known to receive capon, or chicken, as bribes).

After this, man slips even further—not because of his own immorality but because of time's wear on his body. He must wear glasses, his body has shrunk from loss of muscle, and his formerly strong voice has become weak, more childlike than manly. In the end he is a shell of what he had been; all is lost, leaving him where he was in the beginning—like a mere child who is completely dependent. But, of course, this final state is worse than early childhood, since a child grows and becomes knowledgeable and strong, while an old man only grows older, weaker, and more infirm as he sees death waiting for him.

The speech is full of imagery, and the repetition of *sans* (meaning *without*) in the last line only reinforces the downward spiral of life. Man is without one thing and another and another until he is dead and, therefore, completely without. In Jaques's view there is no hope of an afterlife either. His descriptions are pitiful and hopeless, and while most audiences would not agree that this is what comprises life, parts of the speech are inarguably true (for example, we do not control when we begin or end life) and cannot be dismissed so easily.

Immediately after the speech, however, something occurs that makes its negativity appear unwarranted. Orlando, who has gone to retrieve the starving

Adam, returns to the group that has offered them food. On his back he carries
Adam, who is grateful to Orlando. Both Orlando and Adam are, in turn, grateful
to the duke, who is even more glad to help the men when he finds out the
identity of Orlando's father. The duke asks for a song, which ends up speaking of
the negative side of men, but the fact that Orlando and the duke live their own
good lives and seem not to notice the lyrics indicates that perhaps the audience
need not pay too much notice to Jaques's perspective here either. Jaques's speech
and the song are just words; what occurs between Orlando, Adam, and the duke
is true loving concern.

Act III, v, 35–63

And why, I pray you? Who might be your mother,
That you insult, exult, and all at once,
Over the wretched? What though you have no beauty
(As, by my faith, I see no more in you
Than without candle may go dark to bed)
Must you be therefore proud and pitiless?
Why, what means this? Why do you look on me?
I see no more in you than in the ordinary
Of nature's sale-work. 'Od's my little life,
I think she means to tangle my eyes too!
No, faith, proud mistress, hope not after it;
'Tis not your inky brows, your black silk hair,
Your bugle eyeballs, nor your cheek of cream
That can entame my spirits to your worship.
You foolish shepherd, wherefore do you follow her,
Like foggy south, puffing with wind and rain?
You are a thousand times a properer man
Than she a woman. 'Tis such fools as you
That makes the world full of ill-favored children.
'Tis not her glass, but you, that flatters her,
And out of you she sees herself more proper
Than any of her lineaments can show her.
But mistress, know yourself. Down on your knees,
And thank heaven, fasting, for a good man's love;
For I must tell you friendly in your ear,
Sell when you can, you are not for all markets.
Cry the man mercy, love him, take his offer;
Foul is most foul, being foul to be a scoffer;
So take her to thee, shepherd. Fare you well.

In this passage Rosalind (as Ganymede) speaks to Phebe and Silvius, criticizing them for how they behave in their relationship. She starts by questioning Phebe's heartless behavior toward Silvius, asking who her mother must be that she feels she has the right to insult and look down upon Silvius. Rosalind's mention of Phebe's mother might be intended to suggest that Phebe has been brought up in an ill-mannered way. The question may also, however, refer to Phebe's heritage. Heritage, after all, can make some people believe they are better than others; although Rosalind has shown that she does not think this way (since even as the daughter of a duke, she wants to marry Orlando rather than someone of privilege), she knows most of society does. When Phebe says she does not come from any heritage other than that of forest dwellers, Rosalind is assured that Phebe is not treating Silvius so poorly due to her social standing.

After mentioning Phebe's mother, Rosalind speaks of Phebe's looks. She bluntly tells the woman that she is not beautiful, since Rosalind knows that beautiful women often can take advantage of men, although women who merely see themselves as beautiful usually cannot. As Rosalind speaks she notices that Phebe seems attracted to her (disguised as Ganymede). Rosalind is confounded because she already has negative feelings toward this woman. Rosalind is also startled; her life has become increasingly more complex due to her seemingly harmless decision to disguise herself as a man. Rosalind sees this new development as yet another sign of Phebe's complete disregard for Silvius. Immediately Rosalind repeats that she does not find Phebe attractive, attempting to quell the woman's desire for her.

Next Rosalind turns to Silvius. Though she has berated Phebe, we assume she will have pity for Silvius, but that is not readily apparent. Instead, she starts by chastising him for being so foolish as to want a woman like Phebe. She tells him he is a much better person by far than Phebe. She warns that if he does end up married to this woman, he will be like so many others who make foolish choices and populate the earth with children who are just as bad as the cruel Phebe. Rosalind goes so far as to tell Silvius that he is responsible for his predicament, for he has enabled Phebe to believe she is beautiful and to have an inflated opinion of herself.

Apparently Rosalind realizes that Silvius is not going to walk away from Phebe. Rosalind then turns her focus back to Phebe. She tells the woman she should be overjoyed and praising God that a man such as Silvius wants her. Rosalind warns her that she must be pragmatic and take advantage of the situation—to ask for Silvius's mercy, love him, and marry him—for there are few men who will want her. Rosalind then tells Silvius to take Phebe and hopes that Phebe will be more bearable.

Act IV, i, 136–152

Rosalind: Now tell me how long you would have her after you have
possessed her.
Orlando: For ever and a day.
Rosalind: Say "a day" without the "ever." No, no, Orlando. Men are
April when they woo, December when they wed. Maids are May when
they are maids, but the sky changes when they are wives. I will be
more jealous of thee than a Barbary cock-pigeon over his hen, more
clamorous than a parrot against rain, more newfangled than an ape,
more giddy in my desires than a monkey. I will weep for nothing, like
Diana in the fountain, and I will do that when you are disposed to be
merry; I will laugh like a hyen, and that when thou art inclined
to sleep.
Orlando: But will my Rosalind do so?
Rosalind: By my life, she will do as I do.
Orlando: O, but she is wise.

This passage occurs in the midst of Rosalind's wooing session with Orlando.
She is disguised as Ganymede but tells Orlando to envision her and speak
to her as if she were Rosalind. Though she has told Orlando that in these
sessions she will make him fall out of love, the sessions actually allow her to
see just how strong Orlando's love is. During the sessions he can more easily
speak truthfully, whereas he might be more hesitant to do so if he thought
he were actually in Rosalind's presence. At this point Rosalind and Orlando
have just had Celia pretend to marry them. Rosalind, no doubt, must be
thrilled to realize that Orlando indeed appears ready to marry her. After the
fake ceremony she asks him how long he will stay with Rosalind; he responds
in the typical manner of a besotted lover: "For ever and a day." "For ever,"
while as long as possible, is still not long enough to the lover, and so "a day"
is added.

Rosalind must poke fun at this exaggeration, but she goes beyond just
poking and tries to disturb Orlando's perception of love further. She tells him
that a day is more likely the only amount of time he will be able to handle
with Rosalind and then explains why. Men, she says, woo their women and
then get married, but women are wooed and then completely transformed
when they are married. Describing what will happen after marriage, she says
Rosalind will first be intensely jealous. She adds other examples of extreme
behavior and explains that these will occur just when her husband is desiring
the opposite—there will be tears from his wife when he wants to be merry

and laughter when he wants to sleep. Nearly all of the behavior that Rosalind warns of is compared to that of animals. In short, it is behavior that would naturally occur in a wild animal—which man, especially man who has not lived in the country, must feel helpless to control.

When Rosalind is done with her long list of what she will do when married, Orlando asks if this is actually what *his* Rosalind will do. In other words, he doubts that his love would act this way. Even more interestingly, his question shows that he does not blindly stay under the spell of Rosalind playing the role of his lover. The playacting has its limits for him. When Rosalind responds that his lover will do just as she has described, he still doubts her, as evidenced by his comment that his Rosalind is "wise." Rosalind's speech, then, has planted the concern that such maddening behavior is possible, but ultimately Orlando does not believe it applies to his lover. In this way he is like the typical lover who cannot think ill of the object of his affection. Still, the reader gets to see him not simply as a stereotypical lover; we realize he is correct, actually, in how he sees Rosalind, and we have seen more of the true Rosalind than he has. We realize she is wildly in love with Orlando; she is unlike the stereotypical female because of her outstanding wit, intelligence, creativity, and daring; and she is pragmatic and obviously someone who has thought about love. In light of these characteristics—and because she so severely chastised Phebe for mistreating her lover—it seems hard to believe Rosalind could become the miserable wife she has described.

Epilogue

It is not the fashion to see the lady the epilogue, but it is no more unhandsome than to see the lord the prologue. If it be true that good wine needs no bush, 'tis true that a good play needs no epilogue; yet to good wine they do use good bushes, and good plays prove the better by the help of good epilogues. What a case am I in then, that am neither a good epilogue, nor cannot insinuate with you in the behalf of a good play! I am not furnished like a beggar; therefore to beg will not become me. My way is to conjure you, and I'll begin with the women. I charge you, O women, for the love you bear to men, to like as much of this play as please you; and I charge you, O men, for the love you bear to women—as I perceive by your simpering none of you hates them—that between you and the women the play may please. If I were a woman, I would kiss as many of you as had beards that pleased me, complexions that liked me, and breaths that defied not; and I am sure, as many as have good beards, or good faces, or sweet breaths, will, for my kind offer, when I make curtsy, bid me farewell.

In the epilogue Rosalind appears onstage by herself and first points out that it is not usual that a lady give the epilogue and that it is not unbecoming either. Considering that the audience has been watching a play with this very strong female character often at center stage, it is not surprising that she would remain the lead here. Rosalind says that a good play truly needs no epilogue but that an epilogue certainly can only make a good play better. She comments that, since she is not dressed like a beggar, she cannot just beg the crowd for approval. It is interesting, though, that she says she is not *dressed* like a beggar rather than simply saying she is not a beggar. The word choice reminds us of all the disguise that has taken place in the play.

Because she cannot beg, Rosalind says she is left to conjure the audience, which seems fitting since she has performed what she's called *conjuring* in the previous act, in which she managed to get all of the couples happily married. She speaks to the women in the audience first, charging that for the love they have for men, they should like the play. Next she turns to the men and gives basically the same message. She throws in a comment to get a chuckle as well, saying that none of the men hate women, she supposes, since none are simpering. Again, the comment seems appropriate, for in the wooing scenes Rosalind has tried to convince Orlando of the madness of women. All along, though, she had hoped he would not be convinced, and her remark here shows that she knows the audience did not believe her comments about women either.

The end of the speech starts "If I were a woman," which completely breaks down the illusion of the female Rosalind; we're reminded that there is no real Rosalind, that she is only an invented character, and that, in fact, a male actor plays her. The actor says he would, if he were a woman, kiss as many of the men as he found pleasing in the audience and that this, then, would drive them to applause. The statement reminds the audience of the tricks they have seen during the play, when a male actor was playing Rosalind, who was pretending to be Ganymede. At times, Ganymede, in turn, was pretending to be Rosalind. The layers of disguise, during the play as in this epilogue, show the audience not just the possibility of pretense in our own lives but also of the need to reexamine sex roles. In the play, for instance, we see how relatively easy it is for the character Rosalind to take on other roles and enjoy them, and we also realize that when she initially decided to dress as Ganymede, it was as a precaution, to help keep Celia and herself safe. Because of the power of men in the society of the play, even when one is only pretending to be a man, there is more opportunity and more safety.

The illusion of Rosalind as character is not the only illusion broken here, for as soon as Rosalind appears on the stage for this epilogue, she comments on epilogues and the desire for the audience to applaud in appreciation once a play is over. This immediately reminds the audience that it has, in fact, its own role, as audience, and that the play tries to illicit responses from the viewers. If the play is good, they will applaud, and if it is very good, they will think about it as they leave the theater and return to their own lives.

LIST OF CHARACTERS IN
As You Like It

❧

Duke Senior is the elder brother of Duke Frederick. He is the rightful duke, yet his brother has banished him to the Forest of Arden, usurping Duke Senior's power and taking over his land as well as the land of the others who have gone into exile with him. Duke Senior is admired by the people; his servants, daughter, and others who come into contact with him respect him and hold him in high esteem as well, which is part of what has made his brother jealous.

Duke Frederick is the evil usurper of the dukedom who has banished his brother, Duke Senior, and taken over his land as well as the land of the others who went into exile with him. Frederick also banishes Duke Senior's daughter, Rosalind, even though Frederick's own daughter loves her greatly. Later he plans to kill his brother, but upon meeting a religious man he undergoes an epiphany and decides to live a good life.

Amiens is a lord attending Duke Senior; he also sings in the play.

Jaques is a lord attending Duke Senior and an outsider. He has taken on affected mannerisms and speech and is an object of ridicule. His perspective is different from that of the others and does not fit with the joyousness at the end of the play.

Le Beau, a courtier, is another who is satirized for his language and airs.

Charles is a powerful wrestler. When he learns that Orlando is to challenge him, Charles warns Oliver that Orlando will most likely be severely hurt. Charles does not realize that Oliver is lying to him about Orlando because Oliver hates his brother and wants Charles to cause him great harm.

Oliver, oldest son of Sir Rowland de Boys, has control of his dead father's money yet does not allow Orlando a proper gentlemanly life. Aside from being selfish, Oliver is brutally wicked, yet late in the play he transforms himself and loses that wickedness when Orlando saves his life.

Jaques de Boys is the second son of Sir Rowland de Boys. Oliver gives him enough money to be properly schooled, thus he is doing well. He appears at the very end of the play to bring good news to the newly married couples and Duke Senior.

Orlando is the youngest son of Sir Rowland de Boys. People like him, yet his brother Oliver mistreats him and then wants to kill him, forcing him to take refuge in the forest. His strength while wrestling, patience with Ganymede, and kind treatment of Adam, among other things, make him an admirable character.

Adam is a servant to Oliver, yet he sees his wickedness. He warns Orlando that Oliver wants him dead, gives Orlando his savings to live on in the forest, and goes with Orlando to the forest to loyally serve him.

Dennis is a servant to Oliver.

Touchstone is the court clown. He goes to the forest with Rosalind and Celia, who see him as a protector and one who will be uplifting during what could be a trying time. His lustful desire for Audrey stands in contrast to the other romantic relationships in the play.

Sir Oliver Martext is a vicar from the next village who comes to the forest to marry Touchstone and Audrey.

Corin is a shepherd who is very knowledgeable about his occupation. He is humble, helpful to Rosalind and Celia, and realistic, a real person of the natural world who contrasts with the pastoral tradition's idealized vision of shepherds.

Silvius is a shepherd but is unlike the realistic and pragmatic Corin. He is madly in love with Phebe. Though there are others in such a state in the play, none of them desires such a seemingly unworthy person as Phebe.

William is a country man, a realistic character rather than one who fits into an idealistic pastoral vision. He wants Audrey yet fears pursuing her after Touchstone says she is his and threatens William.

Rosalind is the daughter of Duke Senior. She is bold enough and smart enough to manage being banished to the forest, where she disguises herself as

Ganymede. She is also quite clever and intensely in love with Orlando, whom she tricks in order to have fun and to see just how much he really loves her.

Celia is the daughter of Duke Frederick and the cousin and close friend of Rosalind. Her love for Rosalind moves her to accompany her cousin into the forest when she is banished, even though Celia's father will be upset. Celia also speaks her mind, telling Rosalind what she thinks is best for her welfare. In the forest, Celia disguises herself as Aliena.

Phebe is the shepherdess that Silvius wildly desires, though she has no interest in him. Rosalind chastises her for the way she treats Silvius, pointing out the woman's flaws and reminding her that there are a limited number of men who will want her.

Audrey is a country girl. She cannot understand all of what Touchstone says but wants to marry him nonetheless.

Hymen is the god of marriage who appears at the very end of the play, when so many are happily married.

CRITICISM
THROUGH THE AGES
❧

As You Like It
IN THE SEVENTEENTH AND
EIGHTEENTH CENTURIES

While it is generally agreed that *As You Like It* was first performed in 1599 or 1600, perhaps for the opening of the Globe Theatre, there is no record of the play being performed again until 1740. From then through the end of the eighteenth century, the play held wide appeal, perhaps for being one of the most delightful of Shakespeare's works.

In the early 1700s, the biographer and editor Nicholas Rowe wrote in admiration of the famous "All the world's a stage" speech. His contemporary, the critic Charles Gildon, in his "Remarks on the Plays of Shakespear," wrote that while the narrative of the play had nothing dramatic about it, still Shakespeare made the best use of the premise. Such remarks about the narrative and genre of the play would be made by many commentators over the years. Gildon also commented on specific scenes in the play, drawing attention to Shakespeare's skill at being able to construct scenes that not only present the action but also provide insight into the characters' relationships. A particular scene that Rowe deemed "artful and natural" is that between the wrestler and Orlando.

The great critic Samuel Johnson also used the word "natural" to describe Shakespeare's character Jaques, although Johnson was concerned about how quickly and seemingly unnaturally both Rosalind and Celia fall in love. Johnson believed that people of Shakespeare's time preferred comedy over tragedy and that comedy was Shakespeare's strength as well. Johnson also remarked that Shakespeare had missed an opportunity at the end of the play to place Duke Frederick and Jaques in a discussion that would have provided a "moral lesson." Johnson may have felt that this would have provided a chance for Shakespeare to comment on the political issue of usurpation, which was on the minds of many, both in Shakespeare's time and Johnson's. As time went on, however, critics became less concerned about political messages in the play.

The editor and critic Edward Capell was concerned not with political messages but with the origins of Shakespeare's play, a topic that would be discussed for many years. In his introduction to the play that was printed in his own edition of the work, Capell referred to a novel by Thomas Lodge as the basis of *As You Like It*.

William Richardson, agreeing with Rowe and Johnson about the naturalness of Shakespeare's characters, gave his detailed perspective on the humanness and complexity of Jaques. He believed Shakespeare did the right thing in making Jaques both melancholy and misanthropic and that this showed Shakespeare's genius in understanding human nature. For the audience, in Richardson's view, while Jaques is severe, he is also amusing and therefore appealing. It would be unnatural for Shakespeare to have created a complete misanthrope, according to Richardson, since this is so seldom found in the real world.

Through the ages, as critics have examined various characters in the play, Jaques and Rosalind have received the most attention.

1709—Nicholas Rowe. "The Argument of *As You Like It*," from *The Works of Mr. William Shakespear*

The Works of Mr. William Shakespear, by Nicholas Rowe (1674–1718), is said to mark the beginning of the modern Shakespeare text. Rowe also wrote a short account of Shakespeare's life, as well as *The Tragedy of Jane Shore; Written in Imitation of Shakespear's Style.*

The Conversation of *Benedick* and *Beatrice*, in *Much ado about Nothing*, and of *Rosalind* in *As you like it*, have much Wit and Sprightliness all along. . . . The Melancholy of *Jaques*, in *As you like it*, is as singular and odd as it is diverting. And if what *Horace* says *Difficile est proprie communia Dicere*, 'Twill be a hard Task for any one to go beyond him in the Description of the several Degrees and Ages of Man's Life, tho' the Thought be old, and common enough.

> All the World's a Stage;
> And all the Men and Women meerly Players;
> They have their Exits and their Entrances,
> And one Man in his time plays many Parts,
> His Acts being seven Ages. At first the Infant
> Mewling and puking in the Nurse's Arms:
> And then, the whining School-boy with his Satchel,
> and shining Morning-face, creeping like Snail
> Unwillingly to School. And then the Lover
> Sighing like Furnace, with a woful Ballad
> Made to his Mistress' Eye-brow. Then a Soldier
> Full of strange Oaths, and bearded like the Pard,

Jealous in Honour, sudden and quick in Quarrel,
Seeking the bubble Reputation
Ev'n in the Cannon's Mouth. And then the Justice
In fair round Belly, with good Capon lin'd,
With Eyes severe, and Beard of formal Cut,
Full of wise Saws and modern Instances;
And so he plays his Part. The sixth Age shifts
Into the lean and slipper'd Pantaloon,
With Spectacles on Nose, and Pouch on Side;
His youthful Hose, well sav'd, a world too wide
For his shrunk Shank; and his big manly Voice
Turning again tow'rd childish treble Pipes,
And Whistles in his Sound. Last Scene of all,
That ends this strange eventful History,
Is second Childishness and meer Oblivion,
Sans Teeth, sans Eyes, sans Tast, sans ev'ry thing.

His Images are indeed ev'ry where so lively, that the Thing he would represent stands full before you, and you possess ev'ry Part of it. I will venture to point out one more, which is, I think, as strong and as uncommon as any thing I ever saw; 'tis an Image of Patience.

1710—Charles Gildon.
"Remarks on the Plays of Shakespear"

Charles Gildon (1665–1724)—translator, biographer, essayist, play-wright, and poet—wrote a series of notes and essays to accompany Rowe's edition of Shakespeare, providing the first extensive commentaries of the plays. He counted among his literary enemies Alexander Pope and Jonathan Swift.

The Story (of *As You Like It*) has nothing Dramatic in it, yet Shakespear has made as good use of it as possible.

The Scene betwixt Orlando and his Brother Oliver in the opening of the Play is well manag'd, discovering something that goes before in the Quarrel between them; and Oliver's Management of the provoking Charles the Wrestler against Orlando is artful and natural. . . .

1765—Samuel Johnson. *As You Like It* (notes), from *The Plays of William Shakespeare*

Samuel Johnson (1709–1784) is thought by many to be the greatest commentator on Shakespeare. He was a poet, critic, prose writer, lexicographer, editor, and celebrated raconteur. His edition of the works of Shakespeare contained some of his famous thoughts on the plays. The following comments are taken from annotations he supplied to his text of *As You Like It*.

Of this play the fable is wild and pleasing. I know not how the ladies will approve the facility with which both Rosalind and Celia give away their hearts. To Celia much may be forgiven for the heroism of her friendship. The character of Jaques is natural and well preserved. The comick dialogue is very sprightly, with less mixture of low buffoonery than in some other plays; and the graver part is elegant and harmonious. By hastening to the end of his work Shakespeare suppressed the dialogue between the usurper and the hermit, and lost an opportunity of exhibiting a moral lesson in which he might have found matter worthy of his highest powers.

1767—Edward Capell. "Introduction," from his edition of *As You Like It*

Edward Capell was an English editor and Shakespeare critic. He produced an edition of Shakespeare's works and also, along with David Garrick, an edition of *Antony and Cleopatra* that the two adapted for the stage.

A novel or rather pastoral romance, entitled "Euphues's Golden Legacy," written in a very fantastical style by Dr. Thomas Lodge, and by him first published in the year 1590, in quarto, is the foundation of *As You Like It*. Besides the fable, which is pretty exactly followed, the outlines of certain principal characters may be observed in the novel; and some expressions of the novelist (few, indeed, and of no great moment) seem to have taken possession of Shakespeare's memory, and thence crept into the play.

1788—William Richardson. "On the Melancholy Jaques," from *Philosophical Analysis and Illustration of Some of Shakespeare's Remarkable Characters*

William Richardson was a professor at the University of Glasgow. He wrote *Essays on Falstaff* and *Essays on Shakespeare's Dramatic Characters*, which has been called one of the first works of psychological criticism of Shakespeare's plays.

. . . Though melancholy rules the mind of Jaques, he partakes of the leaven of human nature, and, moved by a sense of injury and disappointment,

Most invectively he pierceth through
The body of the country, city, court.

Instigated by sentiments of self-respect, if not of pride, he treats the condition of humanity, and the pursuits of mankind, as insignificant and uncertain. His invectives, therefore, are mingled with contempt, and expressed with humour. At the same time, he shows evident symptoms of a benevolent nature. He is interested in the improvement of mankind, and inveighs, not entirely to indulge resentment, but with a desire to correct their depravity. . . .

This mixture of melancholy and misanthropy in the character of Jaques, is more agreeable to human nature than the representation of either of the extremes; for a complete misanthrope is as uncommon an object as a man who suffers injury without resentment. Mankind hold a sort of middle rank, and are in general too good for the one, and too bad for the other. As benevolence and sensibility are manifest in the temper of Jaques, we are not offended with his severity. By the oddity of his manner, by the keenness of his remarks, and shrewdness of his observations, while we are instructed, we are also amused. He is precisely what he himself tells us, "often wrapped in a most humourous sadness." His sadness, of a mild and gentle nature, recommends him to our regard; his humour amuses.

A picture of this kind shews the fertility of Shakespeare's genius, his knowledge of human nature, and the accuracy of his pencil, much more than if he had represented in striking colours either of the component parts. By running them into one another, and by delineating their shades where they are gradually and almost imperceptibly blended together, the extent and delicacy of his conceptions, and his amazing powers of execution are fully evident.

As You Like It
IN THE NINETEENTH CENTURY
೫೨

William Hazlitt, whose book *Characters of Shakespeare's Plays* was first published in 1817, was one of the great critics of his time. Like other Romantics
of the early nineteenth century, he saw *As You Like It* as providing moral lessons. He also agreed with the Romantics' general ideas that society is evil and
that the natural world is good. Coming from this perspective, then, he viewed
Shakespeare's play as a pastoral drama.

Place and nature were emphasized not only by critics but also by some of
the play's producers. By the mid-nineteenth century, one of the most famous
productions of the play featured elaborate "natural" scenery—a brook gurgled,
sheep bells tinkled, birds sang, and old gnarled and knotted trees stood by; there
was even a lodge covered in vines. In yet another production, the play was moved
outside in order to surround the audience with nature.

Hazlitt also saw the play as most memorable not for its relatively aimless plot
but for its characters and sentiments. The German critic A.W. Schlegel agreed
with Hazlitt about the lack of a plan behind the play. In his view Shakespeare
created a world in which complete freedom makes up for everything that the
characters have left behind. Similarly, but taking Schlegel's view slightly further,
Hermann Ulrici saw the play as totally fantastic.

Yet at least two critics found the land that Shakespeare created in Arden not
to be thoroughly idyllic. Richard Moulton, for instance, saw the play's pastoral
life as being in competition with three types of humor, not all completely
positive: Rosalind's healthy humor, Touchstone's professional humor, and
Jaques's morbid humor. The Danish critic Georg Brandes considered the forest
tainted, as evidenced by Jaques. Brandes also called Jaques the voice of "a
Shakespeare of the future, a Hamlet in germ." William Maginn saw Jaques
much more negatively, as a gentleman with nothing better to do than to spew
criticism. Even regarding Jaques's famous speech about the seven ages of man,
for example, Maginn said that Jacques's complaints are unjustified, since each
man named has been taken care of and is not really suffering in comparison to
what some others must endure.

Other critics examined Jaques not so much as an individual but in relation to other characters in the play. Ulrici, for example, saw Jaques and Touchstone as completing each other and adding a new dimension to the play. (Keep in mind that these characters did not exist in Shakespeare's source for the play.) A. Wilson Verity, too, remarked not so much on Jaques as his own character but rather on his differences with Rosalind.

Rosalind continued to receive significant critical attention, with more female critics remarking on her as well as on other aspects of the play. Lady Martin, an actress at the time, saw Rosalind as so complex as to never be completely known. She found Rosalind fascinating, charming, and happy and envied her having the unusual opportunity to put her lover to the test while in disguise. Martin categorized Rosalind as the "presiding genius" in Arden. She saw Rosalind as so thoroughly realistic as to be outside the action of the play, imagining all her positive traits as helping her when her husband becomes prince.

Another female critic, Anna Jameson, saw Rosalind in a similar vein, believing it impossible to analyze her and finding her completely enchanting. From Jameson's perspective, we forget that Rosalind is a princess since we never see her with her "artificial appendages" and she is so thoroughly free and frolicsome in the pastoral Arden setting. She is fresh, youthful, witty, and sweet, even when she gives her few chastising speeches.

The playwright George Bernard Shaw also enumerated reasons why Rosalind is so appealing—for one, she woos the man she loves rather than waiting for him to woo her. He also reveled in the play's storytelling, fun, poetry, drama, and prose. However, he criticized other aspects of *As You Like It*, as he did much of Shakespeare's work, railing against Shakespeare's attempt to be a "social philosopher."

Critics in the nineteenth century also saw Celia's character in new ways. Jameson described Celia as giving in to Rosalind rather than being eclipsed by her and as being as sweet, kind, intelligent, and almost as witty as Rosalind. Charles Cowden Clarke described Celia's love at first sight as "managed with Shakespeare's masterly skill" and wrote that Celia's goodness not only makes her a fine person but also inspires Oliver to become worthy of her.

1809—August Wilhelm Schlegel.
"Criticisms on Shakspeare's Comedies," from *Lectures on Dramatic Art and Literature*

August Wilhelm Schlegel was a scholar, critic, poet, and professor at the University of Bonn. He translated a number of Shakespeare's plays

into the German language and was one of the most influential dissemi-
nators of the ideas of the German Romantic movement.

It would be difficult to bring the contents (of *As You Like It*) within the compass
of an ordinary narrative; nothing takes place, or rather what is done is not so
essential as what is said; even what may be called the *denouement* is brought
about pretty arbitrarily. Whoever can perceive nothing but what can as it were
be counted on the fingers, will hardly be disposed to allow that it has any plan
at all. Banishment and flight have assembled together, in the forest of Arden, a
strange band: a Duke dethroned by his brother, who, with the faithful companions
of his misfortune, lives in the wilds on the produce of the chase; two disguised
Princesses, who love each other with a sisterly affection; a witty court fool; lastly,
the native inhabitants of the forest, ideal and natural shepherds and shepherdesses.
These light-sketched figures form a motley and diversified train; we see always the
shady dark-green landscape in the background, and breathe in imagination the
fresh air of the forest. The hours are here measured by no clocks, no regulated
recurrence of duty or of toil: they flow on unnumbered by voluntary occupation
or fanciful idleness, to which, according to his humour or disposition, every one
yields himself, and this unrestrained freedom compensates them all for the lost
conveniences of life. One throws himself down in solitary meditation under a tree,
and indulges in melancholy reflections on the changes of fortune, the falsehood
of the world, and the self-inflicted torments of social life; others make the woods
resound with social and festive songs, to the accompaniment of their hunting-
horns. Selfishness, envy, and ambition, have been left behind in the city; of all the
human passions, love alone has found an entrance into this wilderness, where it
dictates the same language alike to the simple shepherd and the chivalrous youth,
who hangs his love-ditty to a tree. A prudish shepherdess falls at first sight in
love with Rosalind, disguised in men's apparel; the latter sharply reproaches her
with her severity to her poor lover, and the pain of refusal, which she feels from
experience in her own case, disposes her at length to compassion and requital. The
fool carries his philosophical contempt of external show, and his raillery of the
illusion of love so far, that he purposely seeks out the ugliest and simplest country
wench for a mistress. Throughout the whole picture, it seems to be the poet's
design to show that to call forth the poetry which has its indwelling in nature and
the human mind, nothing is wanted but to throw off all artificial constraint, and
restore both to mind and nature their original liberty. In the very progress of the
piece, the dreamy carelessness of such an existence is sensibly expressed: it is even
alluded to by Shakspeare in the title. Whoever affects to be displeased, if in this
romantic forest the ceremonial of dramatic art is not duly observed, and ought
in justice to be delivered over to the wise fool, to be led gently out of it to some
prosaical region.

1817—William Hazlitt. *"As You Like It,"* from *Characters of Shakespear's Plays*

William Hazlitt (1778–1830) was an English essayist and one of the finest Shakespeare critics of the nineteenth century. He also examined the work of poets, dramatists, essayists, and novelists of his own and earlier times. His essays appeared in such volumes as *English Poets, English Comic Writers*, and *A View of the English Stage*.

Shakespear has here converted the forest of Arden into another Arcadia, where they "fleet the time carelessly, as they did in the golden world." It is the most ideal of any of this author's plays. It is a pastoral drama, in which the interest arises more out of the sentiments and characters than out of the actions or situations. It is not what is done, but what is said, that claims our attention. Nursed in solitude, "under the shade of melancholy boughs," the imagination grows soft and delicate, and the wit runs riot in idleness, like a spoiled child, that is never sent to school. Caprice and fancy reign and revel here, and stern necessity is banished to the court. The mild sentiments of humanity are strengthened with thought and leisure; the echo of the cares and noise of the world strikes upon the ear of those "who have felt them knowingly," softened by time and distance. "They hear the tumult, and are still." The very air of the place seems to breathe a spirit of philosophical poetry: to stir the thoughts, to touch the heart with pity, as the drowsy forest rustles to the sighing gale. Never was there such beautiful moralising, equally free from pedantry or petulance.

> And this their life, exempt from public haunts,
> Finds tongues in trees, books in the running brooks,
> Sermons in stones, and good in every thing.

Jaques is the only purely contemplative character in Shakespear. He thinks, and does nothing. His whole occupation is to amuse his mind, and he is totally regardless of his body and his fortunes. He is the prince of philosophical idlers; his only passion is thought; he sets no value upon any thing but as it serves as food for reflection. He can "suck melancholy out of a song, as a weasel sucks eggs"; the motley fool, "who morals on the time," is the greatest prize he meets with in the forest. He resents Orlando's passion for Rosalind as some disparagement of his own passion for abstract truth; and leaves the Duke, as soon as he is restored to his sovereignty, to seek his brother out who has quitted it, and turned hermit.

> Out of these convertites
> There is much matter to be heard and learnt.

Within the sequestered and romantic glades of the forest of Arden, they find leisure to be good and wise, or to play the fool and fall in love. Rosalind's character is made up of sportive gaiety and natural tenderness: her tongue runs the faster to conceal the pressure at her heart. She talks herself out of breath, only to get deeper in love. The coquetry with which she plays with her lover in the double character which she has to support is managed with the nicest address. How full of voluble, laughing grace is all her conversation with Orlando—

In heedless mazes running
With wanton haste and giddy cunning.

How full of real fondness and pretended cruelty is her answer to him when he promises to love her "For ever and a day!"

Rosalind: Say a day without the ever: no, no, Orlando, men are
April when they woo, December when they wed: maids are May
when they are maids, but the sky changes when they are wives: I will
be more jealous of thee than a Barbary cock-pigeon over his hen; more
clamorous than a parrot against rain; more new-fangled than an ape;
more giddy in my desires than a monkey; I will weep for nothing like
Diana in the fountain, and I will do that when you are disposed to be
merry; I will laugh like a hyen, and that when you are inclined
to sleep.
Orlando: But will my Rosalind do so?
Rosalind: By my life she will do as I do.

The silent and retired character of Celia is a necessary relief to the provoking loquacity of Rosalind, nor can anything be better conceived or more beautifully described than the mutual affection between the two cousins:

We still have slept together,
Rose at an instant, learn'd, play'd, eat together,
And wheresoe'r we went, like Juno's swans,
Still we went coupled and inseparable.

The unrequited love of Silvius for Phebe shews the perversity of this passion in the commonest scenes of life, and the rubs and stops which nature throws in its way, where fortune has placed none. Touchstone is not in love, but he will have a mistress as a subject for the exercise of his grotesque humour, and to shew his contempt for the passion, by his indifference about the person. He is a rare fellow. He is a mixture of the ancient cynic philosopher with the modern buffoon, and turns folly into wit, and wit into folly, just as the fit takes him. His courtship of Audrey not only throws a degree of ridicule on the state of wedlock itself, but he is equally an enemy to the prejudices of opinion in other respects. The lofty tone of enthusiasm, which the Duke and his companions in exile spread over the stillness and solitude of a country life, receives a pleasant shock from Touchstone's sceptical determination of the question.

> *Corin:* And how like you this shepherd's life, Mr. Touchstone?
> *Clown:* Truly, shepherd, in respect of itself, it is a good life; but in respect that it is a shepherd's life, it is naught. In respect that it is solitary, I like it very well; but in respect that it is private, it is a very vile life. Now in respect it is in the fields, it pleaseth me well; but in respect it is not in the court, it is tedious. As it is a spare life, look you, it fits my humour; but as there is no more plenty in it, it goes much against my stomach.

Zimmerman's celebrated work on Solitude discovers only *half* the sense of this passage.

There is hardly any of Shakespear's plays that contains a greater number of passages that have been quoted in books of extracts, or a greater number of phrases that have become in a manner proverbial. If we were to give all the striking passages, we should give half the play. . . .

━◆◆◆━　━◆◆◆━　━◆◆◆━

1833—Anna Jameson. "Rosalind," from *Characteristics of Women: Moral, Poetical, & Historical*

Anna Murphy Brownell Jameson (1794–1860), born in Dublin, is best remembered for her character studies of Shakespeare's heroines.

Rosalind

. . . Though Rosalind is a princess, she is a princess of Arcady; and notwithstanding the charming effect produced by her first scenes, we scarcely ever think of her with a reference to them, or associate her with a court, and the artificial appendages of her rank. She was not made to "lord it o'er a fair mansion," and take state upon her like the all-accomplished Portia; but to breathe the free air of heaven, and frolic among green leaves.

Though sprightliness is the distinguishing characteristic of Rosalind, as of Beatrice, yet we find her much more nearly allied to Portia in temper and intellect. The tone of her mind is, like Portia's, genial and buoyant: she has something too of her softness and sentiment; there is the same confiding abandonment of self in her affections; but the characters are otherwise as distinct as the situations are dissimilar. The age, the manners, the circumstance in which Shakespeare has placed his Portia, are not beyond the bounds of probability; nay, have a certain reality and locality. But Rosalind is surrounded with the purely ideal and imaginative; the reality is in the characters and in the sentiments, not in the circumstances or situation. While Portia is splendid and romantic, Rosalind is pastoral and picturesque.

Rosalind is like a compound of essences, so volatile in their nature, and so exquisitely blended, that on any attempt to analyze them, they seem to escape us. To what else shall we compare her, all enchanting as she is?—to the silvery summer clouds which, even while we gaze on them, shift their hues and forms, dissolving into air, and light, and rainbow showers?—to the May-morning, flush with opening blossoms and roseate dews, and "charm of earliest birds"?—to some wild and beautiful melody, such as some shepherd-boy might "pipe to Amaryllis in the shade"?—to a mountain streamlet, now smooth as a mirror in which the skies may glass themselves, and anon leaping and sparkling in the sunshine—or rather to the very sunshine itself? for so her genial spirit touches into life and beauty whatever it shines on.

Everything about Rosalind breathes of "youth and youth's sweet prime." She is fresh as the morning, sweet as the dew-awakened blossoms, and light as the breeze that plays among them. She is as witty, as voluble, as sprightly as Beatrice; but in a style altogether distinct. In both, the wit is equally unconscious; but in Beatrice it plays about us like the lightning, dazzling but also alarming; while the wit of Rosalind bubbles up and sparkles like the living fountain, refreshing all around. Her volubility is like the bird's song; it is the outpouring of a heart filled to overflowing with life, love, and joy, and all sweet and affectionate impulses. She has as much tenderness as mirth, and in her most petulant raillery there is a touch of softness—"By this hand it will not hurt a fly!" As her vivacity never lessens our impression of her sensibility, so she wears her masculine attire without the slightest impugnment of her delicacy—Rosalind has in truth "no doublet and hose in her disposition." How her heart seems to throb and flutter under her page's vest! What depth of love in her passion for Orlando! whether disguised beneath a saucy playfulness, or breaking forth with a fond impatience, or half betrayed in that beautiful scene where she faints at the sight of the 'kerchief stained with his blood! Here her recovery of her self-possession—her fears lest she should have revealed her sex—her presence of mind, and quick-witted excuse—

"I pray you, tell your brother how well I counterfeited"—

and the characteristic playfulness which seems to return so naturally with her recovered senses,—are all as amusing as consistent. Then how beautifully is the dialogue managed between herself and Orlando! how well she assumes the airs of a saucy page, without throwing off her feminine sweetness! How her wit flutters free as air over every subject! With what a careless grace, yet with what exquisite propriety!

"For innocence hath a privilege in her
To dignify arch jests and laughing eyes."

And if the freedom of some of the expressions used by Rosalind or Beatrice be objected to, let it be remembered that this was not the fault of Shakespeare or the women, but generally of the age.

The impression left upon our hearts and minds by the character of Rosalind is like a delicious strain of music. There is a depth of delight, and a subtlety of words to express that delight, which is enchanting. Yet when we call to mind particular speeches and passages, we find that they have a relative beauty and propriety, which renders it difficult to separate them from the context without injuring their effect. She says some of the most charming things in the world, and some of the most humorous; but we apply them as phrases rather than as maxims, and remember them rather for their pointed felicity of expression and fanciful application, than for their general truth and depth of meaning.

Rosalind has not the impressive eloquence of Portia, nor the sweet wisdom of Isabella. Her longest speeches are not her best; nor is her taunting address to Phebe, beautiful and celebrated as it is, equal to Phebe's own description of her. The latter, indeed, is more in earnest.

. . .

Celia

Celia is more quiet and retired: but she rather yields to Rosalind than is eclipsed by her. She is as full of sweetness, kindness, and intelligence, quite as susceptible, and almost as witty, though she makes less display of wit. She is described as less fair and less gifted; yet the attempt to excite in her mind a jealousy of her lovelier friend by placing them in comparison—

"Thou art a fool; she robs thee of thy name;
And thou wilt show more bright, and seem more virtuous,
When she is gone"—

fails to awaken in the generous heart of Celia any other feeling than an increased tenderness and sympathy for her cousin. To Celia, Shakespeare has given some of the most striking and animated parts of the dialogue; and in particular, that exquisite description of the friendship between her and Rosalind—

> "If she be a traitor,
> Why, so am I; we have slept together,
> Rose at an instant, learn'd, play'd, eat together,
> And wheresoe'er we went, like Juno's swans,
> Still we were coupled and inseparable."

The feeling of interest and admiration thus excited for Celia at the first follows her through the whole play. We listen to her as to one who has made herself worthy of our love; and her silence expresses more than eloquence. . . .

Phebe

Phebe is quite an Arcadian coquette; she is a piece of pastoral poetry. Audrey is only rustic. A very amusing effect is produced by the contrast between the frank and free bearing of the two princesses in disguise, and the scornful airs of the real shepherdess. In the speeches of Phebe, and in the dialogue between her and Silvius, Shakespeare has anticipated all the beauties of the Italian pastoral. We find two among the most poetical passages of the play appropriated to Phebe: the taunting speech of Silvius, and the description of Rosalind in her page's costume.

1839—Hermann Ulrici. *"As You Like It,"* from *Shakspeare's Dramatic Art*

Hermann Ulrici (1806–1884) was a German scholar, professor of philosophy at the University of Halle, and author of works on Greek poetry and Shakespeare. He wrote books that severely criticized Hegel's ideas and later explored the relationship of philosophy to science.

As You Like It

This charming comedy is also one of the mixed species, but with a decided preponderance of the fanciful element. Even a summary estimate of the contents of the piece will, I think, prove this most clearly.

We have two royal dukes, one of whom has unlawfully (we are not told how) driven the other from the throne; the exiled Duke has thereupon fled into the Forest of Arden where, with his followers, he leads a free and fantastic sort of life; two other aristocratic brothers, the elder of whom so persecutes the younger that he seeks refuge with the exiled Duke in the Forest of Arden; two princesses, the daughters of the two dukes, deeply attached to one another, one of whom is exiled and is accompanied by the other, likewise wend their way to the Forest; two fools, a merry one and a melancholy one; and lastly shepherds and shepherdesses described according to an idealised view of nature—such are the principal characters of the play. Their graceful groupings and the contrast in which they stand to one another enliven the romantic wildernesses of the Forest, and their various situations, relations and characters determine all that takes place in the play. Taken singly nothing that happens is actually contrary to nature, there are no extraordinary or unusual beings or phenomena; taken singly every character, every situation and action might belong to ordinary reality. It is only the introduction of lions and serpents into the mountainous scenery of Europe which gives us a gentle intimation that we are standing upon the ideal soil of poetic fancy. And still more emphatically is this expressed in the development and the composition—the style and the tone, the spirit and the character of the piece in general, and in the position and relation of the individual parts in particular—in short, in the totality of the circumstances and situations, actions and events. We are clearly given to understand that the drama is not a picture of common experience, but that it conceives life from a peculiarly poetical point of view, and that it is intended to exhibit a fantastic reflex of life in the mirror of caprice and humour. For if we consider the whole somewhat more closely, we shall at once have to admit that such things as the play presents, do not and could not happen in actual experience; that such a romantic mode of life in the loneliness of a forest is but a poetical dream; that, in fact, real life cannot be carried on or treated in the manner in which it is by almost all the persons represented; that the good Duke, Orlando, Rosalind, Celia, Jaques and Touchstone, are figures which the realistic mind would call oddities, enthusiasts, romancists; that, in reality, a character like the unrighteous Duke would not readily be converted by a recluse hermit, or a man like Oliver de Boys be wholly changed by a single magnanimous action on the part of his persecuted brother.[1]

It may, therefore, be asked wherein, amid this apparent unreality, lies the poetical truth of the piece? And which is the internal bond that gathers together all the confused and strangely involved threads, forming them into one harmonious whole? We must bear in mind that it is the comic view of life which here forms the basis of the drama, and accordingly that the truth of human life is not represented directly, but by means of contrast, that is, by accident, caprice and waywardness paralysing one another, and by the true agent of human life—the eternal order of things—being brought vividly into view. This becomes clearly evident when we consider how the unrighteous caprice (whatever may have been its motive), which suddenly drove the good old Duke into exile, as suddenly reverts against itself, destroying its own work and restoring what it had wrongfully appropriated; how, in like manner, by a similar change of sentiment, the right relation between the two brothers de Bois is also brought about; how the love between Orlando and Rosalind, between Celia and Oliver—which arose suddenly by the concurrence of circumstances—attains its object by an equally sudden change of circumstances and relations; and lastly, how the coyness of the shepherdess Phoebe is overcome much in the same way, and she is in the end united to her faithful, good-natured simpleton of a lover.

Thus the general comic view of life is reflected throughout the whole play, and forms the foundation and platform upon which the action moves. If, however, it be now asked what is the special standpoint from which the poet has here taken his view of life, or—what is the same thing—where is the central point of unity which gives the play its peculiar stamp, we shall again find that the title furnishes us with some clue. For the title is so striking, so original, so completely without any reference to the action represented, as such, that we have to declare it to be, either utterly senseless and meaningless, or assign to it a concealed reference to the internal significance and to the ideal meaning of the whole.[2] Like the similar title of 'What You Will,' it has been referred to the relation between the play and the public (A.W. von Schlegel), and has been so interpreted as to convey the meaning that the piece was intended to present itself to the spectators in any form they pleased. But this, in fact, as already pointed out, is not and cannot be the case. On the other hand, it is perhaps possible (as Tieck thinks) that the title alludes to a passage in Ben Jonson's 'Cinthia's Revels,' and to the interspersed sallies it contains against the easy and apparently irregular and arbitrary compositions of Shakspeare and the earlier School. But the allusion does not exactly hold good, for the only words in B. Jonson's comedy that can be meant are 'If you like it,' whereas the heading to Shakspeare's play is 'As you like it,' and thus even Tieck's interpretation: 'If you like it, then it is a comedy, that is, a comedy *par excellence*,' is rendered meaningless. The same applies to the equally far-fetched reference to the words: 'If you like it, so, and yet I will be yours in dutie, if you be mine in favours,' in the Preface to Lodge's pastoral and chivalrous romance,[3] from which Shakspeare drew the subject of this play? Shakspeare perhaps intended by means of the title to smile at the vain endeavours of his opponents to bring his fanciful comedies (which certainly differed very widely from Ben Jonson's) into discredit; but even the circumstance of his changing the *If* into *As* proves that he would not have chosen the title, had it not borne within itself some independent significance, some reference to the meaning and spirit of the play itself. Such a reference, I think, it is not difficult to find upon a more careful examination. In the first place it is evident that 'As You Like It,' both in style and character, stands in close affinity to 'What You Will.' The difference in reality is only that in the latter case the element of intrigue plays a prominent part while it is wholly wanting in the first case. The motives which in the present case set the whole in motion are merely chance, the unintentional encounter of persons and incidents, and the freaks, caprices and humours, the sentiments, feelings and emotions to which the various personages recklessly give way in what they do and leave undone. Nowhere does the representation treat of conscious plans, definite resolves, decided aims and objects; nowhere do we find preconsidered, or, in fact, deeper motives proceeding from the inmost nature of the characters. The characters themselves—even though clearly and correctly delineated—are generally drawn in light, hurried outlines—but are full of life, gay and bold in action, and quick in decision; they appear, as already said, either inconstant, variable, going from one extreme to the other, or possess such a vast amount of imagination, sensitiveness and love for what is romantic and adventurous, that their conduct to a prosaic mind can only appear thoughtless, capricious and arbitrary, and such a mind would be inclined to declare them all fools, oddities and fantastic creatures (in the same way as Sir Oliver Martext in the play itself, iii. 3, calls the whole company in the forest 'fantastical knaves'). And, in fact, all do exactly what and as they please; each gives him or herself up, in unbridled wilfulness, to good or evil, according to his or her own whims, moods or impulses whatever the consequences may prove to be. Each looks upon, and turns and shapes life as it pleases him or herself. The Forest of Arden is their stage, and with its fresh and free atmosphere, its mysterious chiaroscuro, its idyllic scenery for huntsmen and shepherds, is, at the same time, the fitting scene for the realisation of a mode and conception of life such as is here described. It is a life such as not only must please the dramatic personages themselves, but would please every one, were such a life only possible; it is the poetical reflex of a life *as you like it*, light and smooth in its flow, unencumbered by serious tasks, free from the fetter of definite objects, and from intentions difficult to realise; an amusing play of caprice, of imagination, and of wavering sensations and feelings. A life like this, however, is possible only in the Forest of Arden, in the midst of similar scenery, under similar circumstances and conditions, and with similar companions and surroundings. At court, in more complicated relations, in a state of impure feelings and selfish endeavours, it would lose its poetical halo, its innocence and gaiety, and become untruth, hypocrisy, injustice and violence, as is proved by the reigning Duke, his courtiers and Oliver de Bois. The point of the piece seems to me to lie in this contrast; but care had to be taken not to make the point too pointed, not to make it a serious moral conflict. If Shakspeare wished to give the play a humorous character, the gay appearance of 'as you like it,' he could not solve the contrast except by allowing selfish injustice and violent arbitrariness to become untrue to themselves, and to turn into their opposites—of course, in perfect accordance with the plan, the meaning and spirit of the whole, but nevertheless entirely without motives. This, at the same time, unravels the other complications into which the play of accident and caprice and their own 'as we like it,' have involved the dramatic personages, and the piece closes in perfect harmony inasmuch as what is right and rational is everywhere happily brought about. Thus the dominion, and the very ground hitherto held by accident and caprice, excessive imagination and adventurous romance, is entirely withdrawn from them.[4]

Shakspeare's intention—that is, the sense in which he conceived Lodge's narrative and transformed it into a drama—which, as I think, is clearly enough manifested in the spirit and character of the whole, as well as reflected in the several parts, is concentrated, and, so to say, condensed in the second and more personal contrast in which the two fools of the piece stand to one another. They and the unimportant figure of the shepherdess whom Touchstone chooses as his sweetheart, are the only persons whom Shakspeare did not find in Lodge's narrative, but freely invented. This addition, however, is in so far of great importance as it alone gives the original subject-matter a different character and colouring, and, so to say, forms the ideal norm, which determines the other alterations introduced by Shakspeare. The two fools, by virtue of the contrast in which they stand to each other, mutually complete each other. The melancholy Jaques is not the fool by profession, he appears rather to be simply a comic character *par excellence*; but his meditative superficiality, his witty sentimentality, his merry sadness have taken so complete a hold of his nature, that it seems to contradict itself, and therefore upon a closer examination distinctly bears the impress of folly, although it certainly is an original kind of folly. The contradiction into which he has fallen, he involuntarily and unconsciously carries about with him, for it is rooted in his very life and character. Of good birth and education, and not without the taste for what is good and noble, but easily led, weak, wanting in independence, and a slave to his easily-excited feelings, he had in his day been a profligate, who in indulging his caprices, desires and passions, had drained the enjoyments of life to the very dregs. And because he found no lasting satisfaction in them, he has withdrawn himself from the world—not having strength or inclination to conceive life from its other and right side—but continues to cherish and foster his inclinations, caprices and humours; these, however, have now taken the form of sentimental melancholy, and express themselves more in speeches full of black views of life, than in actions. This melancholy, this contempt of life and men, this sentimental slander and slanderous sentimentality not only please and amuse himself, but he carries them ostentatiously about, and has found a fitting soil for them in the company around the good Duke. In reality he only acts the melancholy misanthrope, the world-despising hermit, he is himself unconscious of the part he is playing, is not conscious that he is wearing a mere mask behind which lie concealed his old love of life, his old caprices, inclinations and sympathies. His observations therefore are in most cases certainly meditative and profound, and he fancies that on their wings he will be able to rise far above the sphere of ordinary mortals; but he is not aware that this meditation when carefully examined is after all very superficial in its contradictory one-sidedness. His effeminate sentimentality he considers to be genuine, deep feeling, and yet it is not only full of witty points, but, so to say, the bow from which he shoots forth the arrows of his scorn and slander. His melancholy does not call forth tears of sorrow but of joy, and these cause more merriment than the most exuberant frolic, not only to others but in reality to himself also. While the other characters in the foreground look upon life more or less in the light of a gay and festive game of humour and of frolic, he apparently regards it as a sombre funeral procession, where every mourner, in tears and lamentations, is advancing towards his own grave. However, while in the case of the other personages, the merriment of the play bears within itself a hidden seriousness, in his case, on the contrary, the solemn funeral procession changes insensibly into a merry procession of fools. Thus he is always his own counterpart, and at the same time always the very thing which he attacks and combats. In a word, he is exactly like the fool by profession, the personification of capriciousness, as well as of the love of wit and ridicule, except that he unconsciously and involuntarily wears a cloak of melancholy and sentimentality. Hence his honest admiration of the real, acknowledged fool, and his wish to be able himself to play the part of the privileged fool.

The fool whom Jaques so envies, who is his counterpart and mental kinsman, is the merry clown Touchstone. He is a genuine old English clown— in the Shakspearian form—such as we have already met with in 'What You Will'; a fool with the jingling cap and bells, one who is and wishes to be a fool; the same personification of caprice and ridicule, and with the same keen perception of the faults and failings of mankind as Jaques, but a fool with his own knowledge and consent, and not merely passive but active also. He speaks, acts and directs his whole life in accordance with the capricious folly and foolish capriciousness which he considers to be the principles of human existence. While therefore the other lovers are in pursuit of their high ideals of beauty, amiability and virtue, and yet do not in reality attain anything beyond the common human standard, he takes to himself quite an ordinary, silly, ugly, peasant girl; he loves her, in fact, just because she pleases him, and she pleases him just because he loves her. This is the obstinacy of love in its full force, as conceived by Shakspeare in his comedies. And yet this capriciousness which apparently ridicules itself, at the same time, contains a significant trait in which he exhibits his inmost nature, a trait of what is simple, natural, and common to all men, in contrast to what is exaggerated and unnatural, and to all that which is sentimental, eccentric and fantastic—a genuine human trait which, however, he had hitherto been unable to show. While, further, all the other characters have chosen the secluded free life of the Forest of Arden on account of their outward circumstances or inward impulse, in short, with good reason or free will, he alone has gone there without any occasion or reason whatever; he has even done so against his own inclination as the good cheer at court suited him far better; in other words he has done so deliberately in the actual sense of the word. And yet it is just in this that he again, under the mask of folly, shows a trait of genuine human nature, noble unselfishness and fidelity. Lastly, while all the other characters appear more or less like the unconscious play-balls of their own caprices and whims, feelings and impulses, he proves himself to be the one that makes game both of himself and of all the others; by this very means, however, he shows his true independence and freedom. And inasmuch as he consciously and intentionally makes himself a fool and gives free reins to his caprices, freaks and humours, he, at least, shows that he possesses the first necessary elements of true freedom, the consciousness of, and sovereignty over himself. He the professed Fool may frankly be declared the most rational person of the whole curious company, for he alone invariably knows his own mind; in regarding everything as sheer folly, he, at the same time takes it up in the humour in which it is meant to be understood. Accordingly, in Touchstone (who, as it were, personifies the humour which pervades the whole), we find all the perversities and contradictions of a life and mode of life *as you like it* reflected in a concave mirror; but this exterior, at the same time, conceals the poetic truth of the reverse side of the whole. Therefore we find a striking contrast to him in Sir Oliver Martext, the very embodiment of common prose, who will not suffer anything to lead him from his own teat, but in doing this thoroughly perverts the teat of true living reality, the ideal, poetical substance of the book of life.

The other characters also are conceived, arranged and grouped in as significant a manner, in as pure a harmony, and in as vivid a contrast. In 'Twelfth Night' Viola was the heroine, here we have Rosalinde. In comedies, Shakspeare is especially fond of assigning the principal parts to the female sex. Thus in 'The Winter's Tale,' 'Love's Labour Lost,' 'All's Well That Ends Well,' 'The Merchant of Venice,' and in 'Much Ado About Nothing,' etc. Woman, with her natural tendency to intrigue and equally great capriciousness, thoughtlessness, and inconsistency is, in fact, particularly suited to be the bearer of the comic action according to his idea of comedy. In the case of Rosalinde, Shakspeare has made the dangerous attempt of embodying humour—the comic in its capriciousness or fancifulness—in the form of a *woman*, or rather, which is still more venturesome, in that of a *girl*. Rosalinde possesses all the qualities with which we became acquainted in Viola, except that her nature is freer, gayer, and more frank. It is only at times that mischievous ideas come into Viola's head, otherwise she is absorbed in dreamy, serious and melancholy thoughts. Rosalinde, on the other hand, is absolute mischief, absolute caprice, and exuberance of spirits; she even makes fantastic game of her serious love for Orlando. Her playfulness, however, is not like that of a well-bred princess, but the innate grace and *naïveté* of a free child of nature, whose very freedom gives her noble and beautiful nature all the charms of genuine good-breeding. She possesses as little practical cleverness as Viola, and in this respect is inferior to Portia, because described more as a girl than the latter, who, although unmarried, and presented to us in the full bloom of youth, can be imagined only as a mature and complete woman in contrast to the budding girl Rosalinde. However, she is less in need of such cleverness, because, owing to her bold frankness, her gaiety and *naïveté*, she is not easily embarrassed and would not readily enter into any complicate business where cleverness and practical intelligence were required. For in spite of her brilliant, inexhaustible wit, she nevertheless does not possess a spark of that knowledge of the world which is able to grapple with the affairs of common life. Her wit and her judgment are rooted wholly in the poetical soil of a rich imagination, and in a delicate, pure state of feeling out of which her whole being has, so to say, sprung forth. When severed from this soil, her nature becomes withered and stunted like a tender flower that has been taken from its native earth and transplanted into a foreign land. At her uncle's court, Rosalinde appears inclined to be melancholy; for her nature, in spite of the fulness of the natural truth of her womanly heart, is, in regard to mind, so ethereal, so romantically poetic, so genially eccentric that the rude breath of prosaic reality could not but destroy its loveliest blossoms. On this very account it would be useless to endeavour, in a detailed delineation, to point out the several delicate outlines with which Shakspeare's masterly skill and genial hand has sketched the charming picture. I fear that even the few gentle allusions I have already given may have rather damaged than benefited the picture which the reader's own imagination had formed.

The same may be said of the other characters; their fundamental traits—the noble frankness and candour, and the imperishable force of a good disposition as exhibited in Orlando—the pure feeling for humanity, the greatness of mind and goodness of heart, in the amiable, jovial old Duke, whom misfortune has made but the nobler, the happier, and the more cheerful—the simple, touching fidelity of Adam—the self-sacrificing, heartfelt friendship of Celia—in short, all, in spite of their strangeness, thoughtlessness, and perversity, reflect so much of what is beautiful in humanity, and are so clearly brought forward, that a closer analysis would only destroy the delicate, poetical fragrance with which the whole is imbued. It must, however, be obvious to every reader that the characters are all conceived and worked out entirely in keeping with the meaning of *as you like it*, which, indeed, is the fundamental theme of the whole. The fantastic capriciousness which shows itself either as the inner motive or the outward impulse to their resolves and actions, rules the best and noblest, as well as the worst and lowest characters in the most manifold modifications. This is clearly evident from the course of the *action*. The arbitrary, unlawful dethronement of the good Duke forms the basis of the plot, the unreasonable persecution of Orlando by his brother—which is founded on a completely indefinite and undefinable cause of hate—his whim to fight the king's wrestler, likewise, the equally unreasonable banishment of Rosalinde—whom her uncle had long tolerated at his court, and suddenly drives into exile without any cause—are the first and chief motives of its advance. In the Forest of Arden all then abandon themselves to the most unrestrained and most diversified play of caprice and fancy. The play proceeds in this way till the wicked brother and the unlawful Duke are brought to see their transgressions and are converted, and Rosalinde throws aside her disguise. Thus even the mainsprings of the action are in perfect accordance with the meaning and spirit of the play. All the various parts form one perfect harmony, round which play the most graceful melodies; all is so delicate and ingenious, so free, so fresh and gay, so full of bantering humour and genial exuberance of spirits, that everyone who possesses the sense and understanding for the poetical chord here struck, must acknowledge this comedy as deserving the first prize; those who do not possess these requisites for its appreciation will pass it by with indifference or wholly misunderstand it.

Most critics assign the play to the year 1600. That it did not appear till after 1598 is certain, not only from the fact that Meres does not mention it in the often-quoted passage in his *Palladis Tamia*, but also from a line occurring in the play itself (act iii. s. 5.) taken from Marlowe's 'Hero and Leander,' which did not appear in print till 1598. Edm. Capell's supposition that 'As You Like It' belongs to the year 1605, is an arbitrary one, and is proved untenable by the fact that the play is entered at Stationers' Hall as early as August 4th, 1600.[5] The edition which he supposes to have existed, may have actually appeared, but it has been wholly lost. Probably, however, obstacles were placed in the way of its being printed—perhaps by Shakspeare's own theatrical company, which would testify to the unusually great popularity of the piece. It presumably did not appear in print till in the folio of 1623.

NOTES

1. Gervinus, *Shakespeare Commentaries*, finds both cases quite natural and in accordance with the characters. But even though internal motives and inducements might be imagined for such changes, still they are not given in the piece itself, not even intimated in the faintest manner; the change of sentiment takes place suddenly without either preparation or development. Therefore, if we take the two characters, not in the sense in which Gervinus conceives them, but as Shakspeare presents them to us, they appear inconstant, changeable, and slaves to their caprices and inclinations.

2. Gervinus decides in favour of the first alternative, because the title does not suit his conception and interpretation of the drama, so that either his conception

or the title must be meaningless. But why Shakspeare—quite contrary to his usual habit, and contrary to the theatrical custom of the day (which was fond of a very elaborate title, describing the contents of the piece)—should be supposed to give just this play (which Gervinus thinks preaches a serious moral) a completely senseless and unmeaning title, when, in fact, he did not readily pen an unmeaningless word, and why he should be supposed to stick such at the head of one of his plays, is to my mind perfectly unintelligible.

3. *Rosalynde: Euphues' Golden Legacy, etc., 1590*, re-issued in 1592 and 1598, and again recently reprinted in Collier's *Shakespeare's Library*, vol. i.

4. Gervinus, in his moralising tendency burdens even this light creation of Shakspeare's humour (which, as it were, itself plays with its deeply-hidden meaning) with a highly important and dull moral. According to him it is self-control, equanimity, and calmness in external suffering and internal passion, the value of which has to be set forth. But it is impossible to discuss such subjects with him, for in fact he is naturally wanting in all sense for what is humorous, fantastic, and romantic. Shakspeare is dear to him only because he finds his works to contain a solid, historico-political moral, such as he (justly) delights in. But, however right he may be in this, he nevertheless overlooks the fact that Shakspeare is a poet as well, and that consequently he delights in what is poetical even in the form of what is humorous, fantastic and romantic. This, in my opinion, is so clearly evident in *As You Like It*, that there is no necessity to give any special refutation of Gervinus' opinion.

5. In the case of this entry which includes two others of Shakspeare's pieces, *Henry V.* and *Much Ado About Nothing*, the year is indeed not specified, but obviously only because the writer wished to spare himself the trouble of repeating the date which was given at the head of the preceding entry.

—◁◊▷— —◁◊▷— —◁◊▷—

1856—William Maginn. "Jaques," from *Shakespeare Papers*

William Maginn was an Irish writer. In 1830 he became one of the leading supporters of Hugh Fraser's *Fraser's Magazine*, for which he wrote literary sketches, satires, and parodies in both verse and prose, as well as translations.

As he passed through the fields, and saw the animals around him—"Ye," said he, "are happy, and need not envy me that walk thus among you burthened with myself; nor do I, ye gentle beings, envy your felicity, for it is not the felicity of man. I have many distresses from which ye are free; I fear pain when I do not feel it; I sometimes shrink at evils recollected, and sometimes start at evils anticipated. Surely the equity of Providence has balanced peculiar sufferings with peculiar enjoyments."

With observations like these the prince amused himself as he returned, uttering them with a plaintive voice, yet with a look that discovered him to feel some complacence in his own perspicacity, and to receive some solace of the miseries of life from a consciousness of the delicacy with which he felt, and the eloquence with which he bewailed them."

—*Rasselas,* Chap. II.

This remark of Dr. Johnson on the consolation derived by his hero from the eloquence with which he gave vent to his complaints is perfectly just, but just only in such cases as those of Rasselas. The misery that can be expressed in flowing periods can not be of more importance than that experienced by the Abyssinian prince enclosed in the Happy Valley. His greatest calamity was no more than that he could not leave a place in which all the luxuries of life were at his command, but, as old Chremes says in the *Heautontimorumenos,*

> Miserum? quem minus credere 'st?
> Quid reliqui 'st, quin habeat, quae quidem in homine
> dicuntur bona?
> Parentes, patriam incolumem, amicos, genu', cognatos, divitias:
> Atque hae perinde sunt ut illius animus qui ea possidet;
> Qui uti scit, ei bona; illi, qui non utitur rectè, mala.[1]

On which, as

> Plain truth, dear Bentley, needs no arts of speech,

I can not do better than transcribe the commentary of Hickie, or some other grave expositor from whose pages he has transferred it to his own: "'Tis certain that the real enjoyment arising from external advantages depends wholly upon the situation of the mind of him who possesses them; for if he chance to labor under any secret anguish, this destroys all relish; or, if he know not how to use them for valuable purposes, they are so far from being of any service to him, that they often turn to real misfortunes." It is of no consequence that this profound reflection is nothing to the purpose in the place where it appears, because Chremes is not talking of any secret anguish, but of the use or abuse made of advantages according to the disposition of the individual to whom they have been accorded; and the anguish of Clinia was by no means secret. He feared the perpetual displeasure of his father, and knew not whether absence might not have diminished or alienated the affections of the lady on whose account he had abandoned home and country; but the general proposition of the sentence can not be denied. A "fatal remembrance"—to borrow a phrase from one of the most beautiful of Moore's melodies—may render a life, apparently abounding in prosperity, wretched and unhappy, as the vitiation of a single humor of the eye casts a sickly and unnatural hue over the gladsome meadow, or turns to a lurid light the brilliancy of the sunniest skies.

Rasselas and Jaques have no secret anguish to torment them, no real cares to disturb the even current of their tempers. To get rid of the prince first:— His sorrow is no more than that of the starling in the *Sentimental Journey*. He can not get out. He is discontented, because he has not the patience of Wordsworth's nuns, who fret not in their narrow cells; or of Wordsworth's muse, which murmurs not at being cribbed and confined to a sonnet. He wants the philosophy of that most admirable of all jail-ditties—and will not reflect that

> Every island is a prison,
> Close surrounded by the sea;
> Kings and princes, for that reason,
> Prisoners are as well as we.

And as his calamity is, after all, very tolerable—as many a sore heart or a wearied mind, buffeting about amid the billows and breakers of the external world, would feel but too happy to exchange conditions with him in his safe haven of rest—it is no wonder that the weaving of the sonorous sentences of easily-soothed sorrow should be the extent of the mental afflictions of Rasselas, Prince of Abyssinia.

Who or what Jaques was before he makes his appearance in the forest, Shakespeare does not inform us—any farther than that he had been a *roué* of considerable note, as the Duke tells him when he proposes to

> Cleanse the foul body of the infected world,
> If they will patiently receive my medicine.
> *Duke:* Fie on thee! I can tell what thou wouldst do.
> *Jaques:* What, for a counter, would I do but good?
> *Duke:* Most mischievous foul sin, in chiding sin;
> For thou thyself hast been a libertine
> As sensual as the brutish sting itself;
> And all the embossed sores and headed evils
> That thou with license of free foot hast caught,
> Wouldst thou disgorge into the general world.

This, and that he was one of the three or four loving lords who put themselves into voluntary exile with the old Duke, leaving their lands and revenues to enrich the new one, who therefore gave them good leave to wander, is all we know about him, until he is formally announced to us as the melancholy Jaques. The very announcement is a tolerable proof that he is not soul-stricken in any material degree. When Rosalind tells him that he is considered to be a melancholy fellow, he is hard put to it to describe in what his melancholy consists. "I have," he says:

> Neither the scholar's melancholy, which is emulation; nor the
> musician's, which is fantastical; nor the courtier's, which is proud;
> nor the soldier's, which is ambitious; nor the lawyer's, which is
> politic; nor the lady's, which is nice; nor the lover's, which is all
> these: but it is a melancholy of mine own, compounded of many
> simples, extracted from many objects, and indeed the sundry
> contemplation of my travels, in which my often rumination wraps
> me in a most humorous sadness.[2]

He is nothing more than an idle gentleman given to musing, and making invectives against the affairs of the world, which are more remarkable for the poetry of their style and expression than the pungency of their satire. His famous description of the seven ages of man is that of a man who has seen but little to complain of in his career through life. The sorrows of his infant are of the slightest kind, and he notes that it is taken care of in a nurse's lap. The griefs of his schoolboy are confined to the necessity of going to school; and he, too, has had an anxious hand to attend to him. His shining morning face reflects the superintendence of one—probably a mother—interested in his welfare. The lover is tortured by no piercing pangs of love, his woes evaporating themselves musically in a ballad of his own composition, written not to his mistress, but fantastically addressed to her eyebrow. The soldier appears in all the pride and the swelling hopes of his spirit-stirring trade,

> Jealous in honor, sudden and quick in quarrel,
> Seeking the bubble reputation
> Even in the cannon's mouth.

The fair round belly of the justice lined with good capon lets us know how he has passed in life. He is full of ease, magisterial authority, and squirely dignity. The lean and slippered pantaloon, and the dotard sunk into second childishness, have suffered only the common lot of humanity, without any of the calamities that embitter the unavoidable malady of old age.[3] All the characters in Jaques's sketch are well taken care of. The infant is nursed; the boy educated; the youth tormented with no greater cares than the necessity of hunting after rhymes to please the ear of a lady, whose love sits so lightly upon him as to set him upon nothing more serious than such a self-amusing task; the man in prime of life is engaged in gallant deeds, brave in action, anxious for character, and ambitious of fame; the man in declining years has won the due honors of his rank, he enjoys the luxuries of the table and dispenses the terrors of the bench; the man of age still more advanced is well to do in the world. If his shank be shrunk, it is not without hose and slipper—if his eyes be dim, they are spectacled—if his years have made him lean, they have gathered for him wherewithal to fatten the pouch by his side. And when this strange eventful history is closed by the penalties paid by men who live too long, Jaques does not tell us that the helpless being,

> Sans teeth, sans eyes, sans taste, sans everything,
> is left unprotected in his helplessness.

Such pictures of life do not proceed from a man very heavy at heart. Nor can it be without design that they are introduced into this especial place. The moment before, the famished Orlando has burst in upon the sylvan meal of the Duke, brandishing a naked sword, demanding with furious threat food for himself and his helpless companion,

> Oppressed with two weak evils, age and hunger.

The Duke, struck with his earnest appeal, can not refrain from comparing the real suffering which he witnesses in Orlando with that which is endured by himself and his co-mates, and partners in exile. Addressing Jaques, he says:

> Thou seest we are not all alone unhappy:
> This wide and universal theatre
> Presents more woful pageants than the scene
> Wherein we play in.[4]

But the spectacle and the comment upon it lightly touch Jaques, and he starts off at once into a witty and poetic comparison of the real drama of the world with the mimic drama of the stage, in which, with the sight of well-nurtured youth driven to the savage desperation of periling his own life, and assailing that of others—and of weakly old age lying down in the feeble but equally resolved desperation of dying by the wayside, driven to this extremity by sore fatigue and hunger— he diverts himself and his audience, whether in the forest or theatre, on the stage or in the closet, with graphic descriptions of human life; not one of them, proceeding as they do from the lips of the *melancholy* Jaques, presenting a single point on which true melancholy can dwell. Mourning over what can not be avoided must be in its essence common-place: and nothing has been added to the lamentations over the ills brought by the flight of years since Moses, the man of God,[5] declared the concluding period of protracted life to be a period of labor and sorrow; since Solomon, or whoever else writes under the name of the Preacher, in a passage which, whether it is inspired or not, is a passage of exquisite beauty, warned us to provide in youth, "while the evil days come not, nor the years draw nigh when thou shalt say, I have no pleasure in them; while the sun, or the light, or the moon, or the stars be not darkened, nor the clouds return after the rain: in the day when the keepers of the house shall tremble, and the strong men shall bow themselves, and the grinders cease because they are few, and those that look out of the windows be darkened, and the doors shall be shut in the streets, when the sound of the grinding is low, and he shall rise up at the voice of the bird, and all the daughters of music shall be brought low; also when they shall be afraid of that which is high, and fears shall be in the way, and the almond-tree shall flourish, and the grasshopper shall be a burthen, and desire shall fail: because man goeth to his long home, and the mourners go about the streets: or ever the silver cord be loosed, or the golden bowl be broken, or the pitcher be broken at the fountain, or the wheel broken at the cistern;" or, to make a shorter quotation, since Homer summed up all these ills by applying to old age the epithet of *lygros*—a word which can not be translated, but the force of which must be felt. Abate these unavoidable misfortunes, and the catalogue of Jaques is that of happy conditions. In his visions there is no trace of the child doomed to wretchedness before its very birth; no hint that such a thing could occur as its being made an object of calculation, one part medical, three parts financial, to the starveling surgeon, whether by the floating of the lungs, or other test equally fallacious and fee-producing, the miserable mother may be convicted of doing that which, before she had attempted, all that is her soul of woman must have been torn from its uttermost roots, when in an agony of shame and dread the child that was to have made her forget her labor was committed to the cesspool. No hint that the days of infancy should be devoted to the damnation of a factory, or to the tender mercies of a parish beadle. No hint that philosophy should come forward armed with the panoply offensive and defensive of logic and eloquence, to prove that the inversion of all natural relations was just and wise—that the toil of childhood was due to the support of manhood—that those hours, the very labors of which even the etymologists give to recreation, should be devoted to those wretched drudgeries which seem to split the heart of all but those who derive from them blood-stained money, or blood-bedabbled applause. Jaques sees not Greensmith squeezing his children by the throat until they die. He hears not the supplication of the hapless boy begging his still more hapless father for a moment's respite, ere the fatal handkerchief is twisted round his throat by the hand of him to whom he owed his being. Jaques thinks not of the baby deserted on the step of the inhospitable door, of the shame of the mother, of the disgrace of the parents, of the misery of the forsaken infant. His boy is at school, his soldier in the breach, his elder on the justice-seat. Are these the woes of life? Is there no neglected creature left to himself or to the worse nurture of others, whose trade it is to corrupt—who will teach him what was taught to swaggering Jack Chance, found on Newgate steps, and educated at the venerable seminary of St. Giles's Pound, where

> They taught him to drink, and to thieve, and fight,
> And everything else but to read and write.

Is there no stripling short of commons, but abundant in the supply of the strap or the cudgel?—no man fighting through the world in fortuneless struggles, and occupied by cares or oppressed by wants more stringent than those of love?—or in love itself does the current of that bitter passion never run less smooth than when sonnets to a lady's eyebrow are the prime objects of solicitude?—or may not even he who began with such sonneteering have found something more serious and sad, something more heart-throbbing and soul-rending, in the progress of his passion? Is the soldier melancholy in the storm and whirlwind of war? Is the gallant confronting of the cannon a matter to be complained of? The dolorous flight, the trampled battalion, the broken squadron, the lost battle, the lingering wound, the ill-furnished hospital, the unfed blockade, hunger and thirst, and pain, and fatigue, and mutilation, and cold, and rout, and scorn, and slight—services neglected, unworthy claims preferred, life wasted, or honor tarnished—are all passed by! In peaceful life we have no deeper misfortune placed before us than that it is not unusual that a justice of peace may be prosy in remark and trite in illustration. Are there no other evils to assail us through the agony of life? And when the conclusion comes, how far less tragic is the portraiture of mental imbecility, if considered as a state of misery than as one of comparative happiness, as escaping a still worse lot! Crabbe is sadder far than Jaques, when, after his appalling description of the inmates of a workhouse—(what would Crabbe have written *now?*)—he winds up by showing to us amid its victims two persons as being

> *happier* far than they,
> The moping idiot, and the madman gay.

If what he here sums up as the result of his life's observations on mankind be all that calls forth the melancholy of the witty and eloquent speaker he had not much to complain of. Mr. Shandy lamenting in sweetly-modulated periods, because his son has been christened Tristram instead of Trismegistus, is as much an object of condolence. Jaques has just seen the aspect of famine, and heard the words of despair; the Duke has pointed out to him the consideration that more woful and practical calamities exist than even the exile of princes and the downfall of lords; and he breaks off into a light strain of satire, fit only for jesting comedy. Trim might have rebuked him as he rebuked the prostrate Mr. Shandy, by reminding him that there are other things to make us melancholy in the world: and nobody knew it better, or could say it better, than he in whose brain was minted the hysteric passion of Lear choked by his button—the farewell of victorious Othello to all the pomp, pride, and circumstance of glorious war—the tears of Richard over the submission of roan Barbary to Bolingbroke—the demand of Romeo that the Mantuan druggist should supply him with such soon-speeding gear that will rid him of hated life

> As violently as hasty powder fired
> Doth hurry from the fatal cannon's womb

—the desolation of Antony—the mourning of Henry over sire slain by son, and son by sire—or the despair of Macbeth. I say nothing of the griefs of Constance, or Isabel, or Desdemona, or Juliet, or Ophelia, because in the sketches of Jaques he passes by all allusion to women; a fact which of itself is sufficient to prove that his melancholy was but in play—was nothing more than what Arthur remembered when he was in France, where

> Young gentlemen would be as sad as night,
> Only for wantonness.

Shakespeare well knew that there is no true pathetic, nothing that can permanently lacerate the heart, and embitter the speech, unless a woman be concerned. It is the legacy left us by Eve. The tenor of man's woe, says Milton, with a most ungallant and grisly pun, is still from *wo*-man to begin; and he who will give himself a few moments to reflect will find that the stern trigamist is right. On this, however, I shall not dilate. I may perhaps have something to say, as we go on, of the ladies of Shakespeare. For the present purpose, it is enough to remark with Trim, that there are many real griefs to make a man lie down and cry, without troubling ourselves with those which are put forward by the poetic mourner in the forest of Arden.

Different indeed is the sight set before the eyes of Adam in the great poem just referred to, when he is told to look upon the miseries which the fall of man has entailed upon his descendants. Far other than the scenes that flit across this melancholy man by profession are those evoked by Michael in the visionary lazar-house. It would be ill-befitting, indeed, that the merry note of the sweet bird warbling freely in the glade should be marred by discordant sounds of woe, cataloguing the dreary list of disease,

> All maladies
> Of ghastly spasm, or racking torture, qualms
> Of heartsick agony, all feverous kinds,
> Convulsions, epilepsies, fierce catarrhs,
> Intestine stone and ulcer, colic pangs,
> Demoniac frenzy, moping melancholy,
> Marasmus, and wide-wasting pestilence,
> Dropsies, and asthmas, and joint-racking rheums;

while, amid the dire tossing and deep groans of the sufferers,

> Despair
> Tended the sick, busiest from couch to couch;
> And over them triumphant Death his dart
> Shook, but delayed to strike.

And equally ill-befitting would be any serious allusion to those passions and feelings which in their violence or their anguish render the human bosom a lazar-house filled with maladies of the mind as racking and as wasting as those of the body, and call forth a supplication for the releasing blow of Death as the final hope, with an earnestness as desperate, and cry as loud as ever arose from the tenement, sad, noisome, and dark, which holds the joint-racked victims of physical disease. Such themes should not sadden the festive banquet in the forest. The Duke and his co-mates and partners in exile, reconciled to their present mode of life ["I would not change it," says Amiens, speaking, we may suppose, the sentiments of all], and successful in having plucked the precious jewel, Content, from the head of ugly and venomous Adversity, are ready to bestow their woodland fare upon real suffering, but in no mood to listen to the heart-rending descriptions of sorrows graver than those which form a theme for the discourses which Jaques in mimic melancholy contributes to their amusement.

Shakespeare designed him to be a maker of fine sentences—a dresser forth in sweet language of the ordinary common-places or the common-place mishaps of mankind, and he takes care to show us that he did not intend him for anything beside. With what admirable art he is confronted with Touchstone. He enters merrily laughing at the pointless philosophizing of the fool in the forest. His lungs crow like chanticleer when he hears him moralizing over his dial, and making the deep discovery that ten o'clock has succeeded nine, and will be followed by eleven. When Touchstone himself appears, we do not find in his own discourse any touches of such deep contemplation. He is shrewd, sharp, worldly, witty, keen, gibing, observant. It is plain that he has been mocking Jaques; and, as is usual, the mocked thinks himself the mocker. If one has moralized the spectacle of a wounded deer into a thousand similes, comparing his weeping into the stream to the conduct of worldlings in giving in their testaments the sum of more to that which had too much—his abandonment, to the parting of the flux of companions from misery—the sweeping by of the careless herd full of the pasture, to the desertion of the poor and broken bankrupt by the fat and greasy citizens—and so forth; if such have been the common-places of Jaques, are they not fitly matched by the common places of Touchstone upon his watch? It is as high a stretch of fancy that brings the reflection how

> from hour to hour we ripe and ripe,
> And then from hour to hour we rot and rot,
> And thereby hangs a tale,

which is scoffed at by Jaques, as that which dictates his own moralizings on the death of the deer. The motley fool is as wise as the melancholy lord whom he is parodying. The shepherd Corin, who replies to the courtly quizzing of Touchstone by such apophthegms as that "it is the property of rain to wet, and of fire to burn," is unconsciously performing the same part of the clown, as *he* had been designedly performing to Jaques. Witty nonsense is answered by dull nonsense, as the emptiness of poetry had been answered by the emptiness of prose. There was nothing sincere in the lamentation over the wounded stag. It was only used as a peg on which to hang fine conceits. Had Falstaff seen the deer, his imagination would have called up visions of haunches and pastries, preluding an everlasting series of cups of sack among the revel riot of boon companions, and he would have instantly ordered its throat to be cut. If it had fallen in the way of Friar Lawrence, the mild-hearted man of herbs would have endeavored to extract the arrow, heal the wound, and let the hart ungalled go free. Neither would have thought the hairy fool a subject for reflections, which neither relieved the wants of man nor the pains of beast. Jaques complains of the injustice and cruelty of killing deer, but unscrupulously sits down to dine upon venison, and sorrows over the suffering of the native burghers of the forest city, without doing anything farther than amusing himself with rhetorical flourishes drawn from the contemplation of the pain which he witnesses with professional coolness and unconcern.

It is evident, in short, that the happiest days of his life are those which he is spending in the forest. His raking days are over, and he is tired of city dissipation. He has shaken hands with the world, finding, with Cowley, that "he and it would never agree." To use an expression somewhat vulgar, he has had his fun for his money; and he thinks the bargain so fair and conclusive on both sides, that he has no notion of opening another. His mind is relieved of a thousand anxieties which beset him in the court, and he breathes freely in the forest. The iron has not entered into his soul; nothing has occurred to chase sleep from his eyelids; and his fantastic reflections are, as he himself takes care to tell us, but general observations on the ordinary and outward manners and feelings of mankind—a species of taxing which

> like a wild-goose flies,
> Unclaimed of any man.

Above all, in having abandoned station, and wealth, and country, to join the faithful few who have in evil report clung manfully to their prince, he knows that he has played a noble and an honorable part; and they to whose lot it may have fallen to experience the happiness of having done a generous, disinterested, or self-denying action—or sacrificed temporary interests to undying principle—or shown to the world without, that what are thought to be its great advantages can be flung aside, or laid aside, when they come in collision with the feelings and passions of the world within—will be perfectly sure that Jaques, reft of land, and banished from court, felt himself exalted in his own eyes, and therefore easy of mind, whether he was mourning in melodious blank verse, or weaving jocular parodies on the canzonets of the good-humored Amiens.

He was happy "under the greenwood tree." Addison I believe it is who says, that all mankind have an instinctive love of country and woodland scenery, and he traces it to a sort of dim recollection imprinted upon us of our original haunt, the garden of Eden. It is at all events certain, that, from the days when the cedars of Lebanon supplied images to the great poets of Jerusalem, to that in which the tall tree haunted Wordsworth "as a passion," the forest has caught a strong hold of the poetic mind. It is with reluctance that I refrain from quoting; but the passages of surpassing beauty which crowd upon me from all times and languages are too numerous. I know not which to exclude, and I have not room for all; let me then take a bit of prose from one who never indulged in poetry, and I think I shall make it a case in point. In a little book called *Statistical Sketches of Upper Canada, for the use of Emigrants, by a Backwoodsman,* now lying before me, the author, after describing the field-sports in Canada with a precision and a *gout* to be derived only from practice and zeal, concludes a chapter, most appropriately introduced by a motto from the *Lady of the Lake*,

> Us merry, 'tis merry in good greenwood,
> When the mavis and merle are singing,
> When the deer sweep by, and the hounds are in cry,
> And the hunter's horn is ringing, by saying:

"It is only since writing the above that I fell in with the first volume of Moore's *Life of Lord Edward Fitzgerald;* and I can not describe the pleasure I received from reading his vivid, spirited, and accurate description of the feelings as he experienced on first taking on him the life of a hunter. At an earlier period of life than Lord Edward had then attained, I made my debut in the forest, and first assumed the blanket-cloak and the rifle, the moccasin and the snow-shoe; and the ecstatic feeling of Arab-like independence, and the utter contempt for the advantage and restrictions of civilization, which he describes, I then felt in its fullest power. And even now, when my way of life, like Macbeth's, is falling 'into the sere, the yellow leaf,' and when a tropical climate, privation, disease, and thankless toil, are combining with advancing years to unstring a frame the strength of which once set hunger, cold, and fatigue at defiance, and to undermine a constitution that once appeared iron-bound, still I can not lie down by a fire in the woods without the elevating feeling which I experienced formerly returning, though in a diminished degree. This must be human nature; for it is an undoubted fact, that no man who associates with and follows the pursuits of the Indian, for any length of time, ever voluntarily returns to civilized society.

"What a companion in the woods Lord Edward must have been! and how shocking to think that, with talents which would have made him at once the idol and the ornament of his profession, and affections which must have rendered him an object of adoration in all the relations of private life—with honor, with courage, with generosity, with every trait that can at once ennoble and endear— he should never have been taught that there is a higher principle of action than the mere impulse of the passions—that he should never have learned, before plunging his country into blood and disorder, to have weighed the means he possessed with the end he proposed, or the problematical good with the certain evil!—that he should have had Tom Paine for a tutor in religion and politics, and Tom Moore for a biographer, to hold up as a pattern, instead of warning, the errors and misfortunes of a being so noble—to subserve the revolutionary purposes of a faction, who, like Samson, are pulling down a fabric which will bury both them and their enemies under it."

Never mind the aberrations of Lord Edward Fitzgerald, the religion or the politics of Tom Paine, or the biography of Tom Moore. On all these matters I may hold my own opinions, but they are not wanted now; but have we not here the feelings of Jaques? Here are the gloomy expressions of general sorrow over climate, privation, disease, thankless toil, advancing years, unstrung frame. But here also we have ecstatic emotions of Arab-like independence, generous reflections upon political adversaries, and high-minded adherence to the views and principles which in his honor and conscience he believed to be in all circumstances inflexibly right, coming from the heart of a forest. The Backwoodsman is Dunlop; and is he, in spite of this sad-sounding passage, melancholy? Not he, in good sooth. The very next page to that which I have quoted is a description of the pleasant mode of travelling in Canada, before the march of improvement had made it comfortable and convenient.[6]

Jaques was just as woe-begone as the Tiger, and no more. I remember when he—Dunlop I mean, not Jaques—used to laugh at the phrenologists of Edinburgh for saying, after a careful admeasurement, that his skull in all points was exactly that of Shakespeare—I suppose he will be equally inclined to laugh when he finds who is the double an old companion has selected for him. But no matter. His melancholy passes away not more rapidly than that of Jaques; and I venture to say that the latter, if he were existing in flesh and blood, would have no scruple in joining the doctor this moment over the bowl of punch which I am sure he is brewing, has brewed, or is about to brew, on the banks of Huron or Ontario.

Whether he would or not, he departs from the stage with the grace and easy elegance of a gentleman in heart and manners. He joins his old antagonist the usurping Duke in his fallen fortunes; he had spurned him in his prosperity: his restored friend he bequeaths to his former honor, deserved by his patience and his virtue—he compliments Oliver on his restoration to his land, and love, and great allies—wishes Silvius joy of his long-sought and well-earned marriage—cracks upon Touchstone one of those good-humored jests to which men of the world on the eve of marriage must laughingly submit—and makes his bow. Some sage critics have discovered as a great geographical fault in Shakespeare, that he introduces the tropical lion and serpent into Arden, which, it appears, they have ascertained to lie in some temperate zone. I wish them joy of their sagacity. Monsters more wonderful are to be found in that forest; for never yet, since water ran and tall trees bloomed, were there gathered together such a company as those who compose the *dramatis personae* of As You *Like It*. All the prodigies spawned by Africa, *"leonum arida nutrix,"* might well have teemed in a forest, wherever situate, that was inhabited by such creatures as Rosalind, Touchstone, and Jaques.

NOTES

1. It may be thus attempted in something like the metre of the original, which the learned know by the sounding name of Tetrameter Iambic Acatalectic.

2. This is printed as prose, but assuredly it is blank verse. The alteration of a syllable or two, which in the corrupt state of the text of these plays is the slightest of all possible critical licenses, would make it run perfectly smooth. At all events, in the second line, "emulation" should be "emulative," to make it agree with the other clauses of the sentence. The courtier's melancholy is not *pride,* nor the soldier's *ambition,* &c. The adjective is used throughout— *fantastical, proud, ambitious, politic, nice.*

3. "Senectus ipsa est morbus."—Ter. *Phorm.* IV. i. 9.

4. Query *on?* "Wherein we play *in*" is tautological. "Wherein we play on," *i.e.* "continue to play."

5. Psalm xc. "A prayer of Moses, the man of God," v. 10.

6. "Formerly, that is to say, previous to the peace of 1815, a journey between Quebec and Sandwich was an undertaking considerably more tedious and troublesome than the voyage from London to Quebec. In the first place, the commissariat of the expedition had to be cared for; and to that end every gentleman who was liable to travel had, as a part of his appointments, a provision basket, which held generally a cold round of beef, tin plates and drinking-cups, tea, sugar, biscuits, and about a gallon of brandy. These, with your wardrobe and a camp-bed, were stowed away in a batteau, or flat-bottomed boat; and off you set with a crew of seven stout, light-hearted, jolly, lively Canadians, who sung their boat-songs all the time they could spare from smoking their pipes. You were accompanied by a fleet of similar boats, called a brigade, the crews of which assisted each other up the rapids, and at night put into some creek, bay, or uninhabited island, where fires were lighted, tents made of the sails, and the song, the laugh, and the shout, were heard, with little intermission, all the night through; and if you had the felicity to have among the party a fifer or a fiddler, the dance was sometimes kept up all night—for, if a Frenchman has a fiddle, sleep ceases to be a necessary of life with him. This mode of travelling was far from being unpleasant, for there was something of romance and adventure in it; and the scenes you witnessed, both by night and day, were picturesque in the highest degree. But it was tedious; for you were in great luck if you arrived at your journey's end in a month; and if the weather were boisterous, or the wind a-head, you might be an indefinite time longer.

"But your march of improvement is a sore destroyer of the romantic and picturesque. A gentleman about to take such a journey now-a-days, orders his servant to pack his portmanteau, and put it on board the John Molson, or any of his family; and at the stated hour he marches on board, the bell rings, the engine is put in motion, and away you go smoking, and splashing, and walloping along, at the rate of ten knots an hour, in the ugliest species of craft that ever disfigured a marine landscape."

1863—Charles Cowden Clarke. *"As You Like It,"* from *Shakespeare-Characters: Chiefly Those Subordinate*

Charles Cowden Clarke was a famous author and Shakespeare scholar. He published several books, including *Shakespeare's Characters* and *Molière's Characters*, and lectured for more than 20 years on Shakespeare and other literary subjects.

The whole of this 'love at first sight' on Celia's part is managed with Shakespeare's masterly skill. I have always felt those three little speeches to be profoundly true to individual nature, where the ladies are questioning Oliver respecting the incident of the lioness and the snake in the forest, and of Orlando's timely succour. Celia exclaims, in amazement, 'Are you his brother?' Rosalind says, 'Was it you he *rescued*?' And Celia rejoins, 'Was 't you that did so oft contrive to kill him?' Celia's first exclamation is surprised concern to find that this stranger, who interests her, is that unnatural brother of whom she had heard. Rosalind's thought is of her lover,—Orlando's *generosity* in rescuing one who has behaved so unnaturally towards himself; while Celia recurs to the difficulty she has in reconciling the image of one who has acted basely and cruelly with him she sees before her—who is speedily becoming to her the impersonation of all that is attractive, estimable, and lovable in man. Her affectionate nature cannot persuade itself to believe this villainy of him; she, therefore, incredulously reiterates, 'Was 't You that did so oft contrive to kill him?' And his reply is a beautiful evidence of the sweetness which beams transparent in her; since it already influences him, by effecting a confirmation of the virtuous resolves to which his brother's generosity has previously given rise, and by causing him to fall as suddenly in love with her as she with him. He says

> ''Twas I; but 'tis not I;—I do not shame
> To tell you what I was, since my conversion
> So sweetly tastes, being the thing I am.'

It is one of the refined beauties that distinguish Shakespeare's metaphysical philosophy, to show us how a fine nature acting upon an inferior one through the subtle agency of love, operates beneficially to elevate and purify. At one process it proclaims its own excellence, and works amelioration in another. Celia's charm of goodness wins the unkind brother of Orlando (Oliver) to a passionate admiration of herself, at the same time that it excites his emulation to become worthy of her. It begins by teaching him the bravery of a candid avowal of his crime,—the first step towards reformation. Celia's loving-kindness, like all true loving-kindness, hath this twofold virtue and grace: it no less benefits her friends than adorns herself.

⎯⎯ ⎯⎯ ⎯⎯

1884—Helena Faucit, Lady Martin. "Rosalind," from *Shakespeare's Female Characters*

Lady Martin's true name was Helena Faucit. She was a celebrated English actress whose most famous part was that of Rosalind.

When I resolved to make a thorough study of the play, I little thought how long, yet how fascinating a task I had imposed upon myself. With every fresh perusal new points of interest and of charm revealed themselves to me; while, as for Rosalind, "she drew me on to love her" with a warmth of feeling which can only be understood by the artist who has found in the heroine she impersonates that "something never to be wholly known," those suggestions of high qualities answerable to all the contingencies or trials of circumstance, by which we are captivated in real life and which it is her aim and her triumph to bring home to the hearts and imaginations of her audience as they have come home to her own. So it was I came to love Rosalind with my whole heart.

No word escapes from Rosalind's lips as we watch her there [in the last scene, after the entrance of Jaques de Boys], the woman in all her beauty and perfect grace, now calmly happy, beside a father restored to "a potent dukedom," and a lover whom she knows to be wholly worthy to wield that dukedom when in due season she will endow him with it as her husband. Happiest of women I for who else ever had such means of testing that love on which her own happiness depends? In all the days that are before her, all the largeness of heart, the rich imagination, the bright commanding intellect, which made her the presiding genius of the Forest of Arden, will work with no less beneficent sway in the larger sphere of princely duty. With what delight will she recur with her lover-husband to the strange accidents of fortune which "forced sweet love on pranks of saucy boyhood," and to the never-to-be-forgotten hours when he was a second time "o'erthrown" by the wit, the playful wiles, the inexplicable charm of the young Ganymede! How, too, in all the grave duties of the high position to which his alliance will raise him, will he not only possess in her an honoured and admired companion, but will also find wise guidance and support in her clear intelligence and courageous will! It is thus, at least, that I dream of my dear Rosalind and her Orlando.

1893—Richard G. Moulton. "How 'As You Like It' Presents Varied Forms of Humor in Conflict with a Single Conventionality," from *Shakespeare as a Dramatic Artist: A Popular Illustration of the Principles of Scientific Criticism*

Richard G. Moulton was a professor of English at the University of Chicago. He authored *The Moral System of Shakespeare* and *The Literary Study of the Bible*, among other titles.

Love's Labour's Lost is an early play. But in another drama, more complex in its general character, Shakespeare has again introduced the impact of humour upon affectation as a dominant motive. Between the two there is the difference we should expect. The earlier play we have seen resolve as a whole into the central idea, which gives significance to its every part; in *As You Like It* the conflict of humour with convention is only one motive amongst several. Moreover, the idea itself, which is common to the two plays, takes different form in each. In *Love's Labour's Lost* the humour is one and the same throughout, the artificialities with which it is in conflict are many. In *As You Like It*, on the other hand, there are three distinct types of humour: while, for the artificial element, we have that one great conventionality of poetry beside which all others may be called secondary.

I distinguish the *healthy* humour of Rosalind, the *professional* humour of Touchstone, and the *morbid* humour of Jaques. The fun, that plays like sunlit ripples about Rosalind and her friends, Celia and Orlando, there is no need to discuss; every reader drinks it in eagerly, and no one, I imagine, will object to the description of it as 'healthy.' I do not doubt that, as an individual, Touchstone is worthy to be added to this set: but the office he holds gives a different tone to his humour. In connection with another play it has been pointed out that the jester occupied, in the age of court officials, the same position which in this age of newspapers is held by *Punch*: both are national institutions for flashing a comic light on every passing topic. As a professional Fool, Touchstone has privileges: he may attack everything, and every sufferer must applaud his own castigation. But equally he has professional duties: he must use his folly as a stalking-horse under which to present wisdom, or, in other words, he must from time to time hint deep truths as well as keep up a continuous stream of vapid nonsense. The absence of spontaneity is the note which distinguishes this professional folly from natural wit such as Rosalind's. In the course of this play Touchstone has to draw fun on demand from such diverse topics as courtiers' oaths, travellers' complaints, the course of Time, the irregularities of Fortune, shepherd life, court life, music, versification, and his own intended wife—'a poor virgin, sir, an ill-favoured thing, sir, but mine own.' And, to fill up a moment of waiting, he is called upon to exercise his professional function at length, and extemporises a whole system of scientific quarrelling, through its degrees of Retort Courteous,

Quip Modest, Reply Churlish, Reproof Valiant, Countercheck Quarrelsome, Lie with Circumstance, up to the unpardonable Lie Direct.

Of Jaques humour is a prominent feature, no less than of Touchstone and Rosalind: but to determine this third type of humour is much more difficult. The whole character of Jaques is one not easy to define, and one which leaves the most strangely opposite impressions upon different readers. He is a general favourite with audiences in the theatre. Actors, so far as I have observed, seem to form an exalted opinion of him; and it must be difficult for them to do otherwise when they have to speak in his character the most famous of quotations that compares all the world to a stage. On the other hand, Jaques is certainly not a favourite with the personages in the story: he is least liked by the best of them, and the poet himself takes pains to except him from the happy ending which crowns the careers of the rest. The epithet 'philosophical' has stuck to Jaques, and there is good reason for it. We find him everywhere showing, not only seriousness of bent, but also that deep eye to the lessons of life underlying the outward appearances of things which is traditionally associated with wisdom. Yet in the scenes of the play his seriousness is not treated with much respect, and his wisdom by no means gives him the victory when he has to encounter much more unpretentious personages. Interpretation must find some view of him which will be consistent with all this; and we get a hint as to the direction in which we are to look for such a view in the play itself, where the Duke, in answer to Jaques' longing for the Fool's licence of universal satire, says that by such satire he would do—

Most mischievous foul sin, in chiding sin
For thou thyself hast been a libertine,
As sensual as the brutish sting itself;
And all the embossed sores and headed evils,
That thou with license of free foot hast caught,
Wouldst thou disgorge into the general world.

The hypothesis which will make the whole character clear, so far as it can be summed up in a single phrase, might be expressed as the morbid *humour of melancholy.*

Humour is the flower of healthy mental growth; it is mental exertion not for a practical purpose but for its own sake, arbitrary and delighting in its own arbitrariness; it is turned on everything good or bad, great or trivial (for to humour all things are humorous), drawing from everything its sparkling surprises and for ever catching unexpected novelties of aspect; it is an insight into the singularities that lie just below the surface of things, estimated more by their number and the quickness with which they present themselves than by weight and lasting worth; it is further in its sharpest strokes the outcome of the genial good-will which is the normal condition of a well-balanced mind. There is, however, a special Elizabethan view of humour, which emphasised one single element of it,—it was an *arbitrary* assumption of some mental attitude: 'tis my humour' is excuse sufficient for any perverse and unnatural mental condition that Ben Jonson's personages choose to indulge in. Amongst humours in this second sense one of the commonest is 'melancholy'; it was, we find, a specially English affectation, and so much a thing of fashion that in Ben Jonson's *Every Man in his Humour* Stephen practises it before his looking-glass, and in asides asks his mentors whether he is melancholy enough. Yet this fashion rests on a weakness of human nature, that is universal. At all times discontent has been affected as a sign of superiority; a chronic turned-up nose is to the superficial a suggestion of select taste. Every one is familiar with one form of such discontent,—the depreciation of home which travelling almost always produces in a shallow mind, and which is in the play itself alluded to as a characteristic of Jaques.

> Farewell, Monsieur Traveller; look you lisp and wear strange suits, disable all the benefits of your own country, be out of love with your nativity, and almost chide God for making you that countenance you are, or I will scarce think you have swam in a gondola.

Jaques has adopted this Elizabethan humour of melancholy. But more than this, his humour is totally opposed to all that is healthy, and has become morbid; natural emotions have been worn out by his course of dissipation, and discontent supplies their place; with the corruption of his soul his humour, so to speak, has gone bad, and while he retains all the analytic power and insight into unexpected singularities, yet his humour is no longer spontaneous but laboured, no longer genial, but flavoured with malevolence and self-exaltation.

Examined in detail, Jaques' character exhibits the paradox and perversity of view which belongs to humour, but these are gloomy instead of bright, and suggest laborious search, and not involuntary mind-play. He is 'compact of jars'; he can suck melancholy out of a song as a weasel sucks eggs; he speaks of sleeping and railing as of the two sides of his normal condition. We have the Duke throughout by his side as a healthy contrast. The Duke did not seek the artificial life of the forest, though when driven to it by the stubbornness of fortune he can translate it to a quiet and sweet style: Jaques is repelled by his comrades' life as soon as it turns fortunate, and voluntarily flies from dancing measures to get pleasure out of a dethroned convertite. So with regard to the dying stag: the Duke's pity is accidental, rising naturally out of surrounding circumstances—that the brute as a native burgher of the forest should be slaughtered in his own confines. Jaques pours out his pathos as an indulgence; to borrow a word from the vocabulary of funeral sermons, he 'improves' the stag's dying agonies (having first found a comfortable position from which he can watch them) with a thousand ingenious similes, and is so left by his companions weeping and commenting. Similar is Jaques' connection with the celebrated simile of the stage: the brilliant working out of this idea must not blind us to the morbid tone of mind of which it is the outcome. The Duke's reflection which gives rise to the speech is cheerful, inviting to resignation because others have to endure. His accidental use of dramatic imagery is seized upon by Jaques as an opportunity for harping on the hollowness of everything human; it is that *all the world* is no more than a stage, and the men and women *merely* players, which makes the attraction of the theme to Jaques' mind, and his ingenuity catches the lowest view of every phase of life—the mewling and puking infant, the sighing and woeful young man, he characterises a soldier as quick in quarrel, reputation as a bubble, he distinguishes the justice by his creature comforts, old age by its leanness and childish treble, until he reaches a congenial climax in 'sans everything.'

Yet that melancholy is not the real object of this apostle of melancholy some minor touches show. Amiens sings a song in praise of melancholy, Jaques at once turns it into ridicule, for to morbid humour its own pet affectation becomes objectionable when put forward by another. In fact he must have his melancholy to himself, as he is betrayed by Rosalind into avowing—

> I have neither the scholar's melancholy, which is emulation; nor the musician's, which is fantastical; nor the courtier's, which is proud; nor the soldier's, which is ambitious; nor the lawyer's, which is politic; nor the lady's, which is nice; nor the lover's, which is all these: but it is a melancholy of mine own, compounded of many simples, extracted from many objects, and indeed the sundry contemplation of my travels, in which my often rumination wraps me in a most humorous sadness.

It is thus egotism that is at the root of his morbid humour, which is no outcome of social life, but a constant attempt at self-exaltation by the mode of differing from others. He snubs modest excuses for a ragged voice, and compares compliments to the encounter of two dog-apes. He mocks again at 'burdens' and 'stanzos,' and similar technical terms: for your egotist both despises what everybody does as commonplace, and equally regards any distinctive peculiarity he does not share as silly pedantry. Similarly with Jaques' objection to the Duke as too 'disputable': the natural course for one who has information being to impart it, the morbid mind affects reserve; he 'thinks of as many things as others, but gives Heav'n thanks, and makes no boast'—making thus his powers one more difference between himself and his fellow-men. It must not however be supposed that there is no exception to this universal depreciation. Morbid egotism shows its exaltation above ordinary pleasures by a selection of its own, and by vehemence of admiration in proportion as admiration is unexpected. Not only is Jaques merry on hearing a melancholy song, but—like an aesthete with a sunflower—he is raised to a delirious ecstasy by meeting a professional Fool.

A fool, a fool! I met a fool i' the forest,
A motley fool; a miserable world!
As I do live by food, I met a fool.

As the Fool follows his profession of railing Jaques' lungs begin to crow like chanticleer, and he laughs sans intermission an hour by the dial.

It is abundantly clear that malevolence is the inspiration of Jaques' humour. His moralisings on the dying stag are, as the courtiers point out, 'invectively' conceived: he hits the landowners in his reflection on the stag weeping tears into the brook, giving his sum of more to that which has too much; the court come in for their share in the proverb of misery parting the flux of company, and the city when the herd is upbraided for forsaking the broken bankrupt. He envies the Fool's motley for the sake of the Fool's unfettered liberty of attack; and when the Duke points out how ill Jaques is qualified for the jester's office of good-natured censor, his answer shows that Jaques believes the world to be as bad as he wishes to paint it. If Rosalind's humour is a tribute to the delightful oddities of things in general, and Touchstone's humour is a tribute to his professional office, Jaques' morbid humour is a tribute only to himself.

Into these three contrasted types has the simple humour of *Love's Labour's Lost* been expanded. On the other hand, for the elaborate and varied artificialities of that play we have substituted one single conventionality which has maintained its ground in the world of imagination from Theocritus to Watteau—Pastoral Life. The traditional life of the old eclogues is lived again in the forest of Arden by the banished Duke and his followers: with no worse ill than Adam's penalty, the seasons' difference; with hunting of the stag for enterprise, and presentation of him who killed the deer for triumph; with feasts *al fresco*, and songs under the greenwood tree. The simplicity of bucolic life is sufficiently represented in William and Audrey; and, if pastoral lovers are wanted, Phoebe for the fair unkind, Silvius as the despairing lover, with Corin as the Old Shepherd to soothe him, are types that the Sicilian Muses could not surpass. To the end of time, I suppose, shepherd life will be the traditional form in which the more elementary moods of the quiet passions will be enshrined, and Shakespeare is paying his footing as a universal poet when he makes the middle acts of *As You Like It* a dramatised idyl.

Upon this accepted and most unmitigated conventionality the three founts of humour in the drama are continually playing. To draw out in detail the resulting effects would be to turn into dull prose half the play. Rosalind is pitted mainly against the pastoral lovers, and for the soft and sleepy tenderness of such love there can be no more wholesome tonic than the bright audacity and overwhelming flood of high spirits that belong to our heroine.

> What though you have no beauty,—
> As, by my faith, I see no more in you
> Than without candle may go dark to bed—
> Must you be therefore proud and pitiless!
> . . . . Od's my little life,
> I think she means to tangle my eyes too! . . .
> I pray you, do not fall in love with me,
> For I am falser than vows made in wine
> Besides, I like you not.

Moreover, Rosalind in disguise is a humorous situation embodied; and this applied to the hopeless suit of Silvius draws out for the spectators a lengthened irony which finds a happy climax in reconciled impossibilities.

Touchstone also has his fling at the pastoral lovers. When the unhappy Silvius paints the true idyllic passion—

> If thou remember'st not the slightest folly
> That ever love did make thee run into,
> Thou hast not loved—

the professional Fool seconds him with instances

> I remember, when I was in love I broke my sword upon a stone and
> bid him take that for coming a-night to Jane Smile; and I remember
> the kissing of her batlet and the cow's dugs that her pretty chopt
> hands had milked . . . We that are true lovers run into strange capers;
> but as all is mortal in nature, so is all nature in love mortal
> in folly.

> *Rosalind.* Thou speakest wiser than thou art ware of.
> *Touchstone.* Nay, I shall ne'er be ware of mine own wit till I break my
> shins against it.

But Touchstone's license roams more widely over all the denizens of the woodland. He woos the rustic Audrey with folly, with folly he frightens away his rival William; he plays a match with Corin of court folly against pastoral wit, and when this model Shepherd, getting the worse, falls back upon his dignity—

> Sir, I am a true labourer: I earn that I eat, get that I wear, owe no
> man hate, envy no man's happiness, glad of other men's good, content

with my harm, and the greatest of my pride is to see my ewes graze and
my lambs suck—

Touchstone swoops upon this idyllic picture with a demonstration in theology
that Corin's occupation is a simple sin involving him in a parlous state:

> If thou beest not damned for this, the devil himself will have no
> shepherds.

Finally the Fool gets an opportunity for one of his set discourses on this theme
of the pastoral life:

> Truly, shepherd, in respect of itself, it is a good life; but in respect
> that it is a shepherd's life, it is naught. In respect that it is solitary, I like
> it very well; but in respect that it is private, it is a very vile life. Now, in
> respect it is in the fields, it pleaseth me well; but in respect it is not in
> the court, it is tedious. As it is a spare life, look you, it fits my humour
> well; but as there is no more plenty in it, it goes much against my
> stomach.

If the conventionalities of pastoral poetry are to be taken literally, I do not
know that the merits of that phase of existence could be more profoundly
summed up.

As to the third type of humour, I have in describing it indicated sufficiently
how the morbid melancholy of Jaques is turned upon every element of the life
around him. But when, by expansion of the treatment in the earlier play, three
distinct humours have been brought to bear upon the conventional, a further
effect is still possible—the three humours can be brought into conflict with one
another.

Touchstone is the comrade and firm friend of Rosalind and her set, and if
he chaffs them, it belongs to his office, and they readily join in the game. But
when the folly is sprung upon them by surprise it is possible for them to be
disconcerted. Celia believes herself alone as she comes reading the lover's verses,
which endow her friend with the 'quintessence of every sprite'—

> Helen's cheek, but not her heart,
>   Cleopatra's majesty,
> Atalanta's better part,
>   Sad Lucretia's modesty.

Touchstone[1] startles her dreaming away—

> O most gentle pulpiter! what tedious homily of love have you wearied
> your parishioners withal, and never cried, 'Have patience, good people!'

Celia. How now! back, friends! Shepherd, go off a little. Go with him, sirrah.

Celia is clearly 'out' in this game of wit, for she has answered pettishly; Touchstone feels he has scored:

Come, shepherd, let us make an honourable retreat; though not with bag and baggage, yet with scrip and scrippage.

A precisely similar encounter takes place with Rosalind: but though surprised she rallies to the game, and puts the Fool himself out. She is indulging in the pastoral to her own praise—

From the east to western Ind
No jewel is like Rosalind.
Her worth, being mounted on the wind,
Through all the world bears Rosalind.
All the pictures fairest lined
Are but black to Rosalind.

The Fool breaks in, offering to rhyme her so for eight years together, dinners and suppers and sleeping-hours excepted: for such false gallop of verses is no more than the right butter-woman's rank to market.

If a hart do lack a hind,
Let him seek out Rosalind.
If the cat will after kind,
So be sure will Rosalind.
Winter garments must be lined,
So must slender Rosalind, &c.

Our heroine is disconcerted, but alert enough to exchange thrust and cut.

Rosalind. Peace, you dull fool! I found them on a tree.
Touchstone. Truly, the tree yields bad fruit.
Rosalind. I'll graff it with you, and then I shall graff it with a medlar: then it will be the earliest fruit i' the country; for you'll be rotten ere you be half ripe, and that's the right virtue of the medlar.

For once the professional jester is unable to come up to time, and he has no repartee ready.

Touchstone. You have said; but whether wisely or no, let the forest judge.

Similarly, although Jaques patronises Touchstone, takes the Fool for his model and his ambition, snubs other discourse in order to draw out his folly, and calls upon others to enjoy it, yet a conflict between the morbid and the professional humours is possible, when Touchstone descends so far from the dignity of his office as to contemplate the step of marrying. Jaques will assist his protégés's insane act by giving Audrey away, but must at all events sneer at the parson.

Will you, being a man of your breeding, be married under a bush like a beggar? . . . . this fellow will but join you together as they join wainscot; then one of you will prove a shrank panel, and, like green timber, warp, warp.

Touchstone is equal to a reply in his most professional style.

I am not in the mind but I were better to be married of him than of another: for he is not like to marry me well; and not being well married, it will be a good excuse for me hereafter to leave my wife.

Professional humour then has clashed with genuine, morbid with professional. The treatment is complete when the unhealthiness of humour in Jaques is accentuated by his being brought into contact with humour that is sound. When the man of melancholy crosses swords with the lover Orlando he does not come off victorious.

Jaques. God be wi' you: let's meet as little as we can.
Orlando. I do desire we may be better strangers.
Jaques. I pray you, mar no more trees with writing love-songs in their barks.
Orlando. I pray you, mar no more of my verses with reading them ill-favouredly.
Jaques. Rosalind is your love's name?
Orlando. Yes, just.
Jaques. I do not like her name.
Orlando. There was no thought of pleasing you when she was christened.
Jaques. What stature is she of?
Orlando. Just as high as my heart.
Jaques. You are full of pretty answers. Have you not been acquainted with goldsmiths' wives, and conned them out of rings?
Orlando. Not so; but I answer you right painted cloth, from whence you have studied your questions.

Jaques admires the nimble wit, and proposes to sit down and rail in duet against 'our mistress the world, and all our misery.' Orlando takes up the position—unintelligible to a being like Jaques—of caring to rail at none but himself, against whom he knows most faults. Jaques retires in disgust.

> *Jaques.* By my troth, I was seeking for a fool when I found you.
> *Orlando.* He is drowned in the brook: look but in, and you shall
> see him.
> *Jaques.* There I shall see mine own figure.
> *Orlando.* Which I take to be either a fool or a cipher.
> *Jaques.* I'll tarry no longer with you: farewell, good Signior Love.
> *Orlando.* I am glad of your departure: adieu, good Monsieur
> Melancholy.

But the supreme touch of delineation for morbid humour is given by the mere contact of Jaques with the essence of health and brightness in the disguised Rosalind. Like evil spirits compelled by the touch of Ithuriel's spear to show themselves in their true shapes, Jaques seems drawn on by Rosalind's presence to call attention to his peculiar qualities with almost infantile complacency:—how he loves melancholy more than laughing, and thinks it good to be sad and say nothing (like a post, Rosalind interjects), and how, in detail, his melancholy has been compounded out of the scholar, the musician, the courtier, and all others he has met on his travels. So far Rosalind seems to have been looking at him quietly, as a curiosity: in the last sentence she finds the clue to understanding him.

> *Rosalind.* A traveller! By my faith, you have great reason to be sad:
> I fear you have sold your own lands to see other men's; then, to have
> seen much and to have nothing, is to have rich eyes and poor hands.
> *Jaques.* Yes, I have gained my experience.
> *Rosalind.* And your experience makes you sad: I had rather have a
> fool to make me merry than experience to make me sad; and to travel
> for it too!

Jaques appears suddenly to wake up to the sort of impression he is making on the attractive youth, and he seizes the first opportunity for retreating in disgust, with the woman's last word following him down the glade.

NOTES

1. The editions give this speech to Rosalind (iii. ii. 163). But this is surely impossible. Not only is Celia's reproof addressed to Touchstone, and he in retiring treats it as such, but when he is gone Celia asks Rosalind, 'Didst thou hear

these verses?'—which would be absurd if Rosalind had spoken the words of satire on them.

—◦◦◦◦— —◦◦◦— —◦◦◦—

1894—A. Wilson Verity. *"As You Like It*: Critical Remarks," from *The Works of William Shakespeare*

A. Wilson Verity edited *The Best Plays of the Old Dramatists: Thomas Heywood.* He also edited the work of John Milton.

As You Like It is not one of Shakespeare's greatest plays; it is merely one of his most delightful works, delightful alike to reader and to critic, if only on account of its perfect simplicity of motive. We are out in the open air; we hear the wind rustling in the fragrant leaves of the fairy-land of Arden; and we are far too lazy and too genially contented to think of purposes, and leading ideas, and things philosophic. We take the play as it is, without peering beneath the surface for subtle significance, and never once does Touchstone's query rise to our lips—"hast my philosophy in thee?" only the most Teutonic of Teutons would look for a *tendenz* in this fantastic study of an impossible Arcadia, a pastoral Utopia which "never was on sea or land." For As You Like It is, I take it, from beginning to end, purely ideal; the characters, or some of them, we may possibly have met, but their life and environment exist only in the fine frenzy of the poet. And we need not wonder that it should be so, not at any rate if we remember when the play was written. It came immediately after the great historic trilogy. Shakespeare had sounded forth to all the world the silver note of patriotism, had carried men's minds back from a splendid present to an equally splendid and imperishable past, and made an incomparable appeal to the old and eternally fresh sentiment—*pro focis et aris*. And now he hangs up his arms in the temple of the goddess of war, and steeps himself in the freshness and fairness of a life where sorrow and sin are not, where truth is on every shepherd's tongue, where the time fleets by as it did in the golden days of Saturn where destiny herself deigns to smile, where the thought of each and all is—"Come live with me and be my love." Such the *mise-en-scène*, such the atmosphere of careless buoyancy, and with what art is the latter maintained throughout! True, we are told of "the uses of adversity." But Adversity here, as some one has said, is really a fourth Grace, less celebrated by the poets because so seldom seen, but none the less a true sister of the classic Three. She lays the lightest of chastening hands on her children, just revealing "the humorous sadness" of existence, and no more; she is not the pitiless goddess whose stoney glare chills and kills the gazer; she is in perfect harmony with the tone of a play in which no deep chord of passion is ever struck.

Of the characters who live and move in this fairy and fantastic world of romance, a world all touched with the tints of young desire and the purple light of love; it is difficult to speak; they are so familiar to us. Yet a word must be said; and first of Rosalind. She is wit and womanliness in equal proportions; and her womanliness is the spiritualized tenderness that Thackeray gives us. Hence the difficulty of rendering the part aright. It is so easy for an actress to sink the intellectual side of the character and emphasize merely the *abandon* and buoyancy which find vent in the forest scenes; it is so easy, too, to make those scenes a series of boisterous romps. Thus the last-century Rosalind appears to have been a touselled hoyden, for whom the part was pure comedy, and comedy of no very dignified type; and when Mrs. Siddons restored that element of intellectual refinement and sobriety which is essential to the character, the verdict of critics and public was: "cold, unemotional; we prefer Mrs. Jordan." Yet this swash-buckler Rosalind, forever reminding us of her hose and doublet, though too often, perhaps, the stage Rosalind, is emphatically not the Rosalind of Shakespeare. The latter is never a mere boy, a "moonish youth, longing and liking, proud, changeable, fantastic;" under the mask of careless abandonment to every passing freak of fancy she preserves gracious and intact her perfect womanliness and dignity; so that when at last the little comedy has played to its close, and the time comes for all disguise to be laid aside, she moves quite naturally into her new position as bride and princess. She was at home in the forest glade. She will be no less so at the court.

The contrast between Rosalind and Aliena is too obvious to require comment: who runs may read; Shakespeare in his earlier plays is fond of placing two characters in striking antithesis. Far more interesting, because less natural, is the distinction between Rosalind and Jaques. Each represents an aspect of wit: only Jaques' is the wit of the scoffer. He is intellectual and endowed with a keen capacity to feel; but he lacks moral soundness, and sensibility minus morality too often ends in cynicism. The cynicism of Jaques, partly conscious and exaggerated, partly unconscious and quasi-constitutional, is the cynicism of men like Heine. The duke, indeed, charges Jaques with having been a mere libertine, and Gervinus dismisses him as "a *blasé* man, an epicurean." But the duke was not a great judge of character—he was not great at anything except mild moralities—and perhaps the Heidelberg philosopher-critic went equally stray. I think we shall be much nearer the truth if we regard Jaques as typical of the emotional man who is offended by the incongruities and injustices of life, by the sight of evils which he cannot explain, and who, for lack of faith and firmness, takes refuge in what is the last resource of the witty and unwise, indiscriminate mocking. Rosalind has all the wit of Jaques, but she has something more, a something that keeps her intellect clear and trustful. Rosalind and Jaques—these are the central figures of the play, or rather those on which the poet has mainly expended the resources of his art. But throughout the characterization is fine. Orlando is simply the ideal lover; the dainty, delicate, imperious Phebe we have often met, now on a piece of Dresden china, now in a *fête champêtre* by Watteau; Touchstone is an elder brother of the clown in the Comedy of Errors and The Two Gentlemen, only his fooling has an uncomfortable amount of wisdom about it; and Audrey, Adam, William—these may have lived, and their counterparts be still living, not a hundred miles from Stratford.

It is a just criticism that Shakespeare is always "at the height of the particular situation;" that whatever he writes he writes, not merely well, but perfectly; that every dramatic style comes naturally to him. As You Like it admirably illustrates this maxim: from the first page to the last there is nothing, nothing at any rate of significance, to which we can point and say: "Were not this best away?"

1896—George Bernard Shaw. "Toujours Shakespeare," from *Dramatic Opinions and Essays with an Apology by Bernard Shaw*

George Bernard Shaw, one of the great dramatists of his time, was also known for his sometimes idiosyncratic criticism. Among his most famous plays are *Saint Joan*, *Pygmalion* (later adapted into the musical and film *My Fair Lady*), *Man and Superman*, and *Caesar and Cleopatra*.

As You Like It. St. James's Theatre, 2 December, 1898.

The irony of Fate prevails at the St. James's Theatre. For years we have been urging the managers to give us Shakespeare's plays as he wrote them, playing them intelligently and enjoyingly as pleasant stories, instead of mutilating them, altering them, and celebrating them as superstitious rites. After three hundred years Mr. George Alexander has taken us at our words, as far as the clock permits, and given us "As You Like It" at full four hours' length. And, alas! it is just too late: the Bard gets his chance at the moment when his obsolescence has become unendurable. Nevertheless, we were right; for this production of Mr. Alexander's, though the longest, is infinitely the least tedious, and, in those parts which depend on the management, the most delightful I have seen. But yet, what a play! It was in "As You Like It" that the sententious William first began to openly exploit the fondness of the British Public for sham moralizing and stage "philosophy." It contains one passage that specially exasperates me. Jaques, who spends his time, like Hamlet, in vainly emulating the wisdom of Sancho Panza, comes in laughing in a superior manner because he has met a fool in the forest, who

> "Says very wisely, It is ten o'clock.
> Thus we may see [quoth he] how the world wags.
> 'Tis but an hour ago since it was nine;
> And after one hour more, 't will be eleven.
> And so, from hour to hour, we ripe and ripe;
> And then, from hour to hour, we rot and rot;
> And thereby hangs a tale."

Now, considering that this fool's platitude is precisely the "philosophy" of Hamlet, Macbeth ("Tomorrow and to-morrow and to-morrow," &c.), Prospero, and the rest of them, there is something unendurably aggravating in Shakespeare giving himself airs with Touchstone, as if he, the immortal, ever, even at his sublimest, had anything different or better to say himself. Later on he misses a great chance. Nothing is more significant than the statement that "all the world's a stage." The whole world is ruled by theatrical illusion. Between the Caesars, the emperors, the Christian heroes, the Grand Old Men, the kings, prophets, saints, heroes and judges, of the newspapers and the popular imagination, and the actual Juliuses, Napoleons, Gordons, Gladstones, and so on, there is the same difference as between Hamlet and Sir Henry Irving. The case is not one of fanciful similitude, but of identity. The great critics are those who penetrate and understand the illusion: the great men are those who, as dramatists planning the development of nations, or as actors carrying out the drama, are behind the scenes of the world instead of gaping and gushing in the auditorium after paying their taxes at the doors. And yet Shakespeare, with the rarest opportunities of observing this, lets his pregnant metaphor slip, and, with his usual incapacity for pursuing any idea, wanders off into a grandmotherly Elizabethan edition of the advertisement of Cassell's "Popular Educator." How anybody over the age of seven can take any interest in a literary toy so silly in its conceit and common in its ideas as the Seven Ages of Man passes my understanding. Even the great metaphor itself is inaccurately expressed; for the world is a playhouse, not merely a stage; and Shakespeare might have said so without making his blank verse scan any worse than Richard's exclamation, "All the world to nothing!"

And then Touchstone, with his rare jests about the knight that swore by his honor they were good pancakes! Who would endure such humor from any one but Shakespeare?—an Eskimo would demand his money back if a modern author offered him such fare. And the comfortable old Duke, symbolical of the British villa dweller, who likes to find "sermons in stones and good in everything," and then to have a good dinner! This unvenerable impostor, expanding on his mixed diet of pious twaddle and venison, rouses my worst passions. Even when Shakespeare, in his efforts to be a social philosopher, does rise for an instant to the level of a sixth-rate Kingsley, his solemn self-complacency infuriates me. And yet, so wonderful is his art, that it is not easy to disentangle what is unbearable from what is irresistible. Orlando one moment says:

> "Whate'er you are
> That in this desert inaccessible
> Under the shade of melancholy boughs
> Lose and neglect the creeping hours of time,"

which, though it indicates a thoroughly unhealthy imagination, and would have been impossible to, for instance, Chaucer, is yet magically fine of its kind. The next moment he tacks on lines which would have revolted Mr. Pecksniff:

> "If ever you have looked on better days,
> If ever been where bells have knolled to church,
>   [*How perfectly the atmosphere of the rented pew
>   is caught in this incredible line!*]
> If ever sat at any good man's feast,
> If ever from your eyelids wiped—"

I really shall get sick if I quote any more of it. Was ever such canting, snivelling, hypocritical unctuousness exuded by an actor anxious to show that he was above his profession, and was a thoroughly respectable man in private life? Why cannot all this putrescence be cut out of the play, and only the vital parts—the genuine story-telling, the fun, the poetry, the drama, be retained? Simply because, if nothing were left of Shakespeare but his genius, our Shakespearolaters would miss all that they admire in him.

Notwithstanding these drawbacks, the fascination of "As You Like It" is still very great. It has the overwhelming advantage of being written for the most part in prose instead of in blank verse, which any fool can write. And such prose! The first scene alone, with its energy of exposition, each phrase driving its meaning and feeling in up to the head at one brief, sure stroke, is worth ten acts of the ordinary Elizabethan sing-song. It cannot be said that the blank verse is reserved for those passages which demand a loftier expression, since Le Beau and Corin drop into it, like Mr. Silas Wegg, on the most inadequate provocation; but at least there is not much of it. The popularity of Rosalind is due to three main causes. First, she only speaks blank verse for a few minutes. Second, she only wears a skirt for a few minutes (and the dismal effect of the change at the end to the wedding-dress ought to convert the stupidest champion of petticoats to rational dress).

Third, she makes love to the man instead of waiting for the man to make love to her—a piece of natural history which has kept Shakespeare's heroines alive, whilst generations of properly governessed young ladies, taught to say "No" three times at least, have miserably perished. . .

The production at this Christmas season could not be more timely. The children will find the virtue of Adam and the philosophy of Jaques just the thing for them; whilst their elders will be delighted by the pageantry and the wrestling.

<hr />

1898—Georg Brandes. "'As You Like It,'" from *William Shakespeare: A Critical Study*

Georg Brandes, an important Danish critic, wrote extensively on Shakespeare's plays.

<hr />

Never had Shakespeare produced with such rapidity and ease as in this bright and happy interval of two or three years. It is positively astounding to note all that he accomplished in the year 1600, when he stood, not exactly at the height of his poetical power, for that steadily increased, but at the height of his poetical serenity. Among the exquisite comedies he now writes, *As You Like It* is one of the most exquisite.

The play was entered in the Stationers' Register, along with *Much Ado About Nothing*, on the 4th of August 1600, and must in all probability have been written in that year. Meres does not mention it, in 1598, in his list of Shakespeare's plays; it contains a quotation from Marlowe's *Hero and Leander*, published in 1598—

"Who ever lov'd, that lov'd not at first sight?"

a quotation, by the way, which sums up the matter of the comedy; and we find in Celia's words (i. 2), "Since the little wit that fools have was silenced," an allusion to the public and judicial burning of satirical publications which took place on the 1st of June 1599. As there does not seem to be room in the year 1599 for more works than we have already assigned to it, *As You Like It* must be taken as dating from the first half of the following year.

As usual, Shakespeare took from another poet the whole material of this enchanting comedy. His contemporary, Thomas Lodge (who, after leaving Oxford, became first a player and playwright in London, then a lawyer, then a doctor and writer on medical subjects, until he died of the plague in the year 1625), had in 1590 published a pastoral romance, with many poems interspersed, entitled *Euphues golden Legacie, found after his death in his Cell at Silexedra*,[1] which he had written, as he sets forth in his Dedication to Lord Hunsdon, "to beguile the time" on a voyage to the Canary Islands. The style is laboured and exceedingly diffuse, a true pastoral style; but Lodge had that gift of mere external invention in which Shakespeare, with all his powers, was so deficient. All the different stories which the play contains or touches upon are found in Lodge, and likewise all the characters, with the exception of Jaques, Touchstone, and Audrey. Very remarkable to the attentive reader is Shakespeare's uniform passivity with regard to what he found in his sources, and his unwillingness to reject or alter anything, combined as it is with the most intense intellectual activity at the points upon which he concentrates his strength.

We find in *As You Like It*, as in Lodge, a wicked Duke who has expelled his virtuous brother, the lawful ruler, from his domains. The banished Duke, with his adherents, has taken refuge in the Forest of Arden, where they live as free a life as Robin Hood and his merry men, and where they are presently sought out by the Duke's daughter Rosalind and her cousin Celia, the daughter of the usurper, who will not let her banished friend wander forth alone. In the circle of nobility subordinate to the princes, there is also a wicked brother, Oliver, who seeks the life of his virtuous younger brother, Orlando, a hero as modest and amiable as he is brave. He and Rosalind fall in love with each other the moment they meet, and she makes sport with him throughout the play, disguised as a boy. These scenes should probably be acted as though he half recognised her. At last all ends happily. The wicked Duke most conveniently repents; the wicked brother is all of a sudden converted (quite without rhyme or reason) when Orlando, whom he has persecuted, kills a lioness—a lioness in the Forest of Arden!—which is about to spring upon him as he lies asleep. And the caitiff is rewarded (no less unreasonably), either for his villainy or for his conversion, with the hand of the lovely Celia.

This whole story is perfectly unimportant; Shakespeare, that is to say, evidently cared very little about it. We have here no attempt at a reproduction of reality, but one long festival of gaiety and wit, a soulful wit that vibrates into feeling.

First and foremost, the play typifies Shakespeare's longing, the longing of this great spirit, to get away from the unnatural city life, away from the false and ungrateful city folk, intent on business and on gain, away from flattery and falsehood and deceit, out into the country, where simple manners still endure, where it is easier to realise the dream of full freedom, and where the scent of the woods is so sweet. There the babble of the brooks has a subtler eloquence than any that is heard in cities; there the trees and even the stones say more to the wanderer's heart than the houses and streets of the capital; there he finds "good in everything."

The roving spirit has reawakened in his breast—the spirit which in bygone days sent him wandering with his gun through Charlcote Park—and out yonder in the lap of Nature, but in a remoter, richer Nature than that which he has known, he dreams of a communion between the best and ablest men, the fairest and most delicate women, in ideal fantastic surroundings, far from the ugly clamours of a public career, and the oppression of everyday cares. A life of hunting and song, and simple repasts in the open air, accompanied with witty talk; and at the same time a life full to the brim with the dreamy happiness of love. And with this life, the creation of his roving spirit, his gaiety and his longing for Nature, he animates a fantastic Forest of Arden.

But with this he is not content. He dreams out the dream, and feels that even such an ideal and untrammelled life could not satisfy that strange and unaccountable spirit lurking in the inmost depths of his nature, which turns everything into food for melancholy and satire. From this rib, then, taken from his own side, he creates the figure of Jaques, unknown to the romance, and sets him wandering through his pastoral comedy, lonely, retiring, self-absorbed, a misanthrope from excess of tenderness, sensitiveness, and imagination.

Jaques is like the first light and brilliant pencil-sketch for Hamlet. Taine, and others after him, have tried to draw a parallel between Jaques and Alceste—of all Molière's creations, no doubt, the one who contains most of his own nature. But there is no real analogy between them. In Jaques everything wears the shimmering hues of wit and fantasy, in Alceste everything is bitter earnest. Indignation is the mainspring of Alceste's misanthropy. He is disgusted at the falsehood around him, and outraged to see that the scoundrel with whom he is at law, although despised by every one, is nevertheless everywhere received with open arms. He declines to remain in bad company, even in the hearts of his friends; therefore he withdraws from them. He loathes two classes of people:

> "Les uns parcequ'ils sont méchants et malfaisants,
> Et les autres pour être aux méchants complaisants."

These are the accents of Timon of Athens, who hated the wicked for their wickedness, and other men for not hating the wicked.

It is, then, in Shakespeare's Timon, of many years later, that we can alone find an instructive parallel to Alceste. Alceste's nature is keenly logical, classically French; it consists of sheer uncompromising sincerity and pride, without sensibility and without melancholy.

The melancholy of Jaques is a poetic dreaminess. He is described to us
(ii. I) before we see him. The banished Duke has just been blessing the
adversity which drove him out into the forest, where he is exempt from the
dangers of the envious court. He is on the point of setting forth to hunt,
when he learns that the melancholy Jaques repines at the cruelty of the chase,
and calls him in that respect as great a usurper as the brother who drove him
from his dukedom. The courtiers have found him stretched beneath an oak,
and dissolved in pity for a poor wounded stag which stood beside the brook,
and "heaved forth such groans That their discharge did stretch his leathern
coat Almost to bursting." Jaques, they continue, "moralised this spectacle into
a thousand similes:"—

> "Then, being there alone,
> Left and abandon'd of his velvet friends;
> ' 'Tis right,' quoth he; 'thus misery doth part
> The flux of company.' Anon, a careless herd,
> Full of the pasture, jumps along by him,
> And never stays to greet him. 'Ay,' quoth Jaques,
> 'Sweep on, you fat and greasy citizens;
> 'Tis just the fashion: wherefore do you look
> Upon that poor and broken bankrupt there?"

His bitterness springs from a too tender sensibility, a sensibility like that of
Sakya Mouni before him, who made tenderness to animals part of his religion,
and like that of Shelley after him, who, in his pantheism, realised the kinship
between his own soul and that of the brute creation.

Thus we are prepared for his entrance. He introduces himself into the
Duke's circle (ii. 7) with a glorification of the fool's motley. He has encountered
Touchstone in the forest, and is enraptured with him. The motley fool lay
basking in the sun, and when Jaques said to him, "Good morrow, fool!" he
answered, "Call me not fool till heaven have sent me fortune." Then this sapient
fool drew a dial from his pocket, and said very wisely—

> " 'It is ten o'clock:
> Thus may we see,' quoth he, 'how the world wags
> 'Tis but an hour ago since it was nine,
> And after one hour more 'twill be eleven;
> And so from hour to hour we ripe and ripe,
> And then from hour to hour we rot and rot,
> And thereby hangs a tale.' "

"O noble fool!" Jaques exclaims with enthusiasm. "A worthy fool! Motley's the only wear."

In moods of humorous melancholy, it must have seemed to Shakespeare as though he himself were one of these jesters, who had the privilege of uttering truths to great people and on the stage, if only they did not blurt them out directly, but disguised them under a mask of folly. It was in a similar mood that Heinrich Heine, centuries later, addressed to the German people these words: "Ich bin dein Kunz von der Rosen, dein Narr."

Therefore it is that Shakespeare makes Jaques exclaim—

> "O, that I were a fool!
> I am ambitious for a motley coat."

When the Duke answers, "Thou shalt have one," he declares that it is the one thing he wants, and that the others must "weed their judgments" of the opinion that he is wise:—

> "I must have liberty
> Withal, as large a charter as the wind,
> To blow on whom I please; for so fools have
> And they that are most galled with my folly,
> They most must laugh.
> Invest me in my motley: give me leave
> To speak my mind, and I will through and through
> Cleanse the foul body of the infected world,
> If they will patiently receive my medicine."

It is Shakespeare's own mood that we hear in these words. The voice is his. The utterance is far too large for Jaques: he is only a mouthpiece for the poet. Or let us say that his figure dilates in such passages as this, and we see in him a Hamlet *avant la lettre*.

When the Duke, in answer to this outburst, denies Jaques' right to chide and satirise others, since he has himself been "a libertine, As sensual as the brutish sting itself," the poet evidently defends himself in the reply which he places in the mouth of the melancholy philosopher:—

> "Why, who cries out on pride,
> That can therein tax any private party?
> Doth it not flow as hugely as the sea,
> Till that the weary very means do ebb?
> What woman in the city do I name,

When that I say, the city-woman bears
The cost of princes on unworthy shoulders?
Who can come in, and say that I mean her,
When such a one as she, such is her neighbour?"

This exactly anticipates Holberg's self-defence in the character of Philemon
in *The Fortunate Shipwreck*. The poet is evidently rebutting a common prejudice
against his art. And as he makes Jaques an advocate for the freedom which
poetry must claim, so also he employs him as a champion of the actor's
misjudged calling, in placing in his mouth the magnificent speech on the Seven
Ages of Man. Alluding, no doubt, to the motto of *Totus Mundus Agit Histrionem*,
inscribed under the Hercules as Atlas, which was the sign of the Globe Theatre,
this speech opens with the words:—

"All the world's a stage,
And all the men and women merely players;
They have their exits and their entrances;
And one man in his time plays many parts."

Ben Jonson is said to have inquired, in an epigram against the motto of the
Globe Theatre, where the spectators were to be found if all the men and women
were players? And an epigram attributed to Shakespeare gives the simple answer
that all are players and audience at one and the same time. Jaques' survey of the
life of man is admirably concise and impressive. The last line—

"Sans teeth, sans eyes, sans taste, sans everything"—

with its half French equivalent for "without," is imitated from the *Henriade* of
the French poet Garnier, which was not translated, and which Shakespeare must
consequently have read in the original.

This same Jaques, who gives evidence of so wide an outlook over human life, is
in daily intercourse, as we have said, nervously misanthropic and formidably witty.
He is sick of polite society, pines for solitude, takes leave of a pleasant companion
with the words: "I thank you for your company; but, good faith, I had as lief have
been myself alone." Yet we must not take his melancholy and his misanthropy too
seriously. His melancholy is a comedy-melancholy, his misanthropy is only the
humourist's craving to give free vent to his satirical inspirations.

And there is, as aforesaid, only a certain part of Shakespeare's inmost
nature in this Jaques, a Shakespeare of the future, a Hamlet in germ, but not
that Shakespeare who now bathes in the sunlight and lives in uninterrupted
prosperity, in growing favour with the many, and borne aloft by the

admiration and goodwill of the few. We must seek for this Shakespeare in the interspersed songs, in the drollery of the fool, in the lovers' rhapsodies, in the enchanting babble of the ladies. He is, like Providence, everywhere and nowhere.

When Celia says (i. 2), "Let us sit and mock the good housewife, Fortune, from her wheel, that her gifts may henceforth be bestowed equally," she strikes, as though with a tuning-fork, the keynote of the comedy. The sluice is opened for that torrent of jocund wit, shimmering with all the rainbows of fancy, which is now to rush seething and swirling along.

The Fool is essential to the scheme: for the Fool's stupidity is the grindstone of wit, and the Fool's wit is the touchstone of character. Hence his name.

The ways of the real world, however, are not forgotten. The good make enemies by their very goodness, and the words of the old servant Adam (Shakespeare's own part) to his young master Orlando (ii. 3), sound sadly enough:—

"Your praise is come too swiftly home before you.
Know you not, master, to some kind of men
Their graces serve them but as enemies?
No more do yours: your virtues, gentle master,
Are sanctified, and holy traitors to you.
O, what a world is this, when what is comely
Envenoms him that bears it!"

But soon the poet's eye is opened to a more consolatory life-philosophy, combined with an unequivocal contempt for school-philosophy. There seems to be a scoffing allusion to a book of the time, which was full of the platitudes of celebrated philosophers, in Touchstone's speech to William (v. I), "The heathen philosopher, when he had desire to eat a grape, would open his lips when he put it into his mouth, meaning thereby that grapes were made to eat and lips to open;" but no doubt there also lurks in this speech a certain lack of respect for even the much-belauded wisdom of tradition. The relativity of all things, at that time a new idea, is expounded with lofty humour by the Fool in his answer to the question what he thinks of this pastoral life (iii. 2):—

"Truly, shepherd, in respect of itself it is a good life, but in respect that it is a shepherd's life, it is naught. In respect that it is solitary, I like it very well; but in respect that it is private, it is a very vile life. Now, in respect it is in the fields, it pleaseth me well; but in respect it is not in the court, it is tedious. As it is a spare life, look you, it fits my humour well; but as there is no more plenty in it, it goes much against my stomach. Hast any philosophy in thee, shepherd?"

The shepherd's answer makes direct sport of philosophy, in the style of Molière's gibe, when he accounts for the narcotic effect of opium by explaining that the drug possesses a certain *facultas dormitativa*:—

> "*Corin*. No more, but that I know, the more one sickens, the worse at ease he is; and that he that wants money, means, and content, is without three good friends; that the property of rain is to wet, and fire to burn; that good pasture makes fat sheep, and that a great cause of the night is lack of the sun. . . .
> "*Touchstone*. Such a one is a natural philosopher."

This sort of philosophy leads up, as it were, to Rosalind's sweet gaiety and heavenly kindness.

The two cousins, Rosalind and Celia, seem at first glance like variations of the two cousins, Beatrice and Hero, in the play Shakespeare has just finished. Rosalind and Beatrice in particular are akin in their victorious wit. Yet the difference between them is very great; Shakespeare never repeats himself. The wit of Beatrice is aggressive and challenging; we see, as it were, the gleam of a rapier in it. Rosalind's wit is gaiety without a sting; the gleam in it is of "that sweet radiance" which Oehlenschläger attributed to Freia; her sportive nature masks the depth of her love. Beatrice can be brought to love because she is a woman, and stands in no respect apart from her sex; but she is not of an amatory nature. Rosalind is seized with a passion for Orlando the instant she sets eyes on him. From the moment of Beatrice's first appearance she is defiant and combative, in the highest of spirits. We are introduced to Rosalind as a poor bird with a drooping wing; her father is banished, she is bereft of her birthright, and is living on sufferance as companion to the usurper's daughter, being, indeed, half a prisoner in the palace, where till lately she reigned as princess. It is not until she has donned the doublet and hose, appears in the likeness of a page, and wanders at her own sweet will in the open air and the greenwood, that she recovers her radiant humour, and roguish merriment flows from her lips like the trilling of a bird.

Nor is the man she loves, like Benedick, an overweening gallant with a sharp tongue and an unabashed bearing. This youth, though brave as a hero and strong as an athlete, is a child in inexperience, and so bashful in the presence of the woman who instantly captivates him, that it is she who is the first to betray her sympathy for him, and has even to take the chain from her own neck and hang it around his before he can so much as muster up courage to hope for her love. So, too, we find him passing his time in hanging poems to her upon the trees, and carving the name of Rosalind in their bark. She amuses herself, in her page's attire, by making herself his confidant, and pretending, as it were in jest, to be his Rosalind. She cannot bring herself to confess her passion, although she can think and talk (to Celia) of no one but him, and although his delay of a few minutes in keeping tryst with her sets her beside herself with impatience. She is as sensitive as she is intelligent, in this differing from Portia, to whom, in other respects, she bears some resemblance, though she lacks her persuasive eloquence, and is, on the whole, more tender, more virginal. She faints when Oliver, to excuse Orlando's delay, brings her a handkerchief stained with his blood; yet has sufficient self-mastery to say with a smile the moment she recovers, "I pray you tell your brother how well I counterfeited." She is quite at her ease in her male attire, like Viola and Imogen after her. The fact that female parts were played by youths had, of course, something to do with the frequency of these disguises.

Here is a specimen of her wit (iii. 2). Orlando has evaded the page's question what o'clock it is, alleging that there are no clocks in the forest.

> "*Rosalind*. Then, there is no true lover in the forest; else sighing every minute, and groaning every hour, would detect the lazy foot of Time as well as a clock.
>
> "*Orlando*. And why not the swift foot of Time? had not that been as proper?
>
> "*Ros*. By no means, sir. Time travels in divers paces with divers persons. I'll tell you, who Time ambles withal, who Time trots withal, who Time gallops withal, and who he stands still withal.
>
> "*Orl*. I pr'ythee, who doth he trot withal?
>
> "*Ros*. Marry, he trots hard with a young maid, between the contract of her marriage, and the day it is solemnised: if the interim be but a se'nnight, Time's pace is so hard that it seems the length of seven years.
>
> "*Orl*. Who ambles Time withal?
>
> "*Ros*. With a priest that lacks Latin, and a rich man that hath not the gout; for the one sleeps easily, because he cannot study; and the other lives merrily, because he feels no pain. . . .
>
> "*Orl*. Who doth he gallop withal?
>
> "*Ros*. With a thief to the gallows; for though he go as softly as foot can fall, he thinks himself too soon there.
>
> "*Orl*. Who stays it still withal?
>
> "*Ros*. With lawyers in the vacation; for they sleep between term and term, and then they perceive not how Time moves."

She is unrivalled in vivacity and inventiveness. In every answer she discovers gunpowder anew, and she knows how to use it to boot. She explains that she had an old uncle who warned her against love and women, and, from the vantage-ground of her doublet and hose, she declares—

"I thank God, I am not a woman, to be touched with so many giddy offences, as he hath generally taxed their whole sex withal.

"*Orl.* Can you remember any of the principal evils that he laid to the charge of women?

"*Ros.* There were none principal: they were all like one another, as half-pence are; every one fault seeming monstrous, till its fellow fault came to match it.

"*Orl.* I pr'ythee, recount some of them.

"*Ros.* No; I will not cast away my physic but on those that are sick. There is a man haunts the forest, that abuses our young plants with carving Rosalind on their barks; hangs odes upon hawthorns, and elegies on brambles; all, forsooth, deifying the name of Rosalind: if I could meet that fancy-monger, I would give him some good counsel, for he seems to have the quotidian of love upon him."

Orlando admits that he is the culprit, and they are to meet daily that she may exorcise his passion. She bids him woo her in jest, as though she were indeed Rosalind, and answers (iv. 1):—

"*Ros.* Well, in her person, I say—I will not have you.

"*Orl.* Then, in mine own person, I die.

"*Ros.* No, 'faith, die by attorney. The poor world is almost six thousand years old, and in all this time there was not any man died in his own person, *videlicet*, in a love-cause. Troilus had his brains dashed out with a Grecian club; yet he did what he could to die before, and he is one of the patterns of love. Leander, he would have lived many a fair year, though Hero had turned nun, if it had not been for a hot midsummer night; for, good youth, he went but forth to wash him in the Hellespont, and, being taken with the cramp, was drowned, and the foolish chroniclers of that age found it was—Hero of Sestos. But these are all lies: men have died from time to time, and worms have eaten them, but not for love."

What Rosalind says of women in general applies to herself in particular: you will never find her without an answer until you find her without a tongue. And there is always a bright and merry fantasy in her answers. She is literally radiant with youth, imagination, and the joy of loving so passionately and being so passionately beloved. And it is marvellous how thoroughly feminine is her wit. Too many of the witty women in books written by men have a man's intelligence. Rosalind's wit is tempered by feeling.

She has no monopoly of wit in this Arcadia of Arden. Every one in the play is witty, even the so-called simpletons. It is a festival of wit. At some points Shakespeare seems to have followed no stricter principle than the simple one of making each interlocutor outbid the other in wit (see, for example, the conversation between Touchstone and the country wench whom he befools). The result is that the piece is bathed in a sunshiny humour. And amid all the gay and airy wit-skirmishes, amid the cooing love-duets of all the happy youths and maidens, the poet intersperses the melancholy solos of his Jaques:—

"I have neither the scholar's melancholy, which is emulation; nor the musician's, which is fantastical; nor the courtier's, which is proud; nor the soldier's, which is ambitious; nor the lawyer's, which is politic; nor the lady's, which is nice; nor the lover's, which is all these; but it is a melancholy of mine own, compounded of many simples, extracted from many objects."

This is the melancholy which haunts the thinker and the great creative artist; but in Shakespeare it as yet modulated with ease into the most engaging and delightful merriment.

NOTES
1. Reprinted in Hazlitt's Shakespeare's Library, ed. 1875, part i, vol. ii.

—◊◊◊— —◊◊◊— —◊◊◊—

As You Like It
in the Twentieth Century

✖❧

In the twentieth century many commentators focused on the themes of freedom and escape in *As You Like It*. W.H. Auden, for one, in his lecture on the play, spoke of the pastoral and the primitive. In his perspective, nature in the play is not for leisurely pastoral escape but for penance and/or for preparing oneself to return to society. Louis Adrian Montrose had a similar vision. Whereas other critics saw the beginning of the play as a mere means for moving the action into the forest, Montrose saw the play in the reverse. In his view, events take place in the forest that make it possible to repair the damage done at home. Years earlier, the inventive critic and fiction writer G.K. Chesterton wrote, "Rosalind did not go into the wood to look for her freedom; she went into the wood to look for her father."

On the other hand, C.L. Barber felt that the first half of the play focused on portraying the pastoral. Arden, he believed, is a place of freedom. While many in this forest are there because they have been banished, exile ends up not being a punishment after all, since court has come to be an unpleasant place. In Barber's view, the second half of the play is about contrasting attitudes toward love—"romantic participation in love and humorous detachment from its follies." Similarly, Harold C. Goddard saw the play as focused not simply on country versus court but also on the relationship between love and wisdom.

Harold Jenkins believed that *As You Like* It portrays the standard pastoral world and then "duly burlesques it." He wrote of the play in comparison to other Shakespearean comedies and said that in this one "the art of comic juxtaposition is at its subtlest."

Thomas McFarland, in comparing the play to Shakespeare's other comedies, found it more somber. In his view, the play is far from a traditional pastoral. Rather, it struggles to keep its comic balance, containing much less happiness than Shakespeare's two earlier pastorals.

Some critics also considered the play in its Elizabethan context. Jenkins saw Jaques as a version of the Elizabethan melancholy man and disagreed with critics who suggested Jaques was actually the voice of Shakespeare. Montrose discussed the complications of inheritance that are brought up in the play, foreign to many today but familiar to the Elizabethans.

Commentators in the twentieth century continued to be fascinated with the play's most memorable characters. Goddard, who felt that love and wisdom are the key themes in the play, found the character of Jaques both fake and self-involved. Those characters who are in love, such as Rosalind and Orlando, have more humility, insight, and wisdom than Jaques and therefore easily outshine him. Goddard also looked at Touchstone, questioning why some believe that this character is truly wise and witty. Touchstone has neither of these qualities, in Goddard's view, and is also rude, prejudiced, and heartless. Goddard saw Rosalind as mixing wit with love, as someone balanced in body, mind, and spirit, "a sort of universal image of Woman as Sweetheart."

Finally, Harold Bloom examines Rosalind as one of the finest and most likable of Shakespeare's characters: "It seems a miracle that so much wit should be fused with such benignity."

1932—G.K. Chesterton. "The Repetition of Rosalind," from *Chesterton on Shakespeare*

G.K. Chesterton, most famous today for his "Father Brown" detective stories, also wrote novels, treatises on Catholicism, and perceptive works of criticism on such writers as Dickens, Chaucer, and Shakespeare.

... In numberless modern novels and magazine stories, the heroine is apparently complimented by being described as "boyish". Doubtless there will soon be another fashion in fiction, in which the hero will always be described as girlish. Fettered as we are with an antiquated Victorian prejudice of the equality of the sexes, we cannot quite understand why one should be a compliment any more than the other. But, anyhow, the present fashion offers a much deeper difficulty. For the girl is being complimented on her boyishness by people who obviously know nothing at all about boys. Nothing could possibly be more unlike a boy than the candid, confident, unconventional and somewhat shallow sylph who swaggers up to the unfortunate hero of the novel *à la mode*. So far from being unconventional and shallow, the boy is commonly conventional because he is secretive. He is much more sullen outside and much more morbid inside. Who then is this new Pantomime Boy, and where did she come from? In truth she comes out of a very old pantomime.

About three hundred years ago William Shakespeare, not knowing what to do with his characters, turned them out to play in the woods, let a girl masquerade as a boy and amused himself with speculating on the effect of feminine curiosity freed for an hour from feminine dignity. He did it very well, but he could do something else. And the popular romances of today cannot do anything else. Shakespeare took care to explain in the play itself that he did not think that life should be one prolonged picnic. Nor would he have thought that feminine life should be one prolonged piece of private theatricals. But Rosalind, who was then unconventional for an hour, is now the convention of an epoch. She was then on a holiday; she was now very hardworked indeed. She has to act in every play, novel or short story, and always in the same old pert pose. Perhaps she is even afraid to be herself; certainly Celia is now afraid to be herself.

We should think it rather a bore if all tragic youths wore black cloaks and carried skulls in imitation of Hamlet, or all old men waved wands and clasped enormous books in imitation of Prospero. But we are almost as much tied to one type of girl in popular fiction today. And it is getting very tiresome. A huge human success is banking up for anybody bold enough to describe a quiet girl, a girl handicapped by good manners and a habit of minding her own business. Even a sulky girl would be a relief.

The moral is one we often draw; that the family is the real field for personality. All the best Shakespearian dramas are domestic dramas; even when mainly concerned with domestic murders. So far from freedom following on the decay of the family, what follows is uniformity. The Rosalinds become a sort of regiment; if itself a regiment of *vivandières*. They wear uniforms of shingled hair and short skirts; and they seem to stand in a row like chorus girls. Not till we have got back within the four walls of the home shall we have any great tragedy or great comedy. The attempts to describe life in a Utopia of the future are alone enough to prove that there is nothing dramatic about an everlasting picnic.

Men and women must stand in some serious and lasting relation to each other for great passions and great problems to arise; and all this anarchy is as bad for art as it is for morals. Rosalind did not go into the wood to look for her freedom; she went into the wood to look for her father. And all the freedom, and even all the fun of the adventure really arises from that fact. For even an adventure must have an aim. Anyhow, the modern aimlessness has produced a condition in which we are so bored with Rosalind that we almost long for Lady Macbeth.

—◆◆— —◆◆— —◆◆—

1947—W.H. Auden.
"As You Like It," from *Lectures on Shakespeare*

W.H. Auden, one of the most famous poets of the twentieth century, also wrote influential literary criticism. This passage comes from a collection of Auden's lectures given in 1946 and 1947, which were reconstructed and edited years later by Arthur Kirsch.

[22 January 1947]

I don't know how it is in America, but in England students had to read *As You Like It* a good deal in schools and act it too, and at that time I found it dull. The trouble is that it's not a play for kids. It's very sophisticated, and only adults can understand what it's about. You have to be acquainted with what it means to be a civilized person, and a child or adolescent won't have such knowledge. Those who have read William Empson's *Some Versions of Pastoral* will have to excuse me for taking over some of his ideas on pastoral convention—they're very good. Those who haven't read the book should read it.

Any idea of pastoral involves a conception of the primitive. Erwin Panofsky discusses three categories of primitivism: (1) "soft" primitivism, (2) "hard" primitivism, and (3) the Hebraic idea of the Garden of Eden and the Fall. Soft or positivistic primitivism depicted the primitive form of existence as a Golden Age, in comparison with which the subsequent phases of existence were nothing but successive stages of one prolonged fall from grace. The first classical description of the Golden Age is found in Hesiod's *Works and Days*. Hesiod discriminates five ages of man: the age of gold, the age of silver, the age of bronze, the age of the heroic demigods, and the age of iron. Compare Jaques's speech on the seven ages of man (II.vii.139–66). Hesiod says of the "golden race of mortal men" who lived in the first age:

> And they lived like gods without sorrow of heart, remote and free
> from toil and grief: miserable age rested not on them; but with
> legs and arms never failing they made merry with feasting beyond
> the reach of all evils. When they died, it was as though they were
> overcome with sleep, and they had all good things; for the fruitful
> earth unforced bare them fruit abundantly and without stint. They
> dwelt in ease and peace upon their lands with many good things, rich
> in flocks and loved by the blessed gods.

Of the fifth and last age, the Iron Age, Hesiod writes,

> Thereafter, would that I were not among the men of the fifth generation,
> but either had died before or been born afterwards. For now truly is
> a race of iron, and men never rest from labour and sorrow by day, and
> from perishing by night; and the gods shall lay sore trouble upon them.
> But, notwithstanding, even these shall have some good mingled with
> their evils. And Zeus will destroy this race of mortal men also when
> they come to have grey hair on the temples at their birth. The father
> will not agree with his children, nor the children with their father, nor

guest with his host, nor comrade with comrade; nor will brother be dear to brother as aforetime. Men will dishonour their parents as they grow quickly old, and will carp at them, chiding them with bitter words, hard-hearted they, not knowing the fear of the gods. They will not repay their aged parents the cost of their nurture, for might shall be their right: and one man shall sack another's city. There will be no favour for the man who keeps his oath or for the just or for the good; but rather men will praise the evil-doer and his violent dealing. Strength will be right and reverence will cease to be; and the wicked will hurt the worthy man, speaking false words against him, and will swear an oath upon them. Envy, foul-mouthed, delighting in evil, with scowling face, will go along with wretched men one and all. And then Aidôs and Nemesis, with their sweet forms wrapped in white robes, will go from the wide-pathed earth and forsake mankind to join the company of the deathless gods: and bitter sorrows will be left for mortal men, and there will be no help against evil.

In Hesiod, civilization represents a continuous decline.

A modern sophisticated version of this idea is represented in Jean-Jacques Rousseau's conception of the noble savage, who is born good and free, but is corrupted by human institutions. Another version is D.H. Lawrence's opposition of the reflective and destructive mental consciousness to the dark gods of the blood of the instinctive man, who acts naturally. We can see the expression of these feelings in our selves. In an industrial civilization, in the big city, we live a certain type of life. We take summer vacations in the country among comparatively unself-conscious and simple people. We feel that they are happier than we are and think they behave better. We can understand Flaubert's saying of them that "*Ils sont dans le vrai*," that they are right.

"Hard," or negativistic, primitivism, on the other hand, described by such writers as Lucretius, Virgil, and Pliny, as well as Hobbes, imagines the primitive form of existence as a truly bestial state, in which the condition of man in the world was brutal, disorderly, and savage. Through technical and intellectual progress, civilization brings the transformation of the brutal into an orderly, knowing, and civil world. In myth this conception is associated with Vulcan and the coming of fire, and with Hercules, Prometheus, and Demeter.

Would I like to have lived in an earlier period, when there was less knowledge, less power over disease, less plumbing and less police? No, I would not like to have lived then. If one thinks in terms of happiness, or in terms of human love, behavior is worse now. If one thinks in terms of knowledge and power and the potential for good, one can say there has been an advance. The Golden Age view is dangerous. It appeals not to conservatism but to anarchism and nihilism, a feeling that we are all sunk and had better withdraw.

The withdrawal can take the form of an attempt to lead a simple life, to live in a simple way, or it can take the form of drink, whose object is to reduce self-consciousness. There can be a retreat from trying to do anything. A Marxist would point out that the Golden Age view is natural to people like myself who belong to a dying class. The hard view appeals to people, either reactionary or forward-looking, Fascists or Communists, who seek and really enjoy power. They are like Prince Hal. The Falstaffs of the world counter the hard view with a millennial appeal to the recovery of a Golden Age in the future. The soft Hesiodic view and the hard Lucretian view are both historical, though for Hesiod things get worse without reason.

The Hebraic view of the Garden of Eden is Hesiodic, but it is prehistoric and has to be told in mythical as well as historical terms, because the Fall is what conditions history. In Genesis there is not a race of people, there is first a man and a woman. And the first thing they do is eat of the tree of good and evil and get turned out of Eden. Their first act, the act that loses them their innocence, begins history. Like Lucretius, the Hebraic view asserts that all human beings are born bad and have to redeem themselves. But there is a different attitude toward history and civilization in the Hebraic view of primitivism. To the soft Hesiodic view, things are gloomy because every advance is really a decline—the cycle always has to begin with the primitive. This is Spengler's premise. The hard view, that every advance of law and knowledge brings progress, deifies historical process. The Hebraic and Christian view is that civilization is neutral. The knowledge of good and evil increases, but the knowledge in itself is ambiguous. It is a temptation. A man can behave better through understanding, or worse. Neither knowledge nor ignorance has anything to do with the perversion of the will through the love of self, and neither can make you choose good or reject evil. Correspondingly, you cannot have advances in science, including the cure of diseases, without having both good and bad results. One attempt to resolve this problem is to declare, like Hesiod, that it's better not to change anything. The other view, one held by Victorians, is more sure that things will get better and better—but today's history has shown us that such a view is imaginary. But we can't turn to Hesiod completely, because the radius of evil has simply grown too great.

In the Old Irish myth depicted in "The Sea-God's Address to Bran," translated by Kuno Meyer, paradise does not degenerate through historical succession nor is it reclaimed through hard primitivism's promise of the final subjugation of nature. It is, rather, redeemed from the loss imposed by man's sinful quest for independence. Manannan, the sea-god, sings to Bran, who is at sea in his coracle:

Sea-horses glisten in summer
As far as Bran can stretch his glance:

Rivers pour forth a stream of honey
In the land of Manannan, son of Ler.

The sheen of the main on which thou art,
The dazzling white of the sea on which thou rowest about—
Yellow and azure are spread out,
It is a light and airy land.

Speckled salmon leap from the womb
Out of the white sea on which thou lookest:
They are calves, they are lambs of fair hue,
With truce, without mutual slaughter.

Though thou seest but one chariot-rider
In the Pleasant Plain of many flowers,
There are many steeds on its surface,
Though thou dost not see them.

Large is the plain, numerous is the host,
Colours shine with pure glory:
A white stream of silver, stairs of gold
Afford a welcome with all abundance.

An enchanting game, most delicious,
They play over the luscious wine:
Men and gentle women under a bush
Without sin, without transgression.

Along the top of a wood
Thy coracle has swum across ridges:
There is a wood laden with beautiful fruit
Under the prow of thy little skiff.

A wood with blossom and with fruit
On which is the vine's veritable fragrance,
A wood without decay, without defect,
On which is foliage of golden hue.

From the beginning of creation we are
Without old age, without consummation of clay:
Hence we expect not there should be frailty
The sin has not come to us.

An evil day when the serpent came
To the father into his citadel!
He has perverted the ages in this world,
So that there came decay which was not original.

By greed and lust he has slain us,
Whereby he has ruined the noble race:
The withered body has gone to the fold of torment,
An everlasting abode of torture.

It is a law of pride in this world
To believe in the creatures, to forget God:
Overthrow by diseases, and old age,
Destruction of the beguiled soul.

A noble salvation will come
From the King who has created us:
A white law will come over seas
Besides being God, He will be man.

The everlasting garden is the primitive site of the pastoral tradition, but though at the end of Dante's *Purgatorio*, Dante arrives at the Garden of Eden, beyond that is the *Civitas Dei*, the City of God, which is the opposite of the pastoral convention.

The pastoral is an aristocratic form. It begins roughly with Theocritus, and, in a "hard" version, Virgil's *Georgics*. The landscapes of the medieval works of the *Roman de la Rose* and *Pearl* are presented quite differently. The classical form of the pastoral returns in the Renaissance. The greatest Renaissance works in the genre are Góngora's *Soledades* and, in English, Sidney's *Arcadia* and Milton's *Lycidas*. In these works, shepherds speak in extremely formal, sophisticated, and aristocratic language, presenting civilized language in a bucolic setting. These people, as peasants, *sont dans le vrai* in their life. Lao-tse would read them as corrupting their innocence through their speech, since in their simpleness they have the power to be free and are better than their social betters. But in order to be better in the pastoral form, they must speak very well.

On the other side, related to hard primitivism, the shepherds are like the nobles whose words they use. There is the same relation between the governors and the governed, between the shepherd and nature—man is the ruler of nature, the sheep are the ruled. The good shepherd protects the sheep from the wolves, the bad shepherd neglects them.

Other forms of pastoral that Empson deals with include the animal in contrast with man. An animal is undisturbed by self-consciousness, and really acts instinctively—what he wills and what he does are the same. Walt Whitman writes in *Leaves of Grass*:

> I think I could turn and live with animals, they are so placid
>   and self-contain'd,
> I stand and look at them long and long.
>
> They do not sweat and whine about their condition,
> They do not lie awake in the dark and weep for their sins,
> They do not make me sick discussing their duty to God,
> Not one is dissatisfied, not one is demented with the mania of
>   owning things.
> Not one kneels to another, nor to his kind that lived thousands
>   of years ago,
> Not one is respectable or unhappy over the whole earth.

For instance, "If men were as much men as lizards are lizards, / They'd be worth looking at"—the idea of lizards is better.

Children compose another kind of pastoral in their freedom from self-consciousness and sex, and in their detachment. They are incapable of hiding things. If you want to decide whether the Garden of Eden is true, just watch children and you see it work. Both Alice in Wonderland and Jaques can't conceal anything. The fool, the Fool in *King Lear* for example, provides another form of pastoral. The fool is fearless and untroubled by convention—like a child, he isn't even aware of convention. He's not all there, but he is prophetic, because through his craziness he either sees more or dares to say more.

Another pastoral figure is the outlaw, who provides a kind of inverted pastoral, a view from the other side of the tracks: Falstaff, Shylock, and John Gay's *The Beggar's Opera* are examples. So are gangster films and detective stories, though not Mickey Spillane's Mike Hammer series or Chandler's studies of a criminal milieu. The primary interest in the detective story is the identification of the murderer. If all the characters are potential criminals, that interest disappears. The best setting for a detective story is the vicarage or college, both of which correspond to the Edenic pastoral garden. You begin with a discovery of a corpse, and the story then involves guilt, the entry of the law, detection, the apprehension of the murderer, the exit of the law, and the renewal of pastoral peace. False innocence is replaced by true innocence, and the city or court is contrasted with the field or village, a humanized nature that is comparable to that depicted in ordinary pastoral.

Another version of pastoral lumps the village and city together over against nature in the raw. The modern feeling for wild nature is a product of industrialization, in which civilized life is felt to annihilate the individual in the mass. The *idiotes*, the private citizen, is opposed by the *banausos*, the tiny specialist with a nondirected, aimless ambition. Wild nature becomes a place of adventure, in which I can't be a *banausos*, a specialist—wild nature fights me and forces me to become a whole individual, gives me a *raison d'être*. Earlier society saw rough nature as an unpleasant necessity. Wordsworth's description of the city of London in *The Prelude*, presents the modern view of the city as the enemy of the individual:

>   Oh, blank confusion! And a type not false
> Of what the mighty City is itself
> To all except a Straggler here and there,
> To the whole Swarm of its inhabitants;
> An undistinguishable world to men,
> The slaves unrespited of low pursuits,
> Living amid the same perpetual flow
> Of trivial objects, melted and reduced
> To one identity, by differences
> That have no law, no meaning, and no end.

To this we may contrast Sydney Smith's comment: "O it's terrible in the country, one feels that the whole creation is going to expire at tea-time."

Of all of Shakespeare's plays, *As You Like It* is the greatest paean to civilization and to the nature of a civilized man and woman. It is dominated by Rosalind, a triumph of civilization, who, like the play itself, fully embodies man's capacity, in Pascal's words, "to deny, to believe, and to doubt well"—*nier, croire, et douter bien*. The play presents a balance of dialectical opposites: the country versus the court, detachment versus love, honesty versus poetry, nature versus fortune, nature and fortune versus art. We begin in an orchard, a cultivated garden, and the first name we hear is Adam. The resonances are hardly unconscious on Shakespeare's part, since Adam and Orlando are going to be driven out of the garden. At the same time that the garden is parallel to Eden, however, it is different. The biblical Adam shuts himself out of Eden through guilt. Here Orlando is driven out in innocence by an older brother who is jealous of his nicer brother. Orlando complains that Oliver is training him in pastoral rusticity:

> You shall hear me. My father charg'd you in his will to give me good
> education. You have train'd me like a peasant, obscuring and hiding from
> me all gentlemanlike qualities. The spirit of my father grows strong in
> me, and I will no longer endure it. Therefore allow me such exercises as
> may become a gentleman, or give me the poor allottery my father left
> me by testament. (I.i.69–78)

This is an appeal to hard primitivism, to the kind of military exercises recommended for Jesuits by St. Ignatius Loyola.

The other exile is of Duke Senior by Duke Frederick, who possesses what doesn't belong to him and represents the brutal element in civilization. Duke Senior is forced to retire to the pastoral life of the Forest of Arden, which Charles initially describes in terms of soft primitivism:

> They say he is already in the Forest of Arden, and a many merry men
> with him; and there they live like the old Robin Hood of England. They
> say many young gentlemen flock to him every day, and fleet the time
> carelessly as they did in the golden world. (I.i.120–25)

Rosalind and Celia appear, just emerging from the innocence of childhood, another pastoral form. They talk of nature and fortune a little, a bit uncertain as to which is which (I.ii.34–53). Both the Duke and Orlando are in the forest through acts of fortune. But the nature of the people involved is also a concern. Oliver is by nature envious, and there is something in the nice Orlando to arouse his envy. The same is true of Duke Frederick's relation to Duke Senior. Compare Antonio's relation to Prospero in *The Tempest*. Nature gives the characters the wit to flout fortune. There is no distinction, rightly none, between nature and art in human beings, because we are inherently artifice-making creatures and have a psychosomatic constitution in which mind affects matter. The use of nature in *As You Like It* depends first on the characters themselves and then on fortune.

In bidding farewell to Orlando, M. le Beau says, "Hereafter, in a better world than this, / I shall desire more love and knowledge of you" (I.ii.295–96). The court is pictured as an evil from which the good withdraw, either compulsorily, as in the case of Orlando and Rosalind, or voluntarily through love for the exiles, as in the case of Adam and Celia, though to leave even a court represented as evil is exile. Orlando, in the language of soft primitivism, says to Adam,

> O good old man, how well in thee appears
> The constant service of the antique world,
> When service sweat for duty, not for meed!
> Thou art not for the fashion of these times,
> Where none will sweat but for promotion,
> And having that, do choke their service up
> Even with the having. It is not so with thee. (II.iii.56–62)

In the language of hard primitivism, he asks Adam earlier, when Adam tells him he must leave,

What, wouldst thou have me go and beg my food,
Or with a base and boist'rous sword enforce
A thievish living on the common road? (II.iii.31–33)

"O, how full of briers is this working-day world!" Rosalind says to Celia, and Celia responds, "They are but burrs, cousin, thrown upon thee in holiday foolery. If we walk not in the trodden paths, our very petticoats will catch them" (I.iii.12–15). There is a danger in the departure from regular society.

Duke Senior, in the Forest of Arden, first adopts a conventional pastoral posture:

Now, my co-mates and brothers in exile,
Hath not old custom made this life more sweet
Than that of painted pomp? Are not these woods
More free from peril than the envious court?
Here feel we but the penalty of Adam,
The seasons' difference; as, the icy fang
And churlish chiding of the winter's wind,
Which, when it bites and blows upon my body
Even till I shrink with cold, I smile, and say
"This is no flattery; these are counsellors
That feelingly persuade me what I am."
Sweet are the uses of adversity,
Which, like the toad, ugly and venomous,
Wears yet a precious jewel in his head;
And this our life, exempt from public haunt,
Find tongues in trees, books in the running brooks,
Sermons in stones, and good in everything:
I would not change it.

The First Lord immediately puts the Duke's speech in perspective:

.   Happy is your Grace
That can translate the stubbornness of fortune
Into so quiet and so sweet a style. (II.i.1–20)

So the speech of Duke Senior is not priggish—he hasn't chosen his condition.

The first Lord's subsequent description of Jaques's homily on a hunted and wounded deer puts the hardness of life in the wood and in the court together—even other deer abandon the one wounded by hunters, as men abandon someone who is bankrupt:

"Poor deer," quoth he, "thou mak'st a testament
As worldlings do, giving thy sum of more
To that which had too much." Then, being alone,
Left and abandoned of his velvet friends:
"'Tis right!" quoth he, "thus misery doth part
The flux of company." Anon a careless herd,
Full of the pasture, jumps along by him
And never stays to greet him: "Ay," quoth Jaques,
"Sweep on, you fat and greasy citizens!
'Tis just the fashion! Wherefore do you look
Upon that poor and broken bankrupt there?"
Thus most invectively he pierceth through
The body of the country, city, court;
Yea, and of this our life, swearing that we
Are mere usurpers, tyrants, and what's worse,
To fright the animals and to kill them up
In their assign'd and native dwelling place. (II.i.47–63)

Shakespeare treats Petrarchan literary conventions with a sophisticated sensibility in his new pastoral. The love of Silvius and Phoebe, the conventional shepherd and shepherdess, foreshadows that of Orlando and Rosalind, but Rosalind's view of Silvius and Phoebe is, "I must get you out of this madness." On the one hand, she chides Silvius for being too much of a doormat and Phoebe for being vain:

You are a thousand times a properer man
Than she a woman. 'Tis such fools as you
That makes the world full of ill-favour'd children.
'Tis not her glass, but you, that flatters her,
And out of you she sees herself more proper
Than any of her lineaments can show her.
But, mistress, know yourself. Down on your knees,
And thank heaven, fasting, for a good man's love;
For I must tell you friendly in your ear,
Sell when you can! you are not for all markets. (III.v.51–60)

On the other hand, Rosalind is aware that, as Amiens sings in his song, "Most friendship is feigning, most loving mere folly" (II.vii.181). Rosalind tells Orlando, "Love is merely a madness, and, I tell you, deserves as well a dark house and a whip as madmen do; and the reason why they are not so punish'd and cured is that the lunacy is so ordinary that the whippers are in love too" (III.ii.420–24).

"Yet I profess curing it by counsel," Rosalind says, and she describes how she once cured a lover of such lunacy:

> He was to imagine me his love, his mistress; and I set him every day
> to woo me. At which time would I, being but a moonish youth, grieve,
> be effeminate, changeable, longing, and liking, proud, fantastical,
> apish, shallow, inconstant, full of tears, full of smiles; for every passion
> something and for no passion truly anything, as boys and women are for
> the most part cattle of this colour; would now like him, now loathe him;
> then entertain him, then forswear him; now weep for him, then spit at
> him; that I drave my suitor from his mad humour of love to a living
> humour of madness, which was, to forswear the full stream of the
> world and to live in a nook merely monastic. And thus I cur'd him.
> (III.ii.425–42)

A mistaken attachment can lead to a complete withdrawal.

Touchstone says to Audrey, quite correctly, that "the truest poetry is the most feigning, and lovers are given to poetry; and what they swear in poetry may be said, as lovers, they do feign" (III.iii.19–22). In a pastoral reversed, Touchstone stands up both for love, however unfaithful, and for the city: "as a wall'd town is more worthier than a village, so is the forehead of a married man more honourable than the bare brow of a bachelor; and by how much defence is better than no skill, by so much is a horn more precious than to want" (III.iii.59–64).

Jaques is a detached man, as Rosalind sees clearly in the following dialogue:

> *Jaq.* I have neither the scholar's melancholy, which is emulation; nor
> the musician's, which is fantastical; nor the courtier's, which is proud;
> nor the soldier's, which is ambitious; nor the lawyer's, which is politic;
> nor the lady's, which is nice; nor the lover's, which is all these: but it is a
> melancholy of mine own, compounded of many simples, extracted from
> many objects, and indeed the sundry contemplation of my travels, in
> which rumination wraps me in a most humourous sadness.
> *Ros.* A traveller! By my faith, you have great reason to be sad, I fear
> you have sold your own lands to see other men's. Then to have seen
> much and to have nothing is to have rich eyes and poor hands.
> *Jaq.* Yes, I have gain'd my experience.

Rosalind answers, "And your experience makes you sad. I had rather have a fool to make me merry than experience to make me sad—and to travel for it too!" (IV.i.10–29). Jaques is self-exiled.

Rosalind keeps a dialectical balance. When Orlando says that he will die if his love is not requited, Rosalind says,

No, faith, die by attorney. The poor world is almost six thousand years old, and in all this time there was not any man died in his own person, videlicet, in a love cause. Troilus had his brains dash'd out with a Grecian club; yet he did what he could to die before, and he is one of the patterns of love. Leander, he would have liv'd many a fair year though Hero had turn'd nun, if it had not been for a hot midsummer night; for (good youth) he went but forth to wash him in the Hellespont, and being taken with the cramp, was drown'd; and the foolish chroniclers of that age found it was "Hero of Sestos." But these are all lies. Men have died from time to time, and worms have eaten them, but not for love. (IV.i.94–108)

At the same time, Rosalind confesses to Celia how much she loves Orlando: "O coz, coz, coz, my pretty little coz, that thou didst know how many fathom deep I am in love! But it cannot be sounded. My affection hath an unknown bottom, like the Bay of Portugal" (IV.i.209–13).

Touchstone stands up for the similarity of the court and the rustic in his argument with Corin:

Cor. Sir, I am a true labourer; I earn that I eat, get that I wear; owe no man hate, envy no man's happiness; glad of other men's good, content with my harm; and the greatest of my pride is to see my ewes graze and my lambs suck.
Touch. That is another simple sin in you: to bring the ewes and the rams together and to offer to get your living by the copulation of cattle; to be bawd to a bell-wether, and to betray a she-lamb of a twelvemonth to a crooked-pated old cuckoldly ram, out of all reasonable match. If thou beest not damn'd for this, the devil himself will have no shepherds; I cannot see else how thou shouldst scape. (III.ii.77–90)

The representation of wild nature in the lioness contributes to the apparent absurdity of the resolution. Through grace, Oliver overcomes his temptation to let the lioness eat Orlando, and thus converted, he marries Celia. Duke Frederick meets a hermit in the desert—which is important—and is converted by him both from his intention of taking vengeance upon his brother in the forest and "from the world" (V.iv.168). He leaves his crown to Duke Senior. Nature has become a place of repentance, from which the exiles can return. Oliver and Duke Frederick retire to the country not because of its pastoral superiority, but because it is necessary for them to repent—just as, perhaps, the exiles have learned through the suffering of exile. Nature is not a place to retire as *idiotes*, but as a preparation for a return to the world. For others, like Duke Frederick, the retirement to the country is a penance.

Goethe writes, "*Es bildet ein Talent sich in der Stille, / Sich ein Charakter in dem Strom der Welt*," talent builds itself in quietness, character in the stream of the world. Jaques remains in the country. Like Shylock he won't join the dance, like Hamlet his involvement with society is unhappy, like Caliban he is unassimilable. He is too self-conscious, he must go and see things, there is much to be learned—he has an obstinate intellect, as opposed to Caliban's passion. Civilization is a dance between the ocean of barbarism, which is a unity, and the desert of triviality, which is diverse. One must keep a dialectical balance, and keep both faith—through will, and humor—through intellect. Jaques has the latter, Rosalind has both, so she is able to get the returning exiles to join in the rite of dance.

Alice dances so with Tweedledum and Tweedledee:

> ... she took hold of both hands at once: the next moment they were dancing round in a ring. This seemed quite natural (she remembered afterwards), and she was not even surprised to hear music playing: it seemed to come from the tree under which they were dancing, and it was done (as well as she could make it out) by the branches rubbing one across the other, like fiddles and fiddlesticks. ... I don't know when I began it, but somehow I felt as if I had been singing it a long long time!"

———

1951—Harold C. Goddard. *"As You Like It,"* from *The Meaning of Shakespeare*

Harold C. Goddard (1878–1950) was head of the English Department at Swarthmore College. One of the most important twentieth-century books on Shakespeare is his *The Meaning of Shakespeare*, published after his death.

I

As You Like It is far from being one of Shakespeare's greatest plays, but it is one of his best-loved ones. "I know nothing better than to be in the forest," says a character in Dostoevsky, "though all things are good." We are in a forest, the Forest of Arden, during four-fifths of *As You Like It*, but it is a forest that by some magic lets in perpetual sunshine. And not only do we have a sense of constant natural beauty around us; we are in the presence, too, almost continuously, of a number of the other supremely good things of life, song and laughter, simplicity and love; while to guard against surfeit and keep romance within bounds, there is a seasoning of caustic and even cynical wit, plenty of foolishness as a foil for the wisdom, and, for variety, an intermingling of social worlds from courtiers and courtly exiles to shepherds and country bumpkins. In this last respect *As You Like It* repeats the miracle of *A Midsummer-Night's Dream*.

As might be expected of a work that is a dramatized version of a pastoral romance (Lodge's *Rosalynde*), the play is the most "natural" and at the same time one of the most artificial of the author's. Yet we so surrender ourselves after a little to its special tone and atmosphere that there is no other work of Shakespeare's in which coincidences, gods from the machine, and what we can only call operatic duets, trios, and quartettes trouble us less or seem less out of place. The snake and lioness that figure in Oliver's sudden conversion might be thought to be enough for one play, but when on top of that in the twinkling of an eye an old religious man turns the cruel usurping Duke, who is on the march with an army against his enemies, into a humble and forgiving hermit, instead of questioning the psychology we accept it meekly and merely observe inwardly that the magic of the Forest of Arden is evidently even more potent than we had supposed.

It is customary to find the main theme of *As You Like It* in the contrast between court and country. "If we present a pastoral," said Thomas Heywood, "we show the harmless love of shepherds, diversely moralized, distinguishing between the craft of the city and the innocency of the sheep-cote." The play does indeed involve the question of the relative merits of these types of life, and the conclusion implied seems on the surface to be similar to George Meredith's in "Earth's Secret," namely, that wisdom is to be found in residents neither of the country nor of the city but in those rather who "hither thither fare" between the two,

Close interthreading nature with our kind.

But whoever goes no deeper than this does not get very near the heart of *As You Like It*. Shakespeare was the last person to believe that geography makes the man.

There is generally an Emersonian sentence that comes as close to summing up a Shakespearean play as anything so brief as a sentence can. "A mind might ponder its thought for ages and not gain so much self-knowledge as the passion of love shall teach it in a day." There, compressed, is the essence of *As You Like It*, and, positively or negatively, almost every scene in it is contrived to emphasize that truth. As *Love's Labour's Lost*, to which Emerson's sentence is almost equally pertinent, has to do with the relation of love and learning, *As You Like It* has to do with the relation of love and wisdom. Rosalind is the author's instrument for making clear what that relation is.

II

In no other comedy of Shakespeare's is the heroine so all-important as Rosalind is in this one; she makes the play almost as completely as Hamlet does *Hamlet*. She seems ready to transcend the rather light piece in which she finds herself and, if only the plot would let her, to step straight into tragedy. When Celia, in the second scene of the play, begs her cousin to be more merry, Rosalind, in the first words she utters, replies:

> Dear Celia, I show more mirth than I am mistress of; and would
> you yet I were merrier?

> I am not merry; but I do beguile
> The thing I am by seeming otherwise,

says Desdemona on the quay at Cyprus and on the edge of her tragedy. The similarity is startling. It clinches, as it were, the impression Rosalind makes on those who admire her most: that she had it in her, in Cordelia's words, to outfrown a falser fortune's frown than any she is called on to face in this comedy. In so far as she has, she is a transitional figure.

As You Like It has no lack of interesting characters, but most of them grow pretty thin in Rosalind's presence, like match flames in the sun. However less brilliant, Celia suffers less than she otherwise would because of her loyalty and devotion to her cousin and freedom from jealousy of her. Adam, Corin, and Rosalind's father are characters in their own right, but minor ones. Orlando at his best is thoroughly worthy of the woman he loves, but by and large she sets him in the shade. For the rest, Rosalind exposes, without trying to, their one-sidedness or inferiority, whether by actual contact or in the mind of the reader.

> Heaven Nature charg'd
> That one body should be fill'd
> With all graces. . . .

It is this wholeness of hers by which the others are tried, and in the comparison Touchstone himself (so named possibly for that very reason) fades into a mere manipulator of words, while that other favorite of the commentators, Jaques, is totally eclipsed.

III

One way of taking Jaques is to think of him as a picture, duly attenuated, of what Shakespeare himself might have become if he had let experience sour or embitter him, let his critical powers get the better of his imagination, "philosophy" of poetry. As traveler-libertine Jaques has had his day. Now he would turn spectator-cynic and revenge himself on a world that can no longer afford him pleasure, by proving it foul and infected. The more his vision is darkened the blacker, naturally, what he sees becomes in his eyes. He would withdraw from society entirely if he were not so dependent on it for audience. That is his dilemma. So he alternately retreats and darts forth from his retreat to buttonhole anyone who will listen to his railing. But when he tries to rationalize his misanthropy and pass it off as medicine for a sick world, the Duke Senior administers a deserved rebuke. Your very chiding of sin, he tells him, is "mischievous foul sin" itself.

Jaques prides himself on his wit and wisdom. But he succeeds only in proving how little wit and even "wisdom" amount to when indulged in for their own sakes and at the expense of life. His jests and "philosophy" give the effect of having been long pondered in solitude. But the moment he crosses swords with Orlando and Rosalind, the professional is hopelessly outclassed by the amateurs. Extemporaneously they beat him at his own carefully rehearsed game. Being out of love with life, Jaques thinks of nothing but himself. Being in love with Rosalind, Orlando thinks of himself last and has both the humility and the insight that love bequeaths. When the two men encounter, Jaques' questions and answers sound studied and affected, Orlando's spontaneous and sincere.

> Jaq.: Rosalind is your love's name?
> Orl.: Yes, just.
> Jaq.: I do not like her name.
> Orl.: There was no thought of pleasing you when she was christened.
> Jaq.: What stature is she of?
> Orl.: Just as high as my heart.
> Jaq.: You are full of pretty answers. Have you not been acquainted
> with goldsmiths' wives, and conn'd them out of rings?
> Orl.: Not so; but I answer you right painted cloth, from whence you
> have studied your questions.
> Jaq.: You have a nimble wit: I think 'twas made of Atalanta's heels.
> Will you sit down with me? and we two will rail against our mistress the
> world, and all our misery.
> Orl.: I will chide no breather in the world but myself, against whom
> I know most faults.

There is not a trace of any false note in that answer. It has the ring of the true modesty and true wisdom that only true love imparts. Jaques, of course, misses the point diametrically:

JAQ.: The worst fault you have is to be in love.

ORL.: 'Tis a fault I will not change for your best virtue. I am weary
of you.

(To tell the truth we are a bit weary of him too.)

And Rosalind outphilosophizes Jaques as utterly as Orlando has out-
jested him.

JAQ.: I prithee, pretty youth, let me be better acquainted with thee.

Ros.: They say you are a melancholy fellow.

JAQ.: I am so; I do love it better than laughing.

Ros.: Those that are in extremity of either are abominable fellows,
and betray themselves to every modern censure worse than drunkards.

JAQ.: Why, 'tis good to be sad and say nothing.

Ros.: Why, then, 'tis good to be a post.

JAQ.: I have neither the scholar's melancholy, which is emulation; nor
the musician's . . .

and after enumerating seven different types of melancholy, he concludes,

. . . but it is a melancholy of mine own, compounded of many simples,
extracted from many objects; and indeed the sundry contemplation of
my travels, in which my often rumination wraps me in a most humorous
sadness—

Ros.: A traveller! By my faith, you have great reason to be sad. I fear
you have sold your own lands to see other men's; then, to have seen
much, and to have nothing, is to have rich eyes and poor hands.

JAQ.: Yes, I have gained my experience.

Ros.: And your experience makes you sad. I had rather have a fool to
make me merry than experience to make me sad; and to travel for it too!

Love bestows on those who embrace it the experience and wisdom of the
race, compared with which the knowledge schools and foreign lands can offer is
at the worst a mere counterfeit and at the best a mere beginning. What wonder
that Jaques, after being so thoroughly trounced by the pretty youth whose
acquaintance he was seeking a moment before, is glad to sneak away as Orlando
enters (what would they have done to him together?), or that Rosalind, after a
"Farewell, Monsieur Traveller," turns with relief to her lover.

Even Jaques' most famous speech, his "Seven Ages of Man" as it has come to
be called, which he must have rehearsed more times than the modern schoolboy
who declaims it, does not deserve its reputation for wisdom. It sometimes seems
as if Shakespeare had invented Adam (that grand reconciliation of servant

and man) as Jaques' perfect opposite and let him enter this scene, pat, at the exact moment when Jaques is done describing the "last scene of all," as a living refutation of his picture of old age. How Shakespeare loved to let life obliterate language in this way! And he does it here prospectively as well as retrospectively, for the Senior Duke a second later, by his hospitable welcome of Adam and Orlando, obliterates or at least mitigates Amiens' song of man's ingratitude ("Blow, blow, thou winter wind") that immediately follows.

IV

When I read the commentators on Touchstone, I rub my eyes. You would think to hear most of them that he is a genuinely wise and witty man and that Shakespeare so considered him. That Shakespeare knew he could pass him off for that in a theater may be agreed. What he is is another matter. A "dull fool" Rosalind calls him on one occasion. "O noble fool! a worthy fool!" says Jaques on another. It is easy to guess with which of the two Shakespeare came nearer to agreeing. The Elizabethan groundlings had to have their clown. At his best, Touchstone is merely one more and one of the most inveterate of the author's word-jugglers, and at his worst (as a wit) precisely what Rosalind called him. What he is at his worst as a man justifies still harsher characterization.

In her first speech after he enters the play in the first act, Rosalind describes him as "the cutter-off of Nature's wit," and his role abundantly justifies her judgment. "Thou speakest wiser than thou art ware of," she says to him on another occasion, and as if expressly to prove the truth of what she says, Touchstone obligingly replies, "Nay, I shall ne'er be ware of mine own wit till I break my shins against it." Which is plainly Shakespeare's conscious and Touchstone's unconscious way of stating that his wit is low. And his manners are even lower, as he shows when he first accosts Corin and Rosalind rebukes him for his rude tone:

> Touch.: Holla, you clown!
> Ros.: Peace, fool; he's not thy kinsman.
> Cor.: Who calls?
> Touch.: Your betters, sir.
> Cor.: Else are they very wretched.
> Ros.: Peace, I say. Good even to you, friend.

Nothing could show more succinctly Rosalind's "democracy" in contrast to Touchstone's snobbery. (No wonder the people thought highly of her, as they did of Hamlet.) The superiority in wisdom of this "clown" to the man who condescends to him comes out, as we might predict it would, a little later.

> Touch.: Wast ever in court, shepherd?
> Cor.: No, truly.

Touch.: Then thou art damned.
Cor.: Nay, I hope.
Touch.: Truly, thou art damned, like an ill-roasted egg all on
one side.

It is an almost invariable rule in Shakespeare, as it is in life, that when one man damns another, even in jest, he unconsciously utters judgment on himself, and the rest of the scene, like Touchstone's whole role, is dedicated to showing that he himself is his own ill-roasted egg, all "wit" and word-play and nothing else.

Cor.: For not being at court? Your reason.
Touch.: Why, if thou never wast at court, thou never sawest good manners [*We have just had, and are now having, a sample of the manners of this "courtier" who greeted Corin as a "clown."*]; if thou never sawest good manners, then thy manners must be wicked; and wickedness is sin, and sin is damnation. Thou art in a parlous state, shepherd.

Corin may be a "silly" shepherd but he is not taken in by this silly verbal legerdemain. He stands up to his "better" stoutly:

Cor.: Not a whit, Touchstone: those that are good manners at the court, are as ridiculous in the country as the behaviour of the country is most mockable at the court,

and he illustrates by pointing out that the habit of kissing hands at court would be uncleanly among shepherds. Whereupon, as we might expect, Touchstone, forgetting his own rule that he who calls himself wise is a fool, cries "Learn of the wise," and descends to an even lower level of sophistry than before. Corin, sensing that it is futile to argue with such a man, refuses to continue, but refuses with a courtesy at the opposite pole from Touchstone's rudeness, and we suddenly realize that Shakespeare has contrived the whole episode as a refutation on the plane of life of the conclusion for which Touchstone is contending: that good manners are impossible for a countryman.

Cor.: You have too courtly a wit for me; I'll rest.

In reply to which we have an example of courtly wit and manners:

Touch.: Wilt thou rest damned? God help thee, shallow man!

Shallow man! the best possible characterization of Touchstone himself at the moment. And as if to show by way of contrast what a deep man is, Shakespeare lets Corin condense his life into a sentence which, if a sentence ever was, is a perfect blend of modesty and pride:

> COR.: Sir, I am a true labourer: I earn that I eat, get that I wear, owe no man hate, envy no man's happiness, glad of other men's good, content with my harm; and the greatest of my pride is to see my ewes graze and my lambs suck.

It is one of the tersest and one of the finest "creeds" to be found anywhere in Shakespeare, at the farthest possible remove from Touchstone's own which Jaques overheard and quoted. And with all his "wit" the only thing Touchstone can think up by way of retort is the taunt that Corin by his own confession is a "bawd" because, forsooth, he makes his living by the multiplication of his stock. A Hottentot would be ashamed of such reasoning, and as for the jocosity of it, it is close to Touchstone's "low," which is saying a good deal. To the crass animality and ribaldry of this courtier Shakespeare, with another of his sudden switches, instantly opposes the "sanctity" of the man whose very kisses are like "the touch of holy bread": Rosalind, as Ganymede, enters reading snatches of the verses her lover has been hanging or carving on the trees.

> Her worth, being mounted on the wind,
> Through all the world bears Rosalind,

verses which Touchstone, as we would expect, proceeds to parody in such choice lines as:

> If the cat will after kind,
> So be sure will Rosalind.

What wonder that Rosalind rebukes the man as a "dull fool" and tells him that, like a medlar, he will be rotten ere he is ripe. The simile is a manifest double allusion on Shakespeare's part, first, to Touchstone's own "ill-roasted egg" (the same idea under another image), and, second, to Touchstone's summary of human life:

> And so, from hour to hour we ripe and ripe,
> And then from hour to hour we rot and rot.

If we know anything about the man who through the mouth of Edgar in *King Lear* declared that "Ripeness is all," we know what he must have thought of this philosophy of Touchstone's. He must have thought it rotten—rotten not in any modern colloquial sense of the term but rotten in the full implication of the horticultural metaphor.

But even with all this mauling, Shakespeare is not done with Touchstone. Having demonstrated to the hilt that his wit instead of sharpening has dulled his wits, he proceeds to show that his wit has also withered his heart. It is in his interlude with Audrey that we see Touchstone at his moral nadir. It will be said, of course, that this episode is pure farce and that to take it seriously is to show lack of humor. The objection need disturb nobody but the man who makes it. For of all the strange things about this man William Shakespeare one of the most remarkable is the fact that he could contrive no scene so theatrical, no stage effect so comic or dialogue so nonsensical, as to protect himself from the insertion right in the midst of it of touches of nature scientific in their veracity. Such was the grip that truth seems to have had on him.

Audrey is generally dismissed as a country wench expressly set up as a butt for Touchstone. And a theater audience can be duly counted on to roar with laughter at her. She is indeed just a goatherd, plain in appearance (though doubtless not as plain as Touchstone would make out) and so unlettered that most words of more than one syllable bewilder her simple wits. Touchstone's literary and mythological puns and allusions are naturally lost on her. But the attentions of this stranger from the court have awakened unwonted emotions and aspirations in her breast, and nothing could be clearer than her desire to be modest and true and pure. Love is the great leveler as well as the great lifter, and Audrey, perhaps for the first time in her life, feels that even she may have a place in God's world. And this is the way Touchstone deals with the emotion he has awakened:

> TOUCH.: Truly, I would the gods had made thee poetical.
> AUD.: I do not know what "poetical" is. Is it honest in deed and word? Is it a true thing?
> TOUCH.: No, truly, for the truest poetry is the most feigning; and lovers are given to poetry, and what they swear in poetry may be said as lovers they do feign.
> AUD.: Do you wish then that the gods had made me poetical?
> TOUCH.: I do, truly; for thou swearest to me thou art honest; now, if thou wert a poet, I might have some hope thou didst feign.
> AUD.: Would you not have me honest?
> TOUCH.: No, truly, unless thou wert hard-favour'd; for honesty coupled to beauty is to have honey a sauce to sugar.

JAQ.: (*Aside*): A material fool.

AUD.: Well, I am not fair, and therefore I pray the gods make me honest.

TOUCH.: Truly, and to cast away honesty upon a foul slut were to put good meat into an unclean dish.

AUD.: I am not a slut, though I thank the gods I am foul.

TOUCH.: Well, praised be the gods for thy foulness! sluttishness may come hereafter.

As "theater" this is doubtless what a modern director might call "sure-fire stuff." As life it comes close to being the sin against the Holy Ghost. Touchstone of course is planning to marry Audrey ("to take that that no man else will") and abandon her as soon as he is sick of his bargain, and when Sir Oliver Martext, a marrying parson, enters, he is ready to go ahead with the ceremony then and there. Jaques, who has been eavesdropping, coming forward offers at first to "give the woman." But on second thought the scandalous procedure is too much for even him to stomach and he rebukes Touchstone roundly for his conduct, about the best thing Jaques does in the play:

> And will you, being a man of your breeding, be married under a bush
> like a beggar? Get you to church, and have a good priest that can tell
> you what marriage is.

But a good priest and a binding marriage are precisely what Touchstone does not want.

Later, Shakespeare treats us to a little encounter between Touchstone and William, the forest youth who "lays claim" to Audrey. Setting out to make a fool of him, Touchstone asks him if he is wise.

WILL.: Ay, sir, I have a pretty wit.

TOUCH.: Why, thou sayest well. I do now remember a saying, "The fool doth think he is wise, but the wise man knows himself to be a fool."

But in that case Touchstone stands condemned as a fool by his own rule, for about twenty lines back in this same scene he had said, "By my troth, we that have good wits have much to answer for." And about ten lines farther on he again convicts himself by his own rule even more convincingly:

TOUCH.: You do love this maid?

WILL.: I do, sir.

TOUCH.: Give me your hand. Art thou learned?

WILL.: No, sir.

TOUCH.: Then learn this of me. . . .

Whereupon, addressing William as "you clown," he announces that he, Touchstone, is the man who is to marry Audrey, and orders his rival on pain of death to abandon her company, meanwhile drowning him under such a flood of unfamiliar words that the bewildered youth is only too glad to decamp. "Oh, but Touchstone's threats to kill are just jest," it will be said, "and his superiority and condescension just mock-heroics and mock-pedantics. Again you are guilty of taking seriously what is mere fooling, making a mountain out of a molehill of the text, and treating William as if he were a real human being instead of the theatrical puppet that he is." (As if Shakespeare did not make even his most minor characters human beings!) Granted that to Touchstone the whole thing is a huge joke; that does not make his torrent of talk any less perplexing or menacing to William, nor the theft of Audrey any less mean or immoral. It is merely a consummation of what this man in motley has revealed throughout: his snobbery and bad manners, and ultimately his hard heart. Touchstone, if you insist, is making a fool of this rustic simpleton, William. It is another William who is making a fool of Touchstone.

So even the tormented comes off better than the tormentor. Indeed nearly everybody in the play does who comes in contact with Touchstone. "A touchstone," says the dictionary, is "a black siliceous stone used to test the purity of gold and silver by the streak left on the stone when rubbed by the metal." Not precious itself, it reveals preciousness in what touches it. That seems to be precisely the function assigned to Touchstone in this play, so perhaps its author knew what he was doing when he named him. Near the end two of the banished Duke's pages enter and Touchstone asks them for a song. They comply with his request by singing

It was a lover and his lass,

and when they are done Touchstone rewards them by remarking, "Truly, young gentlemen, though there was no great matter in the ditty, yet the note was very untuneable." "You are deceived, sir," the First Page protests, "we kept time; we lost not our time." "By my troth, yes," Touchstone persists, "I count it but time lost to hear such a foolish song." Here again Shakespeare lets Touchstone judge himself in judging others, for though as manikin he will doubtless long continue to entertain the crowd in the theater, as man he is even more empty of both matter and music than the foolish song he counts it time lost to listen to. Touchstone is "wit" without love.

V

And Rosalind is wit with love, which is humor, humor being what wit turns into when it falls in love. But humor is almost a synonym for many-sidedness and reconciliation of opposites, and in her versatility, her balance of body, mind, and spirit, Rosalind reminds us of no less a figure than Hamlet himself, the uncontaminated Hamlet. As there is a woman within the Prince of Denmark, so there is a man within this Duke's daughter, but never at the sacrifice of her dominant feminine nature. "Do you not know I am a woman? when I think, I must speak," she says to Celia. She changes color when she first suspects that the verses on the trees are Orlando's, and cries "Alas the day! what shall I do with my doublet and hose?" when the fact that he is in the Forest is confirmed. And she swoons when she hears he is wounded. Yes, Rosalind is a woman in spite of the strength and courage of the man within her. All of which makes her disguise as a boy immeasurably more than a merely theatrical matter.

> That you are fair or wise is vain,
> Or strong, or rich, or generous;
> You must add the untaught strain
> That sheds beauty on the rose.

So says Emerson (in lines enough in themselves to acquit him of being what he is so often called, a "puritan"). Rosalind is all of these things: fair and wise and strong and rich (except in a worldly sense) and generous. But not in vain. For she has also, as her name betokens, the untaught strain that sheds beauty on a rose. The Forest of Arden, for all its trees, is, as we remarked, forever flooded with sunshine. There is no mystery about it. Rosalind is in the Forest and she supplies it with an internal light. "Be like the sun," says Dostoevsky. Rosalind is. She attracts everything that comes within her sphere and sheds a radiance over it. She is the pure gold that needs no touchstone.

Rosalind has the world at her feet not just for what she is but because, being what she is, she so conducts her love with Orlando as to make it a pattern for all true love-making. Unimaginative love, whether sentimental or overpassionate, overreaches and defeats itself because it cannot keep its secret. Intentionally or otherwise, it spills over—confesses or gives itself away. (Juliet is no exception: she admitted her love so soon only because Romeo had overheard her in soliloquy by accident.) The love of Silvius for Phebe and of Phebe for Ganymede in this play are examples. Imaginative love is wiser. Taking its cue from the arts, of which it is one and perhaps the highest, it creates a hypothetical case in its own image, a kind of celestial trap under cover of which (only the maddest mixture of metaphors can do it justice) it extorts an unconscious confession from the loved one, all the while keeping a line of retreat fully open in case the confession should be unfavorable, in order that no humiliation may ensue.

In this play Rosalind undertakes to cure Orlando of his love by having him come every day to woo her under the illusion that she is just the boy Ganymede impersonating Rosalind. Thus the love between the two is rehearsed in the kingdom of the imagination, where all true love begins, before any attempt is made to bring it down to the level of everyday life, a situation that permits both lovers to speak now as boldly, now as innocently, as though they were angels or children. (The only conceivable situation that could surpass it as a model of right love-making would be one where each of the lovers was simultaneously luring the other into a confession without that other being aware of what was happening.)

Again we are reminded of the Prince of Denmark. In *Hamlet* a literal play within the play becomes a device (inspired or infernal according to your interpretation of the play) whereby to catch the guilty conscience of a murderer. Here a metaphorical "play" within the play becomes a celestial trap in which to expose the tender heart of a lover. Heaven and hell are at opposite poles, but the one is a model of the other. "Upward, downward," says Heraclitus, "the way is the same." It is not chance that *As You Like It* and *Hamlet* were written not far apart in time.

Love between man and woman having the importance that it does in life, what wonder that a drama that depicts it in perfect action under its happiest aspect should be popular, even though not one in a hundred understands the ground of its fascination. How many a woman who sees or reads *As You Like It* either believes in secret that she does resemble Rosalind or wishes that she did! And how many a man projects on its heroine the image of the woman he loves best, or, if not, the memory of some lost first love who still embodies the purest instincts of his youth, and hears her voice instead of the words printed on the page! Which is why the imaginative man will always prefer to read the play rather than to have some obliterating actress come between the text and his heart. And so Rosalind is a sort of universal image of Woman as Sweetheart, just as Cressida is an image of Woman as Seductress, and Cleopatra of Woman, both good and evil, in a still more universal sense.

In her own way, and on a lower level, Rosalind contributes her mite to our understanding of why Dante chose the Rose as a symbol of the ultimate paradise.

1955—Harold Jenkins.
"*As You Like It*," from *Shakespeare Survey*

Harold Jenkins was general editor of the Arden Shakespeare (Second Series). His essays are collected in *Structural Problems in Shakespeare: Lectures and Essays by Harold Jenkins*.

A masterpiece is not to be explained, and to attempt to explain it is apt to seem ridiculous. I must say at once that I propose nothing so ambitious. I merely hope, by looking at one play, even in what must necessarily be a very fragmentary way and with my own imperfect sight, to illustrate something of what Shakespeare's method in comedy may be. And I have chosen *As You Like It* because it seems to me to exhibit, most clearly of all the comedies, Shakespeare's characteristic excellences in this kind. This is not to say that *As You Like It* is exactly a representative specimen. Indeed I am going to suggest that it is not. In this play, what I take to be Shakespeare's distinctive virtues as a writer of comedy have their fullest scope; but in order that they may have it, certain of the usual ingredients of Shakespeare's comedy, or indeed of any comedy, have to be—not of course eliminated, but very much circumscribed. In *As You Like It*, I suggest, Shakespeare took his comedy in one direction nearly as far as it could go. And then, as occasionally happens in Shakespeare's career, when he has developed his art far in one direction, in the comedy which succeeds he seems to readjust his course.

If our chronology is right, after *As You Like It* comes, among the comedies, *Twelfth Night*. And while we may accept that *Twelfth Night* is, as Sir Edmund Chambers says, very much akin to *As You Like It* "in style and temper", in some important respects it returns to the method and structure of the previous comedy of *Much Ado About Nothing*. Sandwiched between these two, *As You Like It* is conspicuously lacking in comedy's more robust and boisterous elements—the pomps of Dogberry and the romps of Sir Toby. More significantly, it has nothing which corresponds to the splendid theatricalism of the church scene in *Much Ado*, nothing which answers to those crucial bits of trickery by which Benedick and Beatrice in turn are hoodwinked into love. Even if, as may be objected, they are not hoodwinked but merely tricked into removing their hoods, still those stratagems in Leonato's orchard are necessary if the happy ending proper to the comedy is to be brought about. These ambushes, if I may call them so—they are really inverted ambushes—are paralleled, or should one say parodied, in *Twelfth Night* in the scene where Malvolio is persuaded that he too is beloved. And this ambush too is necessary if, as the comedy demands, Malvolio is to have his sanity called in question and his authority undermined. The slandering of Hero in *Much Ado* also is to have its counterpart in *Twelfth Night*. For the slandering of Hero, with its culmination in the church scene, forces one pair of lovers violently apart while bringing another pair together. And in *Twelfth Night* the confusion of identities holds one pair of lovers—Orsino and Viola—temporarily apart, yet forces another pair—Olivia and Sebastian—with some violence together. A satisfactory outcome in *Much Ado* and *Twelfth Night* depends on such embroilments; and the same is even more true in an earlier comedy like *A Midsummer Night's Dream*. In *As You Like It* I can hardly say that such embroilments do not occur, but they are not structural to anything like the same degree. Without the heroine's masculine disguise Phebe would not have married Silvius any more than in *Twelfth Night* Olivia would have married Sebastian; but the confusions of identity in *As You Like It* have no influence whatever upon the ultimate destiny of Rosalind and Orlando, or of the kingdom of Duke Senior, or of the estate of Sir Rowland de Boys. Yet these are the destinies with which the action of the play is concerned. It is in the defectiveness of its action that *As You Like It* differs from the rest of the major comedies—in its dearth not only of big theatrical scenes but of events linked together by the logical intricacies of cause and effect. Of comedy, as of tragedy, action is the first essential; but *As You Like It* suggests that action is not, if I may adapt a phrase of Marston's, "the life of these things". It may be merely the foundation on which they are built. And *As You Like It* further shows that on a very flimsy foundation, if only you are skilful enough, a very elaborate structure may be poised. But the method has its dangers, and though Shakespeare's skill conceals these dangers from us, *Twelfth Night*, as I said, returns to a more orthodox scheme.

The story which provides the action for *As You Like It* belongs to the world of fairy-tale or folk-lore. This is a world which supplied the plots of a number of Shakespeare's plays, including the greatest, notably *King Lear*. And fairy-tales have many advantages for the dramatist, among which is their total disregard of practical probabilities. In fairy-tales, for example, evil is always absolute, clearly recognized, and finally overthrown; all of which may have something to do with the Aristotelian theory that while history records what has happened, poetry shows what should happen. Relaxing the more prosaic demands of verisimilitude, the fairy-tale invites the imagination. It can certainly provide a convenient road into the Forest of Arden. And this is not less true for Shakespeare because the road had already been built for him by Lodge.

A man has died and left three sons. Three is the inevitable number, and though Shakespeare, like Lodge, forgets to do much with the middle one, he is not therefore unimportant. The eldest brother is wicked, the youngest virtuous— and does fabulous feats of strength, notably destroying a giant in the shape of Charles the wrestler, who has torn other hopeful youths to pieces. Orlando therefore wins the princess, herself the victim of a wicked uncle, who has usurped her father's throne. This is the *story* of *As You Like It*. And Shakespeare, making the journey of the imagination far more quickly than Lodge, gets most of it over in the first act. That is what is remarkable. By the time we reach the second act Rosalind has already come safe to the Forest of Arden, by the aid of her man's disguise. From this disguise, as everybody knows, springs the principal comic situation of the play. But such is the inconsequential nature of the action that this comic situation develops only when the practical need for the disguise is past. The course of true love has not run smooth. But most of its obstacles have really disappeared before the main comedy begins. It only remains for the wicked to be converted, as they duly are at the end, all in comedy's good but arbitrary time, when the wicked eldest brother makes a suitable husband for the second princess. Or a most *un*suitable husband, as all the critics have complained. But this, I think, is to misunderstand. Instead of lamenting that Celia should be thrown away on Oliver, he having been much too wicked to deserve her, we should rather see that Oliver's getting this reward is a seal set on his conversion, and a sign of how good he has now become.

The first act of *As You Like It* has to supply the necessary minimum of event. But, Quiller-Couch notwithstanding, this first act is something more than mechanical.[2] It is for one thing a feat of compression, rapid, lucid and, incidentally, theatrical. In fifty lines we know all about the three brothers and the youngest is at the eldest's throat. In three hundred more we know all about the banished Duke and where and how he lives, and the giant has been destroyed before our eyes. But there is more to the first act than this. Before we enter Arden, to "fleet the time carelessly, as they did in the golden world", we must be able to contrast its simple life with the brittle refinement of the court. This surely is the point of some of what 'Q' called the "rather pointless chop-logic"; and also of the courtier figure of Le Beau, a little sketch for Osric, with his foppery of diction and his expert knowledge of sport. Le Beau's notion of sport provokes Touchstone's pointed comment on the courtier's values: "Thus men may grow wiser every day: it is the first time that ever I heard breaking of ribs was sport for ladies." This is the callousness one learns at a court ruled by a tyrannous Duke, whose malevolent rage against Rosalind and Orlando not only drives them both to Arden but completes the picture of the world they leave behind.

This first act, then, shows some instinct for dramatic preparation, though we may grant that Shakespeare's haste to get ahead makes him curiously perfunctory. He is in two minds about when Duke Senior was banished; and about which Duke is to be called Frederick; and whether Rosalind or Celia is the taller. He has not quite decided about the character of Touchstone. I do not think these are signs of revision. They simply show Shakespeare plunging into his play with some of its details still but half-shaped in his mind. The strangest of these details is the mysterious middle brother, called Fernandyne by Lodge but merely "Second Brother" in *As You Like It*, when at length he makes his appearance at the end. Yet in the fifth line of the play he was already christened Jaques. And Shakespeare of course afterwards gave this name to someone else. It seems clear enough that these two men with the same name were originally meant to be one. As things turned out Jaques could claim to have acquired his famous melancholy from travel and experience; but I suspect that it really began in the schoolbooks which were studied with such profit by Jaques de Boys. Though he grew into something very different, Jaques surely had his beginnings in the family of De Boys and in such an academy as that in Navarre where four young men turned their backs on love and life in the belief that they could supply the want of experience by study and contemplation.

Interesting as it might be to develop this idea, the important point of comparison between *As You Like It* and *Love's Labour's Lost* is of another kind. And to this I should like briefly to refer before I come to discuss the main part of *As You Like It*. *Love's Labour's Lost* is the one play before *As You Like It* in which Shakespeare sought to write a comedy with the minimum of action. Four young men make a vow to have nothing to do with a woman; each breaks his oath and ends vowing to serve a woman. That is the story; far slighter than in *As You Like It*. Yet, in contrast with *As You Like It*, the careful and conspicuous organization of *Love's Labour's Lost* distributes its thin action evenly through the play. And the characters always act in concert. In the first act the men, all together, make their vow; in the second the ladies, all together, arrive and the temptation begins. The climax duly comes, where you would expect it, in a big scene in Act IV, when each in turn breaks his vow and all together are found out. *Love's Labour's Lost* is the most formally constructed of all the comedies. When the ladies and gentlemen temporarily exchange partners, this is done symmetrically and to order. Indeed the movement of the whole play is like a well-ordered dance in which each of the participants repeats the steps of the others. But this is exactly what does *not* happen in *As You Like It*, where the characters do *not* keep in step. When they *seem* to be doing the same thing they are really doing something different, and if they ever echo one another they mean quite different things by what they say—as could easily be illustrated from the little quartet of lovers in the fifth act ("And so am I for Phebe.—And I for Ganymede.—And I for Rosalind.—And I for no woman"), where the similarity of the tune they sing conceals their different situations. The pattern of *As You Like It* comes not from a mere repetition of steps, but from constant little shifts and changes. The formal parallelisms of *Love's Labour's Lost* are replaced by a more complex design, one loose enough to hold all sorts of asymmetries within it.

But of course the effect of variations upon a theme instead of simple repetitions is not new in *As You Like It*. It is the tendency of Shakespeare's comedy from the start. In *Love's Labour's Lost* itself the courtly gestures of the four young men are burlesqued by those of a fantastic knight, and while the four young men are vowing not to see a woman, Costard the clown is "taken with a wench". Moreover, one of the four, though he goes through the movements with the others, has some trouble to keep in step, and is always threatening to break out of the ring. Even when he makes his vow with the others, he knows that necessity will make him break it. As he joins in their purposes he knows them to be foolish and he mocks at ideals which he at the same time pursues. Human activity offers itself to the dramatist in a large variety of forms and the same individual can play contradictory parts. The drunken tinker in *The Taming of the Shrew* does not know whether he may not really be a noble lord. Although Shakespeare did not invent this situation, it was just the thing to appeal to him. For he knew that a man is very easily "translated".

In the middle of his fairy play he put a man with an ass's head. In perhaps the most remarkable encounter in Shakespeare the daintiest fairy queen caresses a man turned brute, who, with a fairy kingdom around him, can think only of scratching his itch. When the animal appears in a man it may terrify his fellows; it may also attract to it his finest dreams and fancies, corrupting them, or being uplifted by them to a vision of new wonder. Shakespeare of course does nothing as crude as *say* this. He knows as well as the Duke in Arden that sermons may be found in stones, but much better than the Duke that it is tedious to preach them, a thing, incidentally, he does not permit the Duke to do. What Shakespeare characteristically does in his comedy is to set together the contrasting elements in human nature and leave them by their juxtaposition or interaction to comment on one another.

In *As You Like It* the art of comic juxtaposition is at its subtlest. It is to give it fullest scope that the action can be pushed up into a corner, and the usual entanglements of plotting, though not dispensed with altogether, can be loosened. Freedom, of course, is in the hospitable air of Arden, where convenient caves stand ready to receive outlaws, alfresco meals are abundantly provided, with a concert of birds and running brooks, and there is no worse hardship than a salubrious winter wind. This is "the golden world" to which, with the beginning of his second act, Shakespeare at once transports us, such a world as has been the dream of poets since at least the time of Virgil when, wearied with the toilings and wranglings of society, they yearn for the simplicity and innocence of what they choose to think man's natural state.[3] It is of course a very literary tradition that Shakespeare is here using, but the long vogue of the pastoral suggests that it is connected with a universal impulse of the human mind, to which Shakespeare in *As You Like It* gives permanent expression. But this aspect of the play is merely the one which confronts us most conspicuously. There are many others. *As You Like It* has been too often praised for its idyllic quality alone, as though it were some mere May-morning frolic prolonged into a lotos-eating afternoon. A contrast with the ideal state was necessitated by the literary tradition itself, since the poet seeking an escape into the simple life was expected to hint at the ills of the society he was escaping from. That meant especially the courts of princes, where life—it was axiomatic—was at its most artificial. And the vivid sketching in of the courtly half of the antithesis is, as I have shown, an important function of *As You Like It*'s maligned first act. With the first speech of the banished Duke at the opening of the second act, the complete contrast is before us; for, while introducing us to Arden, this speech brings into sharp focus that first act which has just culminated in the usurper's murderous malice. "Are not these woods more free from peril than the envious court?" Though the contrast is traditional, it comes upon us here, like so many things in Shakespeare, with the vitality of fresh experience. The Forest of Arden comes to life in numerous little touches of the country-side, and the heartless self-seeking of the outer world is concentrated into phrases which have the force of permanent truth. The line that 'Q' admired—"And unregarded age in corners thrown"—might have come from one of the sonnets, and when Orlando observes how "none will sweat but for promotion" we recognize the fashion of our times as well as his. As the play proceeds, it is easy enough for Shakespeare to keep us ever aware of the forest, what with Amiens to sing for us, the procession home after the killing of the deer, an empty cottage standing ready for Rosalind and Celia, surrounded by olive-trees beyond a willow stream, and a good supply of oaks for Orlando or Oliver to lie under. It cannot have been quite so easy to keep us in touch with the court life we have now abandoned; but nothing is neater in the construction of the play than those well-placed little scenes which, by despatching first Orlando and then Oliver to the forest, do what is still required by the story and give the illusion that an action is still going briskly forward, while at the same time they renew our acquaintance with the wicked world. After the first scene in the ideal world of Arden and a sentimental discourse on the deer, there is Frederick again in one of his rages, sending for Oliver, who, an act later, when we are well acclimatized to the forest, duly turns up at court. Then occurs a scene of eighteen lines, in which Shakespeare gives as vivid a sketch of the unjust tyrant as one could hope to find. The tyrant prides himself upon his mercy, punishes one man for his brother's sins, and finds in his victim's excuses further cause of offence. Oliver's plaint that he had never loved his brother brings the instant retort, "More villain thou. Well, push him out of doors." As this eruption dies down, there appears in the Forest of Arden the cause of all the trouble quietly hanging his verses on a tree.

The contrast between court and country is thus presented and our preference is very plain. Yet as a counterpoise to all this, there is one man in the country-side who actually prefers the court. Finding himself in Arden, Touchstone decides: "When I was at home, I was in a better place." It is no doubt important that he is a fool, whose values may well be topsy-turvy. But in one word he reminds us that there are such things as domestic comforts. And presently we find that the old man whom society throws into the corner is likely in the "uncouth forest" to die of hunger and exposure to the "bleak air". There is clearly something to be said on the other side; the fool may anatomize the wise man's folly. And there is also Jaques to point out that the natural life in Arden, where men usurp the forest from the deer and kill them in their "native dwelling-place", while deer, like men, are in distress abandoned by their friends, is as cruel and unnatural as the other. When Amiens sings under the greenwood tree and turns "his merry note unto the sweet bird's throat", inviting us to shun ambition and be pleased with what we get, Jaques adds a further stanza to the song which suggests that to leave your "wealth and ease" is the act of an ass or a fool. Most of us, I suppose, have moods in which we would certainly agree with him, and it is a mark of Shakespeare's mature comedy that he permits this criticism of his ideal world in the very centre of it. The triumphal procession after the killing of the deer, a symbolic ritual of the forester's prowess, is accompanied by a mocking song, while the slayer of the deer is given its horns to wear as a somewhat ambiguous trophy.

It is Jaques, mostly, with the touch of the medieval buffoon in him, who contributes this grotesque element to the songs and rituals of Arden. Like Touchstone he is not impressed by Arden, but unlike Touchstone he does not prefer the court. Indeed, as we have seen, he is able to show that they are very much alike, infected by the same diseases. No doubt his is a jaundiced view of life, and it is strange that some earlier critics should have thought it might be Shakespeare's. Shakespeare's contemporaries would hardly have had difficulty in recognizing in Jaques a variant of the Elizabethan melancholy man—the epithet is applied to him often enough—though I remain a little sceptical when I am told by O.J. Campbell that from the first moment they heard Jaques described, the Elizabethans would have perceived "the unnatural melancholy produced by the adustion of phlegm".[4] Whatever its physiological kind, the important thing about his melancholy is that it is not the fatigue of spirits of the man who has found the world too much for him, but an active principle manifesting itself in tireless and exuberant antics. Far from being a morose man, whether he is weeping with the stag or jeering at the huntsman, he throws himself into these things with something akin to passion. His misanthropy is a form of self-indulgence, as is plain enough in his very first words:

> *Jaques.* More, more, I prithee, more.
> *Amiens.* It will make you melancholy, Monsieur Jaques.
> *Jaques.* I thank it. More, I prithee, more. I can suck melancholy out of a song.

His own comparison with a weasel sucking eggs suggests what a ferocious and life-destroying thing this passion is. Shakespeare's final dismissal of Jaques is profound. Far from making Celia a better husband than Oliver, as George Sand apparently thought, he is the one person in the play who could not be allowed to marry anyone, since he can have nothing to do with either love or generation. His attempt to forward the nuptials of Touchstone and Audrey serves only to postpone them. He is of course the one consistent character in the play in that he declines to go back with the others to the court that they have scorned. Yet how *can* he go back when the court has been converted? Jaques's occupation's gone. And he will not easily thrive away from the social life on which he feeds. It is notable that the place he really covets, or affects to, is that of the motley fool, licensed to mock at society, indulged by society but not of it. Yet, seeking for a fool, he has only to look in the brook to find one; and it is the romantic hero who will tell him so.

Shakespeare, then, builds up his ideal world and lets his idealists scorn the real one. But into their midst he introduces people who mock their ideals and others who mock *them*. One must not say that Shakespeare never judges, but one judgement is always being modified by another. Opposite views may contradict one another, but of course they do not cancel out. Instead they add up to an all-embracing view far larger and more satisfying than any one of them in itself.

Now when Orlando tells Jaques that he may see a fool by looking in the brook, this is not the first time that Jaques and Orlando meet; and the relations between the two of them are worth a moment's glance. Their first encounter occurs in public when the Duke and his retinue are met for one of their forest repasts. Jaques has just been eloquent about the vices of mankind and is justifying the satirist who scourges them, when he is confronted with the romantic hero in his most heroic attitude, rushing into the middle of the scene with drawn sword,[5] crying, "Forbear, and eat no more." But Jaques is not the man to be discomposed, even when a sudden interruption throws him off his hobby-horse. When he has inquired, "Of what kind should this cock come of?", the heroic attitude begins to look extravagant. The hero stands his ground: "Forbear, I say: He dies that touches any of this fruit"; at which Jaques nonchalantly helps himself to a grape, saying, "An you will not be answered with reason (raisin), I must die." Heroism now appears thoroughly deflated, or would do if Jaques were attended to by the company at large. The hero is in fact saved by the Duke's "civility"; and their talk of "gentleness" and "nurture" even throws back into perspective Jaques's recent attack upon society. The situation as a whole retains its equilibrium. And yet as a result of this little incident we are bound to feel that the romantic hero is very vulnerable to the ridicule of the satirist, until their duel of wit in the following act readjusts our view by allowing Orlando his retort.

There is a formal point to notice here, easy to miss but full of meaning. The wit-combat between Jaques and the hero is matched an act or so later—there is no strict regularity about these things—by a similar wit-combat between Jaques and the heroine. On each occasion Jaques is worsted and departs, leaving Rosalind and Orlando to come together. In fact the discomfiture of Monsieur Melancholy by one or other of the lovers is the prelude to each of the two big love-scenes of the play. And this arrangement makes a point more prettily than any action-plot involving Jaques could do. The mocking words of Jaques's farewell are in each case illuminating: "Farewell, good Signior Love"; and "Nay, then, God be wi' you, an you talk in blank verse." The gibe at blank verse is not an incidental or decorative jest. It makes it clear that, however we judge of them, the melancholy spirit of Jaques and the romantic emotion of Rosalind and Orlando cannot mingle. Shakespeare dismisses the melancholy man before he gives the lovers their scope. And in this I follow his example.

So far I have dealt only with the immigrants to Arden. There is of course a native population. The natural world of the poet's dreams has always been inhabited by shepherds, who from the time of Theocritus have piped their songs of love. And Rosalind and Celia have been in the forest for only twenty lines when two shepherds appear pat before them. In an earlier comedy perhaps these might have been a similar pair singing comparable love-ditties. But in *As You Like It*—Shakespeare making the most of what is offered him by Lodge—they are a contrasting pair. One is young and one is old, one is in love and one is not. The lover is the standard type. But the notion of love has undergone a change since classical times and the shepherds of Renaissance pastorals have all been bred in the schools of courtly love. So young Silvius is the faithful abject lover who finds disdain in his fair shepherdess's eye and sighs "upon a midnight pillow"— Shakespeare always fixes on a detail in which a whole situation is epitomized. There are of course many other lovers in the play, but the story of Silvius and Phebe is of the pure pastoral world, the familiar literary norm against which all the others may be measured. First against Silvius and Phebe are set Rosalind and Orlando, and the immediate result of this is that Rosalind and Orlando, though they clearly belong to the pastoral world, seem much closer to the ordinary one. Indeed, since Silvius and Phebe relieve them of the necessity of displaying the lovers' more extravagant postures, Rosalind and Orlando are freer to act like human beings. Rosalind need only play at taunting her adorer while allowing her real woman's heart to be in love with him in earnest. In an earlier comedy like *The Two Gentlemen of Verona* the heroes themselves had to undergo those "bitter fasts, with penitential groans, With nightly tears and daily heart-sore sighs", and these are what, as H.B. Charlton says, may make Valentine look a fool. But with Silvius to take this burden from him, Orlando can really be a hero, performing the traditional hero's fabulous feats, and upon occasion may even be a common man like ourselves. He has, for example, the very human trait of unpunctuality; he is twice late for an appointment. And although on one occasion he has the perfect excuse of a bloody accident, on the other he has nothing to say, beyond "My fair Rosalind, I come within an hour of my promise." Such engaging casualness is of course outside Silvius's range. And although Orlando has his due share of lovers' sighs and is indeed the "unfortunate he" who hangs the verses on the trees, in so human a creature these love-gestures appear not as his *raison d'être* but as an aberration. A delightful aberration, no doubt—"I would not be cured, youth", he says—but still an aberration that can be the legitimate subject of our mockery. Lying contemplating his love under an oak, he seems to Celia "like a dropped acorn", and both the ladies smile at his youthful lack of beard. But Orlando is robust enough to stand their mockery and ours, and Shakespeare's superb dramatic tact arranges that Orlando shall draw our laughter towards him so that he may protect the fragile Silvius from the ridicule which would destroy *him*. Rosalind alone is privileged to make fun of Silvius; and that because searching his wounds, she finds her own. The encounters which do not occur have their significance as well as those which do: Touchstone is only once, and

Jaques never, allowed a sight of Silvius before the final scene of the play. Silvius has not to be destroyed or the play will lack something near its centre.

If in a pastoral play the ideal shepherd is satirized it must be indirectly. But that he is, through his complete unreality, a likely target for satire has been commonly recognized by the poets, who have therefore had a habit of providing him with a burlesque counterpart to redress the balance and show that they did know what rustics were like in real life. As Gay was to put it in his proem to *The Shepherd's Week*, the shepherd "sleepeth not under myrtle shades, but under a hedge"; and so when Gay's shepherd makes love it is in a sly kiss behind a haycock to the accompaniment of the lady's yells of laughter. This may have been the method of Shakespeare's William, for, far from inditing verses to his mistress, William is singularly tongue-tied; though he is "five and twenty" and thinks he has "a pretty wit", the biggest of his eleven speeches is only seven words long. And his partner is just as much a contrast to the shepherdess of pastoral legend. She thanks the gods she is not beautiful, does not even know the meaning of "poetical", and her sheep, alas, are goats.

Shakespeare, then, presents the conventional pastoral, and duly burlesques it. But with a surer knowledge of life than many poets have had, he seems to suspect that the burlesque as well as the convention may also miss the truth. Do shepherds really sleep under hedges? In order to be unsophisticated, must they be stupid too? So among his varied array of shepherds, Silvius and Ganymede and William, Shakespeare introduces yet another shepherd, the only one who knows anything of sheep, whose hands even get greasy with handling them. It does not matter that Shakespeare got the hint for Corin from Corydon in Lodge. For Lodge found Corydon in literature and for Corin Shakespeare went to life. Lodge's Corydon, though he may make the king smile with his clownish salutation, has evidently been bred at court himself. Would he ever else accost a lady in distress in strains like these

> If I should not, fair damosel, occasion offence, or renew your griefs by rubbing the scar, I would fain crave so much favour as to know the cause of your misfortunes.

Shakespeare's Corin speaks at once of grazing and shearing and an unkind master; and when he talks about the shepherd's life he shows that he knows the value of money and that fat sheep need good pasture. His greatest pride is to see his ewes graze and his lambs suck. This is the note of his philosophy, and if it has its limitations, it is far from despicable and is splendidly anchored to fact. His attitude to love is that of the fully sane man undisturbed by illusions. Being a man, he has been in love and can still guess what it is like; but it is so long ago he has forgotten all the details. How little he belongs to Arcadia may be discovered from Sidney, whose shepherd-boy went on piping "as though he should never be old". In *As You Like It* perpetual youth is the happiness of Silvius, and his fate.

That much of the difference between Silvius and Corin is apparent from the short dialogue of twenty lines which first introduces them together to us.

In Corin Shakespeare provides us with a touchstone with which to test the pastoral. Corin's dialogue with the Touchstone of the court, dropped into the middle of the play, adds to the conventional antithesis between courtier and countryman a glimpse of the real thing. Our picture of the court as a place of tyranny, ambition and corruption is no doubt true enough. But its colours are modified somewhat when Touchstone gives us the court's plain routine. For him, as he lets us know on another occasion, the court is the place where he has trod a measure, flattered a lady, been smooth with his enemy and undone three tailors. Though Touchstone seeks to entangle Corin in the fantastications of his wit, his arguments to show that the court is better than the sheepfarm have a way of recoiling on himself. What emerges from the encounter of these two realists is that ewe and ram, like man and woman, are put together and that though the courtier perfumes his body it sweats like any other creature's. In city or country, *all* ways of life are at bottom the same, and we recognize a conclusion that Jaques, by a different route, has helped us to reach before.

The melancholy moralizings of Jaques and the Robin Hood raptures of the Duke, though in contrast, are equally the product of man's spirit. There has to be someone in Arden to remind us of the indispensable flesh. It was a shrewd irony of Shakespeare's to give this office to the jester. Whether he is wiser or more foolish than other men it is never possible to decide, but Touchstone is, as well as the most artificial wit, the most natural man of them all; and the most conscious of his corporal needs. After the journey to the forest Rosalind complains of a weariness of spirits, to which Touchstone retorts "I care not for my spirits, if my legs were not weary." And when he displays his wit at the expense of Orlando's bad verses, saying "I'll rhyme you so eight years together", he remembers to add "dinners and suppers and sleeping-hours excepted." A "material fool", as Jaques notes. This preoccupation with the physical makes Touchstone the obvious choice for the sensual lover who will burlesque the romantic dream. So Touchstone not only deprives the yokel William of his mistress, but steals his part in the play, making it in the process of infinitely greater significance. However, Shakespeare from the beginning cast Touchstone for this burlesque role, though he may not have seen at first what form the burlesque would take. When Silvius first exhibits his love to us, and reminds Rosalind of hers, Touchstone completes the trio on his discordant note:

> I remember, when I was in love I broke my sword upon a stone and
> bid him take that for coming a-night to Jane Smile; and I remember the
> kissing of . . . the cow's dugs that her pretty chopt hands had milked.

This sort of extravagance—in the burlesque-chivalrous vein—is not, I think, developed; but an indecent jest about a peascod does point forward to the animal lust which propels him towards Audrey, and his amour with her forms the perfect contrast to the three idealized courtships of the play. If we need a formal juxtaposition of the two kinds of love to point the matter further, I note that it is just when Rosalind has met Orlando in the forest and Orlando has promised to woo her "by the faith of [his] love" and "with all [his] heart" that we see Touchstone courting the goat-girl, regretting that fair women should be honest and talking of sexual desire.

The fool is not only a material touchstone; he is also the time-keeper of the play. At least, in the forest, where "there's no clock", he carries a time-piece with him; and it provokes the reflection: "It is ten o'clock . . . 'Tis but an hour ago since it was nine, And after one hour more 'twill be eleven." The people of Arcadia will do well to take note of this, but if all you can do with your hours is to count them, this undeniable truth may seem a trifle futile. Touchstone, to do him justice, goes on: "And so, from hour to hour, we ripe and ripe, And then, from hour to hour, we rot and rot." He dares to speak in Arcadia, where one can never grow old, of Time's inevitable processes of maturity and decay. By this the ideal life of the banished Duke is mocked, and since Touchstone's words are repeated by Jaques with delighted and uproarious laughter, the mockery is double. Yet, in accordance with the play's principle of countering one view with another, there are two things that may be noted: first, that in a later scene Touchstone, who sums up life as riping and rotting, is compared by Rosalind to a medlar, which is rotten before it is ripe; and second, that it is at this very point, when the ideal life is doubly mocked, that the Duke administers to the mocker Jaques a direct and fierce rebuke, charging the mocker of the world's vices with having lived a vicious life himself.

The satirist, of course, is far from silenced; it is now that he ridicules the romantic hero, and presently he delivers his famous speech on the seven ages of man, brilliantly summing up the course of human life, but omitting to notice anything in it that is noble or even pleasant. However, as has often been observed, though the seven ages speech ends with a description of man's final decrepitude—"sans teeth, sans eyes, sans taste, sans everything"—it has not yet left the speaker's tongue when an aged man appears who is at once addressed as "venerable". There is always this readjustment of the point of view. Senility and venerableness—are they different things or different ways of looking at the same? Certainly the entry of the venerable Adam does not disprove what Jaques says; Shakespeare seeks no cheap antithesis. "Sans teeth"—Adam himself has admitted to being toothless, Orlando has called him "a rotten tree", and his helplessness is only too visible when he is *carried* on to the stage. Yet he *is* carried, tenderly, by the master whom he has followed "to the last gasp, with truth and loyalty". Here is the glimpse of human virtue that the seven ages speech omitted. And then it is upon this moving spectacle of mutual affection and devotion that Amiens sings his song, "Blow, blow, thou winter wind, Thou art not so unkind

As man's ingratitude." Placed here, this lovely lyric, blend of joy and pathos, has a special poignancy.

The arrangement of the play depends upon many such piquant but seemingly casual juxtapositions. *As You Like It* contemplates life within and without Arden, with numerous shifts of angle, alternating valuations, and variations of mood. As for action, incident—life in the Forest of Arden does not easily lend itself to those. I have suggested that Shakespeare does something to supply this want by a glance or two back at what is happening at court. And departures from the court are matched by arrivals in the forest. For events, of course, even in Arden do sometimes occur. Orlando arrives dramatically, even melodramatically. Presently Rosalind learns that he is about. A little later on they meet. Later still Oliver arrives and is rescued from a lioness. Shakespeare still keeps up a sense of things going on. But the manner of the play, when once it settles down in the forest, is to let two people drift together, talk a little, and part, to be followed by two more. Sometimes a pair will be watched by others, who will sometimes comment on what they see. Sometimes of course there is a larger group, once or twice even a crowded stage; but most often two at a time. When they part they may arrange to meet again, or they may not. Through the three middle acts of the play, though there are two instances of love at first sight (one of them only reported), it is rare that anything happens in any particular encounter between these people of the sort that changes the course of their lives, anything, that is to say, that goes to make what is usually called a plot. Yet the meetings may properly be called 'encounters', because of the impact the contrasting characters make on one another and the sparkle of wit they kindle in one another. What is important in each meeting is our impression of those who meet and of their different attitudes to one another or to one another's views of life, an impression which is deepened or modified each time they reappear with the same or different partners. As I describe it, this may all sound rather static, but such is the ease and rapidity with which pairs and groups break up, re-form, and succeed one another on the stage that there is a sense of fluid movement. All is done with the utmost lightness and gaiety, but as the lovers move through the forest, part and meet again, or mingle with the other characters in their constantly changing pairs and groups, every view of life that is presented seems, sooner or later, to find its opposite. Life is "but a flower in spring time, the only pretty ring time", but for the unromantic Touchstone there is "no great matter in the ditty" and he counts it but time lost—his eye no doubt still on his timepiece—"to hear such a foolish song". A quartet of lovers avowing their love is broken up when one of them says

Pray you, no more of this; 'tis like the howling of Irish wolves against the moon.

And the one who says this is she who cannot tell "how many fathom deep" she is in love. Dominating the centre of the play, playing both the man's and woman's parts, counsellor in love and yet its victim, Rosalind gathers up into herself many of its roles and many of its meanings. Around her in the forest, where the banished Duke presides, is the perfect happiness of the simple life, an illusion, much mocked at, but still cherished. She herself, beloved of the hero, has all the sanity to recognize that "love is merely a madness" and that lovers should be whipped as madmen are, but admits that "the whippers are in love too". Heroine of numerous masquerades, she is none the less always constant and never more true than when insisting that she is counterfeiting. For she is an expert in those dark riddles which mean exactly what they say. Though things are rarely what they seem, they may sometimes be so in a deeper sense. What is wisdom and what is folly is of course never decided— you may have it "as you like it". Or, as Touchstone rejoined to Rosalind, after her gibe about the medlar, "You have said; but whether wisely or no, let the forest judge."

It may be possible to suggest that the forest gives its verdict. For if *As You Like It* proclaims no final truth, its ultimate effect is not negative. Longing to escape to our enchanted world, we are constantly brought up against reality; sanity, practical wisdom sees through our illusions. Yet in *As You Like It* ideals, though always on the point of dissolving, are for ever recreating themselves. They do not delude the eye of reason, yet faith in them is not extinguished in spite of all that reason can do. "I would not be cured, youth."

NOTES

1. A lecture delivered to the Shakespeare Conference at Stratford-upon-Avon, 18 August 1953.

2. Quiller-Couch, *Shakespeare's Workmanship* (1918), p. 130. In spite of some radical disagreement, I have got a number of hints from 'Q''s essay.

3. This is not to imply that Shakespeare's 'golden world' is at all the same as the primitive life of the mythical golden age, in which, by contrast with the Forest of Arden, there was no winter wind, sheep went unshorn, and man, at peace with all creatures, neither killed the deer nor was threatened by the snake and lion. Virgil associated the simplicity of pastoral life with the golden age, and the two ideals were frequently combined, not to say confused, by later pastoralists (cf. Roy Walker, *The Golden Feast* (1952), p. 133).

4. *Huntington Library Bulletin*, VIII (1935), 85.

5. "*Enter Orlando*" says the Folio simply, but the dialogue justifies Theobald's "*with Sword drawn.*"

1959—C.L. Barber. "The Alliance of Seriousness and Levity in *As You Like It*," from *Shakespeare's Festive Comedy*

C.L. Barber was a professor of literature at the University of California, Santa Cruz. He also wrote *The Whole Journey: Shakespeare's Power of Development* and *The Story of Language*.

> In a true piece of Wit all things must be
> Yet all things there agree.
> —Cowley, quoted by T.S. Eliot in "Andrew Marvell"

> Then is there mirth in heaven
> When earthly things made even
> Atone together.
> —*As You Like It*

Shakespeare's next venture in comedy after *The Merchant of Venice* was probably in the Henry IV plays, which were probably written in 1597–98. Thus the Falstaff comedy comes right in the middle of the period, from about 1594 to 1600 or 1601, when Shakespeare produced festive comedy. *Much Ado About Nothing*, *As You Like It*, and *Twelfth Night* were written at the close of the period, *Twelfth Night* perhaps after *Hamlet*. *The Merry Wives of Windsor*, where Shakespeare's creative powers were less fully engaged, was produced sometime between 1598 and 1602, and it is not impossible that *All's Well That Ends Well* and even perhaps *Measure for Measure* were produced around the turn of the century, despite that difference in tone that has led to their being grouped with *Hamlet* and *Troilus and Cressida*.[1] I shall deal only with *As You Like It* and *Twelfth Night*; they are the two last festive plays, masterpieces that include and extend almost all the resources of the form whose development we have been following. What I would have to say about *Much Ado About Nothing* can largely be inferred from the discussion of the other festive plays. To consider the various other sorts of comedy which Shakespeare produced around the inception of the period when his main concern became tragedy would require another, different frame of reference.

As You Like It is very similar in the way it moves to *A Midsummer Night's Dream* and *Love's Labour's Lost*, despite the fact that its plot is taken over almost entirely from Lodge's *Rosalynde*. The reality we feel about the experience of love in the play, reality which is not in the pleasant little prose romance, comes from presenting what was sentimental extremity as impulsive extravagance and so leaving judgment free to mock what the heart embraces.[2] The Forest of Arden, like the Wood outside Athens, is a region defined by an attitude of liberty from ordinary limitations, a festive place where the folly of romance can have its day. The first half of *As You Like It*, beginning with tyrant brother and tyrant Duke and moving out into the forest, is chiefly concerned with establishing this sense of freedom; the traditional contrast of court and country is developed in a way that is shaped by the contrast between everyday and holiday, as that antithesis has become part of Shakespeare's art and sensibility. Once we are securely in the golden world, where the good Duke and "a many merry men . . . fleet the time carelessly," the pastoral motif as such drops into the background; Rosalind finds Orlando's verses in the second scene of Act III, and the rest of the play deals with love. This second movement is like a musical theme with imitative variations, developing much more tightly the sort of construction which played off Costard's and Armado's amorous affairs against those of the nobles in Navarre, and which set Bottom's imagination in juxtaposition with other shaping fantasies. The love affairs of Silvius and Phebe, Touchstone and Audrey, Orlando and Rosalind succeed one another in the easy-going sequence of scenes, while the dramatist deftly plays each off against the others.

The Liberty of Arden

The thing that asks for explanation about the Forest of Arden is how this version of pastoral can feel so free when the Duke and his company are so high-minded. Partly the feeling of freedom comes from release from the tension established in the first act at the jealous court:

> Now go we in content
> To liberty, and not to banishment. (I.iii.139–140)

Several brief court scenes serve to keep this contrast alive. So does Orlando's entrance, sword in hand, to interrupt the Duke's gracious banquet by his threatening demand for food. Such behavior on his part is quite out of character (in Lodge he is most courteous); but his brandishing entrance gives Shakespeare occasion to resolve the attitude of struggle once again, this time by a lyric invocation of "what 'tis to pity and be pitied" (II.vii.117).

But the liberty we enjoy in Arden, though it includes relief from anxiety in brotherliness confirmed "at good men's feasts," is somehow easier than brotherliness usually is. The easiness comes from a witty redefinition of the human situation which makes conflict seem for the moment superfluous. Early in the play, when Celia and Rosalind are talking of ways of being merry by devising sports, Celia's proposal is "Let us sit and mock the good housewife Fortune from her wheel" (I.ii.34–35). The two go on with a "chase" of wit that goes "from

Fortune's office to Nature's" (I.ii.43), whirling the two goddesses through many variations; distinctions between them were running in Shakespeare's mind. In Act II, the witty poetry which establishes the greenwood mood of freedom repeatedly mocks Fortune from her wheel by an act of mind which goes from Fortune to Nature:

> A fool, a fool! I met a fool i' th' forest. . . .
> Who laid him down and bask'd him in the sun
> And rail'd on Lady Fortune in good terms, . . .
> "Good morrow, fool," quoth I. "No, sir," quoth he,
> "Call me not fool till heaven hath sent me fortune."
> And then he drew a dial from his poke,
> And looking on it with lack-lustre eye,
> Says very wisely, 'It is ten o'clock.
> Thus we may see.' quoth he, 'how the world wags.
> 'Tis but an hour ago since it was nine,
> And after one more hour 'twill be eleven;
> And so, from hour to hour, we ripe and ripe,
> And then, from hour to hour, we rot and rot;
> And thereby hangs a tale.' (II.vii. 12–28)

Why does Jaques, in his stylish way, say that his lungs "began to crow like chanticleer" to hear the fool "thus moral on the time," when the moral concludes in "rot and rot"? Why do we, who are not "melancholy," feel such large and free delight? Because the fool "finds," with wonderfully bland wit, that nothing whatever happens under the aegis of Fortune. ("Fortune reigns in gifts of the world," said Rosalind at I.ii.44.) The almost tautological inevitability of nine, ten, eleven, says that all we do is ripe and ripe and rot and rot. And so there is no reason not to bask in the sun and "lose and neglect the creeping hours of time" (II.vii.112). . . . Touchstone's "deep contemplative" moral makes the same statement as the spring song towards the close of the play: "How that a life was but a flower." When they draw the moral, the lover and his lass are only thinking of the "spring time" as they take "the present time" when "love is crowned with the prime." (The refrain mocks them a little for their obliviousness, by its tinkling "the only pretty ring time.") But Touchstone's festive gesture is *not* oblivious.

The extraordinary thing about the poised liberty of the second act is that the reduction of life to the natural and seasonal and physical works all the more convincingly as a festive release by including a recognition that the physical can be unpleasant. The good Duke, in his opening speech, can "translate the stubbornness of fortune" into a benefit: he does it by the witty shift which makes the "icy fang / And churlish chiding of the winter wind" into "counsellors / That feelingly persuade me what I am" (II.i.6–11). The two songs make the same gesture of welcoming physical pain in place of moral pain:

> Come hither, come hither, come hither!
>> Here shall he see
>> No enemy
> But winter and rough weather. (II.v.5–8)

They are patterned on holiday drinking songs, as we have seen already in considering the Christmas refrain, "Heigh-ho, sing heigh-ho, unto the green holly,"[3] and they convey the free solidarity of a group who, since they relax in physical pleasures together, need not fear the fact that "Most friendship is feigning, most loving mere folly."

Jaques' speech on the seven ages of man, which comes at the end of Act II, just before "Blow, Blow, thou winter wind," is another version of the liberating talk about time; it expands Touchstone's "And thereby hangs a tale." The simplification, "All the world's a stage," has such imaginative reach that we are as much astonished as amused, as with Touchstone's summary ripe and rot. But simplification it is, nevertheless; quotations (and recitations) often represent it as though it were dramatist Shakespeare's "philosophy," his last word, or one of them, about what life really comes to. To take it this way is sentimental, puts a part in place of the whole. For it only is *one* aspect of the truth that the roles we play in life are settled by the cycle of growth and decline. To face this part of the truth, to insist on it, brings the kind of relief that goes with accepting folly—indeed this speech is praise of folly, superbly generalized, praise of the folly of living in time (or is it festive abuse? the poise is such that relish and mockery are indistinguishable). Sentimental readings ignore the wit that keeps reducing social roles to caricatures and suggesting that meanings really are only physical relations beyond the control of mind or spirit:

>   Then a soldier, . . .
> Seeking the bubble reputation
> Even in the cannon's mouth. And then the justice,
> In fair round belly with good capon lin'd . . . (III.vii.149–154)

Looking back at time and society in this way, we have a detachment and sense of mastery similar to that established by Titania and Oberon's outside view of "the human mortals" and their weather.

Counterstatements

That Touchstone and Jaques should at moments turn and mock pastoral contentment is consistent with the way it is presented; their mockery makes explicit the partiality, the displacement of normal emphasis, which is implicit in the witty advocacy of it.

> If it do come to pass
> That any man turn ass,
> Leaving his wealth and ease
> A stubborn will to please . . . (II.v.52–55)

The folly of going to Arden has something about it of Christian humility, brotherliness and unworldliness ("Consider the lilies of the field . . ."), but one can also turn it upside down by "a Greek invocation to call fools into a circle" and find it stubbornness. Touchstone brings out another kind of latent irony about pastoral joys when he plays the role of a discontented exile from the court:

> *Corin.* And how like you this shepherd's life, Master Touchstone?
> *Touchstone.* Truly, shepherd, in respect of itself, it is a good life; but
> in respect that it is a shepherd's life, it is naught. In respect that it is
> solitary, I like it very well; but in respect that it is private, it is a very vile
> life. Now in respect it is in the fields, it pleaseth me well; but in respect
> it is not in the court, it is tedious. As it is a spare life, look you, it fits my
> humour well; but as there is no more plenty in it, it goes much against
> my stomach. (III.ii.12–22)

Under the apparent nonsense of his self-contradictions, Touchstone mocks the contradictory nature of the desires ideally resolved by pastoral life, to be at once at court and in the fields, to enjoy both the fat advantages of rank and the spare advantages of the mean and sure estate. The humor goes to the heart of the pastoral convention and shows how very clearly Shakespeare understood it.

The fact that he created both Jaques and Touchstone out of whole cloth, adding them to the story as it appears in Lodge's *Rosalynde*, is an index to what he did in dramatizing the prose romance. Lodge, though he has a light touch, treats the idyllic material at face value. He never makes fun of its assumptions, but stays safely within the convention, because he has no securely grounded attitude towards it, not being sure of its relation to reality. Shakespeare scarcely changes the story at all, but where in Lodge it is presented in the flat, he brings alive the dimension of its relation to life as a whole. The control of this dimension makes his version solid as well as delicate.

Although both Jaques and Touchstone are connected with the action well enough at the level of plot, their real position is generally to mediate between the audience and something in the play, the same position Nashe assigns to the court fool, Will Summers, in *Summer's Last Will and Testament*.[4] Once Jaques stands almost outside the play, when he responds to Orlando's romantic greeting: "Good day and happiness, dear Rosalind!" with "Nay then, God b'wi'you, and you talk in blank verse!" (IV.i.31). Jaques' factitious melancholy, which critics have made too much of as a "psychology," serves primarily to set him at odds both with society and with Arden, and so motivate contemplative mockery. Touchstone is put outside by his special status as a fool. As a fool, incapable, at least for professional purposes, of doing anything right, he is beyond the pale of normal achievements. In anything he tries to do he is comically disabled, as, for example, in falling in love. All he achieves is a burlesque of love. So he has none of the illusions of those who try to be ideal, and is in a position to make a business of being dryly objective. "Call me not fool till heaven hath sent me fortune." Heaven sends him Audrey instead, "an ill-favour'd thing, sir, but mine own" (V.iv.60)—not a mistress to generate illusions. In *As You Like It* the court fool for the first time takes over the work of comic commentary and burlesque from the clown of the earlier plays; in Jaques' praise of Touchstone and the corrective virtues of fooling, Shakespeare can be heard crowing with delight at his discovery. The figure of the jester, with his recognized social role and rich traditional meaning, enabled the dramatist to embody in a character and his relations with other characters the comedy's purpose of maintaining objectivity.

The satirist presents life as it is and ridicules it because it is not ideal, as we would like it to be and as it should be. Shakespeare goes the other way about: he represents or evokes ideal life, and then makes fun of it because it does not square with life as it ordinarily is. If we look for social satire in *As You Like It*, all we find are a few set pieces about such stock figures as the traveller and the duelist. And these figures seem to be described rather to enjoy their extravagance than to rebuke their folly. Jaques, in response to a topical interest at the time when the play appeared, talks a good deal about satire, and proposes to "cleanse the foul body of th' infected world" (II.vii.60) with the fool's medicine of ridicule. But neither Jaques, the amateur fool, nor Touchstone, the professional, ever really gets around to doing the satirist's work of ridiculing life as it is, "deeds, and language, such as men do use."[5] After all, they are in Arden, not in Jonson's London: the infected body of the world is far away, out of range. What they make fun of instead is what they can find in Arden—pastoral innocence and romantic love, life as it might be, lived "in a holiday humour." Similar comic presentation of what is not ideal in man is characteristic of medieval fool humor, where the humorist, by his gift of long ears to the long-robed dignitaries, makes the point that, despite their pageant perfection, they are human too, that "stultorum numerus infinitus est." Such humor is very different from modern satire, for its basic affirmation is not man's possible perfection but his certain imperfection. It was a function of the pervasively formal and ideal cast of medieval culture, where what should be was more present to the mind than what is: the humorists' natural recourse was to burlesque the pageant of perfection, presenting it as a procession of fools, in crowns, mitres, caps, and gowns. Shakespeare's point of view was not medieval. But his clown and fool comedy is a response, a counter-movement, to artistic idealization, as medieval burlesque was a response to the ingrained idealism of the culture.

"all nature in love mortal in folly"

I have quoted [previously] a riddling comment of Touchstone which moves from acknowledging mortality to accepting the folly of love:

> We that are true lovers run into strange capers; but as all is mortal in nature, so is all nature in love mortal in folly. (II.iv.53–56)

The lovers who in the second half of the play present "nature in love" each exhibit a kind of folly. In each there is a different version of the incongruity between reality and the illusions (in poetry, the hyperboles) which love generates and by which it is expressed. The comic variations are centered around the seriously-felt love of Rosalind and Orlando. The final effect is to enhance the reality of this love by making it independent of illusions, whose incongruity with life is recognized and laughed off. We can see this at closer range by examining each affair in turn.

All-suffering Silvius and his tyrannical little Phebe are a bit of Lodge's version taken over, outwardly intact, and set in a wholly new perspective. A "courting eglogue" between them, in the mode of Lodge, is exhibited almost as a formal spectacle, with Corin for presenter and Rosalind and Celia for audience. It is announced as

> a pageant truly played
> Between the pale complexion of true love
> And the red glow of scorn and proud disdain. (III.iv.55–57)

What we then watch is played "truly"—according to the best current convention: Silvius, employing a familiar gambit, asks for pity; Phebe refuses to believe in love's invisible wound, with exactly the literal-mindedness about hyperbole which the sonneteers imputed to their mistresses. In Lodge's version, the unqualified Petrarchan sentiments of the pair are presented as valid and admirable. Shakespeare lets us feel the charm of the form; but then he has Rosalind break up their pretty pageant. She reminds them that they are nature's creatures, and that love's purposes are contradicted by too absolute a cultivation of romantic liking or loathing: "I must tell you friendly in your ear, / Sell when you can! you are not for all markets" (III.v.59–60). Her exaggerated downrightness humorously underscores the exaggerations of conventional sentiment. And Shakespeare's treatment breaks down Phebe's stereotyped attitudes to a human reality: he lightly suggests an adolescent perversity underlying her resistance to love. The imagery she uses in disputing with Silvius is masterfully squeamish, at once preoccupied with touch and shrinking from it:

> 'Tis pretty, sure, and very probable
> That eyes, which are the frail'st and softest things,
> Who shut their coward gates on atomies,
> Should be call'd tyrants, butchers, murtherers!
>   . . . lean but upon a rush,
> The cicatrice and capable impressure
> Thy palm some moment keeps; but now mine eyes,
> Which I have darted at thee, hurt thee not, . . . (III.v.11–25)

Rosalind, before whom this resistance melts, appears in her boy's disguise "like a ripe sister," and the qualities Phebe picks out to praise are feminine. She has, in effect, a girlish crush on the femininity which shows through Rosalind's disguise; the aberrant affection is happily got over when Rosalind reveals her identity and makes it manifest that Phebe has been loving a woman. "Nature to her bias drew in that" is the comment in *Twelfth Night* when Olivia is fortunately extricated from a similar mistaken affection.

Touchstone's affair with Audrey complements the spectacle of exaggerated sentiment by showing love reduced to its lowest common denominator, without any sentiment at all. The fool is detached, objective and resigned when the true-blue lover should be

> All made of passion, and all made of wishes,
> All adoration, duty, and observance. (V.ii.101–102)

He explains to Jaques his reluctant reasons for getting married:

> *Jaques.* Will you be married, motley?
> *Touchstone.* As the ox hath his bow, sir, the horse his curb, and the
> falcon her bells, so man hath his desires; and as pigeons bill, so wedlock
> would be nibbling. (III.iii.79–83)

This reverses the relation between desire and its object, as experienced by the other lovers. They are first overwhelmed by the beauty of their mistresses, then impelled by that beauty to desire them. With Touchstone, matters go the other way about: he discovers that man has his troublesome desires, as the horse his curb; then he decides to cope with the situation by marrying Audrey:

> Come, sweet Audrey.
> We must be married, or we must live in bawdry. (III.iii.98–99)

Like all the motives which Touchstone acknowledges, this priority of desire to attraction is degrading and humiliating. One of the hall-marks of chivalric and Petrarchan idealism is, of course, the high valuation of the lover's mistress, the assumption that his desire springs entirely from her beauty. This attitude of the poets has contributed to that progressively-increasing respect for women so fruitful in modern culture. But to assume that only one girl will do is, after all, an extreme, an ideal attitude: the other half of the truth, which lies in wait to mock sublimity, is instinct—the need of a woman, even if she be an Audrey, because "as pigeons bill, so wedlock would be nibbling." As Touchstone put it on another occasion:

> If the cat will after kind,
> So be sure will Rosalinde. (III.ii.109–110)

The result of including in Touchstone a representative of what in love is unromantic is not, however, to undercut the play's romance: on the contrary, the fool's cynicism, or one-sided realism, forestalls the cynicism with which the audience might greet a play where his sort of realism had been ignored. We have a sympathy for his downright point of view, not only in connection with love but also in his acknowledgment of the vain and self-gratifying desires excluded by pastoral humility; he embodies the part of ourselves which resists the play's reigning idealism. But he does not do so in a fashion to set himself up in opposition to the play. Romantic commentators construed him as "Hamlet in motley," a devastating critic. They forgot, characteristically, that he is ridiculous: he makes his attitudes preposterous when he values rank and comfort above humility, or follows biology rather than beauty. In laughing at him, we reject the tendency in ourselves which he for the moment represents. The net effect of the fool's part is thus to consolidate the hold of the serious themes by exorcising opposition. The final Shakespearean touch is to make the fool aware that in humiliating himself he is performing a public service. He goes through his part with an irony founded on the fact (and it is a fact) that he is only making manifest the folly which others, including the audience, hide from themselves.

Romantic participation in love and humorous detachment from its follies, the two polar attitudes which are balanced against each other in the action as a whole, meet and are reconciled in Rosalind's personality. Because she remains always aware of love's illusions while she herself is swept along by its deepest currents, she possesses as an attribute of character the power of combining wholehearted feeling and undistorted judgment which gives the play its value. She plays the mocking reveller's role which Berowne played in *Love's Labour's Lost*, with the advantage of disguise. Shakespeare exploits her disguise to permit her to furnish the humorous commentary on her own ardent love affair, thus keeping comic and serious actions going at the same time. In her pretended role of saucy shepherd youth, she can mock at romance and burlesque its gestures while playing the game of putting Orlando through his paces as a suitor, to "cure" him of love. But for the audience, her disguise is transparent, and through it they see the very ardor which she mocks. When, for example, she stages a gayly overdone take-off of the conventional impatience of the lover, her own real impatience comes through the burlesque; yet the fact that she makes fun of exaggerations of the feeling conveys an awareness that it has limits, that there is a difference between romantic hyperbole and human nature:

> *Orlando.* For these two hours, Rosalind, I will leave thee.
> *Rosalind.* Alas, dear love, I cannot lack thee two hours!
> *Orlando.* I must attend the Duke at dinner. By two o'clock I will be
> with thee again.
> *Rosalind.* Ay, go your ways, go your ways! I knew what you would
> prove. My friends told me as much, and I thought no less. That
> flattering tongue of yours won me. 'Tis but one cast away, and so, come
> death! Two o'clock is your hour? (IV.i.181–190)

One effect of this indirect, humorous method of conveying feeling is that Rosalind is not committed to the conventional language and attitudes of love, loaded as these inevitably are with sentimentality. Silvius and Phebe are her foils in this: they take their conventional language and their conventional feelings perfectly seriously, with nothing in reserve. As a result they seem naïve and rather trivial. They are no more than what they say, until Rosalind comes forward to realize their personalities for the audience by suggesting what they humanly are beneath what they romantically think themselves. By contrast, the heroine in expressing her own love conveys by her humorous tone a valuation of her sentiments, and so realizes her own personality for herself, without being indebted to another for the favor. She uses the convention where Phebe, being unaware of its exaggerations, abuses it, and Silvius, equally naïve about hyperbole, lets it abuse him. This control of tone is one of the great contributions of Shakespeare's comedy to his dramatic art as a whole. The discipline of comedy in controlling the humorous potentialities of a remark enables the dramatist to express the relation of a speaker to his lines, including the relation of naïveté: The focus of attention is not on the outward action of saying something but on the shifting, uncrystallized life which motivates what is said.

The particular feeling of headlong delight in Rosalind's encounters with Orlando goes with the prose of these scenes, a medium which can put imaginative effects of a very high order to the service of humor and wit. The comic prose of this period is first developed to its full range in Falstaff's part, and steals the show for Benedict and Beatrice in *Much Ado About Nothing*. It combines the extravagant linguistic reach of the early clowns' prose with the sophisticated wit which in the earlier plays was usually cast, less flexibly, in verse. Highly patterned, it is built up of balanced and serial clauses, with everything linked together by alliteration and kicked along by puns. Yet it avoids a stilted, Euphuistic effect because regular patterns are set going only to be broken to underscore humor by asymmetry. The speaker can rock back and forth on antitheses, or climb "a pair of stairs" (V.ii.42) to a climax, then slow down meaningly, or stop dead, and so punctuate a pithy reduction, bizarre exaggeration or broad allusion. T.S. Eliot has observed that we often forget that it was Shakespeare who wrote the greatest prose in the language. Some of it is in *As You Like It*. His control permits him to convey the constant shifting of attitude and point of view which expresses Rosalind's excitement and her poise. Such writing, like the brushwork and line of great painters, is in one sense everything. But the whole design supports each stroke, as each stroke supports the whole design.

The expression of Rosalind's attitude towards being in love, in the great scene of disguised wooing, fulfills the whole movement of the play. The climax comes when Rosalind is able, in the midst of her golden moment, to look beyond it and mock its illusions, including the master illusion that love is an ultimate and final experience, a matter of life and death. Ideally, love should be final, and Orlando is romantically convinced that his is so, that he would die if Rosalind refused him. But Rosalind humorously corrects him, from behind her page's disguise:

> . . . Am I not your Rosalind?
>
> *Orlando*. I take some joy to say you are, because I would be talking
> of her.
>
> *Rosalind*. Well, in her person, I say I will not have you.
>
> *Orlando*. Then, in mine own person, I die.
>
> *Rosalind*. No, faith, die by attorney. The poor world is almost six
> thousand years old, and in all this time there was not any man died in
> his own person, videlicet, in a love cause. Troilus had his brains dash'd
> out with a Grecian club; yet he did what he could to die before, and
> he is one of the patterns of love. Leander, he would have liv'd many
> a fair year though Hero had turn'd nun, if it had not been for a hot
> midsummer night; for (good youth) he went but forth to wash him in
> the Hellespont, and being taken with the cramp, was drown'd; and the
> foolish chroniclers of that age found it was 'Hero of Sestos.' But these
> are all lies. Men have died from time to time, and worms have eaten
> them, but not for love.

Orlando. I would not have my right Rosalind of this mind, for I
protest her frown might kill me.
   Rosalind. By this hand, it will not kill a fly! (IV.i.90–108)

A note almost of sadness comes through Rosalind's mockery towards the
end. It is not sorrow that men die from time to time, but that they do not
die for love, that love is not so final as romance would have it. For a moment
we experience as pathos the tension between feeling and judgment which is
behind all the laughter. The same pathos of objectivity is expressed by Chaucer
in the sad smile of Pandarus as he contemplates the illusions of Troilus' love.
But in *As You Like It* the mood is dominant only in the moment when the last
resistance of feeling to judgment is being surmounted: the illusions thrown up
by feeling are mastered by laughter and so love is reconciled with judgment.
This resolution is complete by the close of the wooing scene. As Rosalind
rides the crest of a wave of happy fulfillment (for Orlando's behavior to the
pretended Rosalind has made it perfectly plain that he loves the real one) we
find her describing with delight, almost in triumph, not the virtues of marriage,
but its fallibility:

Say 'a day' without the 'ever.' No, no, Orlando! Men are April when
they woo, December when they wed. Maids are May when they are
maids, but the sky changes when they are wives. (IV.i.146–150)

Ordinarily, these would be strange sentiments to proclaim with joy at such a
time. But as Rosalind says them, they clinch the achievement of the humor's
purpose. (The wry, retarding change from the expected cadence at "but the sky
changes" is one of those brush strokes that fulfill the large design.) Love has
been made independent of illusions without becoming any the less intense; it
is therefore inoculated against life's unromantic contradictions: To emphasize
by humor the limitations of the experience has become a way of asserting
its reality. The scenes which follow move rapidly and deftly to complete the
consummation of the love affairs on the level of plot. The treatment becomes
more and more frankly artificial, to end with a masque. But the lack of realism
in presentation does not matter, because a much more important realism in
our attitude towards the substance of romance has been achieved already by
the action of the comedy.
     In writing of Marvell and the metaphysical poets, T.S. Eliot spoke of an
"alliance of levity and seriousness (by which the seriousness is intensified)." What
he has said about the contribution of wit to this poetry is strikingly applicable
to the function of Shakespeare's comedy in *As You Like It*: that wit conveys "a
recognition, implicit in the expression of every experience, of other kinds of
experience which are possible."[6] The likeness does not consist simply in the fact

that the wit of certain of Shakespeare's characters at times is like the wit of the metaphysicals. The crucial similarity is in the way the humor functions in the play as a whole to implement a wider awareness, maintaining proportion where less disciplined and coherent art falsifies by presenting a part as though it were the whole. The dramatic form is very different from the lyric: Shakespeare does not have or need the sustained, inclusive poise of metaphysical poetry when, at its rare best, it fulfills Cowley's ideal:

> In a true piece of Wit all things must be
>   Yet all things there agree.

The dramatist tends to show us one thing at a time, and to realize that one thing, in its moment, to the full; his characters go to extremes, comical as well as serious; and no character, not even a Rosalind, is in a position to see all around the play and so be completely poised, for if this were so the play would cease to be dramatic. Shakespeare, moreover, has an Elizabethan delight in extremes for their own sake, beyond the requirements of his form and sometimes damaging to it, an expansiveness which was subordinated later by the seventeenth century's conscious need for coherence. But his extremes, where his art is at its best, are balanced in the whole work. He uses his broad-stroked, wide-swung comedy for the same end that the seventeenth-century poets achieved by their wire-drawn wit. In Silvius and Phebe he exhibits the ridiculous (and perverse) possibilities of that exaggerated romanticism which the metaphysicals so often mocked in their serious love poems. In Touchstone he includes a representative of just those aspects of love which are not romantic, hypostatizing as a character what in direct lyric expression would be an irony:

> Love's not so pure and abstract as they use
> To say who have no mistress but their muse.

By Rosalind's mockery a sense of love's limitations is kept alive at the very moments when we most feel its power:

> But at my back I always hear
> Time's winged chariot hurrying near.

The fundamental common characteristic is that the humor is not directed at "some outside sentimentality or stupidity," but is an agency for achieving proportion of judgment and feeling about a seriously felt experience.

As You Like It seems to me the most perfect expression Shakespeare or anyone else achieved of a poise which was possible because a traditional way of living connected different kinds of experience to each other. The play articulates fully the feeling for the rhythms of life which we have seen supporting Nashe's strong but imperfect art in his seasonal pageant. Talboys Dimoke and his friends had a similar sense of times and places when they let holiday lead them to making merry with the Earl of Lincoln; by contrast, the Puritan and/or time-serving partisans of Lincoln could not or would not recognize that holiday gave a license and also set a limit. An inclusive poise such as Shakespeare exhibits in Rosalind was not, doubtless, easy to achieve in any age; no culture was ever so "organic" that it would do men's living for them. What Yeats called Unity of Being became more and more difficult as the Renaissance progressed; indeed, the increasing difficulty of poise must have been a cause of the period's increasing power to express conflict and order it in art. We have seen this from our special standpoint in the fact that the everyday–holiday antithesis was most fully expressed in art when the keeping of holidays was declining.

The humorous recognition, in *As You Like It* and other products of this tradition, of the limits of nature's moment, reflects not only the growing consciousness necessary to enjoy holiday attitudes with poise, but also the fact that in English Christian culture saturnalia was never fully enfranchised. Saturnalian customs existed along with the courtly tradition of romantic love and an ambient disillusion about nature stemming from Christianity. In dramatizing love's intensity as the release of a festive moment, Shakespeare keeps that part of the romantic tradition which makes love an experience of the whole personality, even though he ridicules the wishful absolutes of doctrinaire romantic love. He does not found his comedy on the sort of saturnalian simplification which equates love with sensual gratification. He includes spokesmen for this sort of release in reduction; but they are never given an unqualified predominance, though they contribute to the atmosphere of liberty within which the aristocratic lovers find love. It is the latter who hold the balance near the center. And what gives the predominance to figures like Berowne, Benedict and Beatrice, or Rosalind, is that they enter nature's whirl consciously, with humor that recognizes it as only part of life and places their own extravagance by moving back and forth between holiday and everyday perspectives. Aristophanes provides a revealing contrast here. His comedies present experience entirely polarized by saturnalia; there is little *within* the play to qualify that perspective. Instead, an irony attaches to the whole performance which went with the accepted place of comedy in the Dionysia. Because no such clear-cut role for saturnalia or saturnalian comedy existed within Shakespeare's culture, the play itself had to place that pole of life in relation to life as a whole. Shakespeare had the art to make this necessity into an opportunity for a fuller expression, a more inclusive consciousness.

NOTES

1. For the chronology, see E.K. Chambers, *William Shakespeare* (Oxford, 1930), I, 248–249 and 270–271.

2. I hope that a reader who is concerned only with *As You Like It* will nevertheless read the generalized account of festive comedy in Ch. 1 [of the book *Shakespeare's Festive Comedy*], for that is assumed as a background for the discussion here.

3. See above, pp. 113–116.

4. See above, Ch. 4, pp. 61–67.

5. Ben Jonson, *Every Man in his Humour*, Prologue, 1.21.

6. *Selected Essays, 1917–1932* (New York, 1932), pp. 255 and 262.

———〰—— ——〰—— ——〰——

1972—Thomas McFarland. "For Other Than for Dancing Measures: The Complications of *As You Like It*," from *Shakespeare's Pastoral Comedy*

Thomas McFarland was a professor in the English department at Princeton University. Among his numerous books are *Tragic Meanings in Shakespeare* and *Romanticism and the Forms of Ruin*.

To approach *As You Like It* immediately after *Love's Labour's Lost* and *A Midsummer-Night's Dream* is to encounter a darkening of action and tone. The pastoral realm into which it enters has, in marked contrast to the moonlit forest outside Athens, genuine problems to ameliorate. The moment of pure pastoral celebration in Shakespeare's art is now forever gone. The motif of criminal action, which had been tentatively put forward in *The Two Gentlemen of Verona*, only to be banished from the golden confines of Navarre's park and Oberon's forest, now reasserts itself. *As You Like It* is a play that labors to keep its comic balance, and for this reason the comic reclamation in the Forest of Arden involves complicated character interactions and severe criticisms of behavior. The play exhibits more humor, but much less happiness, than its two great pastoral predecessors.

The situation at the start of *As You Like It* could, indeed, as well serve for a tragedy as for a comedy. The index to the state of moral well-being in Shakespeare's comedies is usually provided by the character and circumstances of the ruler. The mysterious illness of the King in *All's Well* casts that whole play into deviation from an ideal state; the lovesickness of Orsino at the beginning of *Twelfth Night* forebodes maladjustments throughout the Illyrian society. Conversely, the youth and magnanimity of Navarre, the puissance and benignity of Theseus, authenticate a pervasive well-being in their two realms. It is significant, therefore, that the world of *As You Like It* is presented at the outset as severely disfigured, for its ruler has been banished and his power usurped.

Grave though usurpation is, it is rendered still more grave by the fact that the usurper, as in *The Tempest*, is the brother of the true ruler, and the action of usurpation therefore reverberates with the archetypal crime of Cain. When Claudius faces his own offense, he says: "O my offence is rank, it smells to heaven; / It hath the primal eldest curse upon't, / A brother's murder" (*Hamlet*, 3.3.36–38). Neither in *As You Like It* nor in *The Tempest* does the crime of brother against brother proceed to murder; for such an outcome would put the actions of the two plays irrevocably beyond the power of comedy to heal. But usurpation and banishment represent the most serious kind of transgression. We recall the word that, in opening the somber action of *The White Devil*, casts all within that play into a nightmare of alienation: "Banished?" Or we recall Romeo's agony:

> They are free men, but I am banished.
> Hadst thou no poison mix'd, no sharp-ground knife,
> No sudden mean of death, though ne'er so mean,
> But "banished" to kill me?—"banished"?
> O friar, the damned use that word in hell;
> Howling attends it. [*Romeo and Juliet*, 3.3.42–48]

When, therefore, we learn that "the old Duke is banished by his younger brother the new Duke" (1.1.91–92), a mood of intense alienation settles over *As You Like It*. The mood is deepened by its foreshadowing in the relationship of Orlando and Oliver. "He lets me feed with his hinds, bars me the place of a brother," says Orlando (1.1.17–18). Indeed, it is bitter irony that in this play the comic motif of repetition doubles the Cain-and-Abel motif by extending it from Oliver and Orlando to the young Duke and the old Duke. In the supporting trope of Orlando and Oliver, moreover, the trouble between the brothers specifically involves, as does that of Cain and Abel, the relationship between father and son:

> My father charg'd you in his will to give me good education: you have train'd me like a peasant, obscuring and hiding from me all gentleman-like qualities. The spirit of my father grows strong in me, and I will no longer endure it. . . . [1.1.60–65]

Their father being dead, the old servant Adam fills his place in the psychodramatic struggle, his name reinforcing the motif of "primal eldest curse." It can hardly be without significance that Shakespeare here slightly alters his source, for in Lodge's *Rosalynde* the retainer is called "*Adam Spencer*, the olde servaunt of Sir *John* of *Bordeaux*," and is almost always referred to by both given and surname. In changing "Adam Spencer" to simple "Adam" in the struggle of brother against brother, *As You Like It* conveys the sense of old woe ever renewed.

Beset from its beginning by such clouds of gloom and disharmony, the play must stake its claim to comic redemption very early. In the same conversation in which Oliver, fresh from his mistreatment of his brother and old Adam, learns from the wrestler Charles the "old news" of the old Duke's banishment (1.1.90), he, and the cosmos of the play, also learn of the existence of the land of pastoral wonder:

> OLIVER. Where will the old Duke live?
> CHARLES. They say he is already in the Forest of Arden. . . . many
> young gentlemen flock to him every day, and fleet the time carelessly, as
> they did in the golden world. [1.1.104–9]

It is interesting that the play here invokes, instead of the Theocritan iconology of formal pastoral, the separate but intertwined tradition of the Golden Age; for the latter, by being more explicitly paradisal, more explicitly repels tragic possibility. Rapin urges in 1659, in his "Dissertatio de carmine pastorali," that pastoral poetry "is a product of the Golden Age." To Rapin, pastoral itself is "a perfect image of the state of Innocence, of that golden Age, that blessed time, when Sincerity and Innocence, Peace, Ease, and Plenty inhabited the Plains." So, to bring in the golden world so early, and entrust the message to such an unexpected source as Charles, is to go—not historically but semiotically—to the very fountainhead of the pastoral myth and thereby to concede the dire need for alleviation of the alienated mood.

Secure, then, in the promise of Arden's redemption, the play indulges in a still closer approach to tragic irrevocability. "I had as lief thou didst break his neck as his finger," says Oliver to Charles, perverting the latter's honorable intentions in the proposed wrestling match against Orlando (1.1.132). Oliver adorns the malignant proposal by language of studied villainy:

> And thou wert best look to't; for if thou dost him any slight disgrace, or
> if he do not mightily grace himself on thee, he will practise against thee
> by poison, entrap thee by some treacherous device, and never leave thee
> till he hath ta'en thy life by some indirect means or other; for, I assure
> thee, and almost with tears I speak it, there is not one so young and
> so villainous this day living. I speak but brotherly of him; but should I
> anatomize him to thee as he is, I must blush and weep, and thou must
> look pale and wonder. [1.1.132–40]

Such brotherly betrayal prefigures the relationship of Edmund and Edgar. And when Charles departs, Oliver's musing to himself suggests also the selfless dedication of Iago's hatred:

I hope I shall see an end of him; for my soul, yet I know not why, hates nothing more than he. [1.1.144–46]

This play, then, involves the first massive assault of the forces of bitterness and alienation upon the pastoral vision of Shakespeare, and its action glances off the dark borders of tragedy. Indeed, the motif of repeated abandonment of the court, first by Orlando and Adam, then by Rosalind, Celia, and Touchstone, is prophetic of the departings and rejections of Cordelia, Kent, and Edgar at the beginning of *King Lear's* quest for essential being.

It is, accordingly, both fitting and necessary that the second act of *As You Like It* opens with an equally massive attempt to restore comic benignity and to check the tragic tendency. For the rightful ruler, Duke Senior, without preliminary of action, invokes the pastoral vision and the idea of a new society in extraordinarily specific terms. In fact, the social assurance of comedy, the environmental assurance of pastoral, and the religious implication of both, are all established by the Duke's speech:

Now, my co-mates and brothers in exile,
Hath not old custom made this life more sweet
Than that of painted pomp? Are not these woods
More free from peril than the envious court?
Here feel we not the penalty of Adam,
The seasons' difference; as the icy fang
And churlish chiding of the winter's wind,
Which when it bites and blows upon my body,
Even till I shrink with cold, I smile and say,
"This is no flattery; these are counsellors
That feelingly persuade me what I am."
Sweet are the uses of adversity;
Which, like the toad, ugly and venomous,
Wears yet a precious jewel in his head;
And this our life, exempt from public haunt,
Finds tongues in trees, books in the running brooks,
Sermons in stones, and good in everything. [2.1.1–17]

But "good," despite the Duke's statement, is not "in everything" as it is in *Love's Labour's Lost* and *A Midsummer-Night's Dream*; and the early promise of a "golden world" is not entirely fulfilled. The Forest of Arden, though a paradise, is not an unequivocal paradise; the "churlish chiding of the winter's wind," even if not painfully felt, is present. "Arden," as Helen Gardner notes in her well-known essay on *As You Like It*, "is not a place where the laws of nature are abrogated and roses are without their thorns." The gall of the court, before it is flushed away by the Arethusan waters, mingles and dissolves itself into the pastoral limpidity. Hence the existence of natural danger in the forest makes it a place halfway between reality and paradise. As Oliver says of his encounter with Orlando there:

> A wretched ragged man, o'ergrown with hair,
> Lay sleeping on his back. About his neck
> A green and gilded snake had wreath'd itself,
> Who with her head nimble in threats approach'd
> The opening of his mouth; but suddenly,
> Seeing Orlando, it unlink'd itself,
> And with indented glides did slip away
> Into a bush. . . . [4.3.105–12]

The presence of the serpent, potentially dangerous, indicates a certain admixture of harsh reality in this version of a golden world, for of that world Virgil stipulates that "occidet et serpens, et fallax herba veneni occidet"—both the serpent and the false poison plant shall die (*Eclogues*, 4.24–25). And in the Forest of Arden, an unpastoral danger is brought still closer by the lioness that almost kills Oliver:

> A lioness, with udders all drawn dry,
> Lay crouching, head on ground, with catlike watch,
> When that the sleeping man should stir. . . .
> This seen, Orlando did approach the man,
> And found it was his brother, his elder brother. . . .
> . . . kindness, nobler ever than revenge,
> And nature, stronger than his just occasion,
> Made him give battle to the lioness,
> Who quickly fell before him. . . .
> In brief, he led me to the gentle Duke,
> Who gave me fresh array and entertainment,
> Committing me unto my brother's love;
> Who led me instantly into his cave,
> There stripp'd himself, and here upon his arm
> The lioness had torn some flesh away,
> Which all this while had bled. . . . [4.3.113–47]

The function of the serpent and the lioness are clearly revealed in these lines: as figures of venom and fury, they symbolically accept the burden of the venom and fury generated by the Cain and Abel contest of Oliver and Orlando. The two brothers, their rage displaced into the iconic beasts, are ready for reconciliation:

CELIA. Are you his brother?
ROSALIND. Was't you he rescu'd?
CELIA. Was't you that did so oft contrive to kill him?
OLIVER. 'Twas I; but 'tis not I. I do not shame
To tell you what I was, since my conversion
So sweetly tastes, being the thing I am. . . .
When from the first to last, betwixt us two,
Tears our recountments had most kindly bath'd,
As how I came into that desert place—
In brief, he led me to the gentle Duke. [4.3.132–41]

Thus the Cain-against-Abel tragic disharmony gives way to the legendary Roland-for-an-Oliver togetherness implied by the brothers' names.

The seriousness of the deviances to be reclaimed is to be found not only in a slight deterioration in the pastoral environment, but also in the introduction of Jaques, a pastorally untypical character. Jaques is a humor figure representing the type of the malcontent; he is a member of the tribe not only of Marston's Malevole but, in a sense, of Hamlet himself. Like Hamlet, he calls into question all aspects of life that fall below an exalted ideal of human conduct. It is significant that the first mention of his name refers to his awareness of this less-than-ideal pastoral environment. The old Duke says:

Come, shall we go and kill us venison?
And yet it irks me the poor dappled fools,
Being native burghers of this desert city,
Should, in their own confines, with forked heads
Have their round haunches gor'd.
    FIRST LORD. Indeed, my lord,
The melancholy Jaques grieves at that;
And, in that kind, swears you do more usurp
Than doth your brother that hath banish'd you. [2.1.21–28]

It is emphasized that the Forest of Arden is a version of pastoral like Robin Hood's Sherwood Forest (Charles had said at the outset that "in the forest of Arden" the Duke and his retainers "live like the old Robin Hood of England" [1.1.105–9]). The specification not only prefigures Jonson's pastoral variant, whose "scene is Sherwood" (*The Sad Shepherd*, Prologue, line 15), but it also indicates a world somewhat less perfect than Ovid's golden age. Indeed, as Elizabeth Armstrong points out, "Peace between man and the animal creation" was "a traditional feature of the Age of Gold"; and the "existence of this tradition" may have deterred Ronsard "from allowing his Age of Gold people to slay animals for food or sport" (*Ronsard and the Age of Gold* [Cambridge, 1968], p. 189). The continuation of the First Lord's report suggests, in direct ratio to its length, the deficiencies of this only partly golden world:

> To-day my Lord of Amiens and myself
> Did steal behind him as he lay along
> Under an oak whose antique root peeps out
> Upon the brook that brawls along this wood!
> To the which place a poor sequest'red stag,
> That from the hunter's aim had ta'en a hurt,
> Did come to languish; and indeed, my lord,
> The wretched animal heav'd forth such groans
> That their discharge did stretch his leathern coat
> Almost to bursting; and the big round tears
> Cours'd one another down his innocent nose
> In piteous chase; and thus the hairy fool. . . .
> Stood on th' extremest verge of the swift brook,
> Augmenting it with tears.
>   DUKE SENIOR. But what said Jaques?
> Did he not moralize this spectacle?
>   FIRST LORD. O, yes, into a thousand similes. . . .
> swearing that we
> Are mere usurpers, tyrants, and what's worse,
> To fright the animals and to kill them up
> In their assign'd and native dwelling-place.
>   DUKE SENIOR. And did you leave him in this contemplation?
>   SECOND LORD. We did, my lord, weeping and commenting
> Upon the sobbing deer.[1] [2.1.29–66]

The import of the passage can hardly be mistaken: the deer, with its human coordinates of feeling ("The wretched animal. . . the big round tears . . . his innocent nose . . ."), brings the reality of human pain into the forest; and Jaques's moral criticism, by linking the killing of the deer with usurpation and tyranny,[2] indicates that the forest is not completely divorced from the reality of the urban spectacle. Jaques, indeed, links city, court, and pastoral forest together by his criticism.

Although a pastorally atypical figure in the play, Jaques is nevertheless in a sense its central figure, or at least the figure who does most to define the idiosyncratic strain of malaise. But the type of the malcontent can imply not only Hamlet's idealism but Bosola's cynicism, and Jaques's presence threatens as well as criticizes the pastoral environment. It is therefore necessary to provide him a counterweight, so that the unchecked burden of malcontentment may not become so heavy as to break up entirely the fragilities of the pastoral vision. That counterweight the play summons up in the character of Touchstone, the fool. Replacing the "hairy fool / Much marked of the melancholy Jaques" (that is, the deer whose travail brings out Jaques's role as in part the emissary of a realm of more beatific feeling), Touchstone reminds us, perhaps subliminally, of Jaques's compassion and at the same time dissolves the accompanying melancholy into a language of ridicule and jest more fitting to comic aims. The function of the fool is to redeem Jaques from the melancholy that is so dangerous to the comic-pastoral aspiration:

> DUKE SENIOR. What, you look merrily!
> JAQUES. A fool, a fool! I met a fool i' th' forest,
> A motley fool. A miserable world!
> As I do live by food, I met a fool,
> Who laid him down and bask'd him in the sun,
> And rail'd on Lady Fortune in good terms,
> In good set terms—and yet a motley fool.
> "Good morrow, fool," quoth I. "No, sir," quoth he,
> "Call me not fool till heaven hath sent me fortune."
> And then he drew a dial from his poke,
> And, looking on it with lack-lustre eye,
> Says very wisely, "It is ten o'clock;
> Thus we may see," quoth he, "how the world wags;
> 'Tis but an hour ago since it was nine;
> And after one hour more 'twill be eleven;
> And so, from hour to hour, we ripe and ripe,
> And then, from hour to hour, we rot and rot;
> And thereby hangs a tale." When I did hear
> The motley fool thus moral on the time,
> My lungs began to crow like chanticleer,
> That fools should be so deep contemplative;
> And I did laugh sans intermission
> An hour by his dial. O noble fool!
> A worthy fool! Motley's the only wear. [2.7.11–34]

Thus, whilst Jaques criticizes the world, Touchstone gently and unintentionally mocks that criticism. Touchstone's own railing "on Lady Fortune in good set terms" reveals to Jaques the dimension of the absurd in all human seriousness. To hear a "motley fool thus moral on the time" is to suggest that to moral on the time is to be a motley fool. If a fool is "deep contemplative," then perhaps the "deep contemplative" is the foolish. Touchstone is a mirror that not only reflects, but lightens, the malcontentment of Jaques. Indeed, garbed in fool's motley, such criticisms as those of Jaques can safely be allowed in the pastoral realm. "Invest me in my motley," says Jaques:

> give me leave
> To speak my mind, and I will through and through
> Cleanse the foul body of th' infected world. . . . [2.7.58–60]

But only if he accepts the dimension of the ludicrous as supplied by the fool can Jaques fit into the comic scheme:

> JAQUES. Yes, I have gain'd my experience.
> ROSALIND. And your experience makes you sad. I had rather have a
> fool to make me merry than experience to make me sad. . . . [4.1.23–25]

Touchstone himself serves the same large function as his counterpart in *King Lear*, although his role is less wonderfully developed. The fool, in either comedy or tragedy, tends to criticize arrogance and pretense on the part of other characters (he can make no claim to wisdom, but he is, notwithstanding, no less wise than the others). In comedy, moreover, his benign good nature provides an added depth of social criticism of the individual: the fool, who is isolated by his motley garb and supposed mental limitations, refuses to be alienated. Whereas Jaques, the malcontent, endlessly finds the world a woeful place, Touchstone accepts existence as he finds it. And most importantly, either here or in *King Lear*, the fool constantly urges the paradox of St. Paul: "If any man among you seemeth to be wise in this world, let him become a fool, that he may be wise" (I Cor. 3:18).

Thus, as Jaques says, "The wise man's folly is anatomiz'd / Even by the squand'ring glances of the fool" (2.7.56–57). "The more pity," says Touchstone,

> that fools may not speak wisely what wise men do foolishly.
> CELIA. By my troth, thou sayest true; for since the little wit that fools
> have was silenced, the little foolery that wise men have makes a great
> show. [1.2.78–82]

And as Touchstone emphasizes, "'The fool doth think he is wise, but the wise man knows himself to be a fool'" (5.1.20–30). By thus paradoxically collapsing the original juxtaposition of wisdom and folly into a playful equation where they are interchangeable, the fool reinforces those attitudes of Plotinus and Plato, . . . by which we are urged to realize that human life, when all is done, is not a very serious matter.

This implication of the fool's influence is made explicit in the famous speech of Jaques, uttered after he has met Touchstone and expressed the desire "that

I were a fool! / I am ambitious for a motley coat" (2.7.42–43); for the speech constitutes a change from Jaques's customary black melancholy:

> All the world's a stage,
> And all the men and women merely players;
> They have their exits and their entrances;
> And one man in his time plays many parts,
> His acts being seven ages. At first the infant,
> Mewling and puking in the nurse's arms,
> Then the whining school-boy, with his satchel
> And shining morning face, creeping like snail
> Unwillingly to school. And then the lover,
> Sighing like furnace, with a woeful ballad
> Made to his mistress' eyebrow. Then a soldier,
> Full of strange oaths, and bearded like the pard,
> Jealous in honour, sudden and quick in quarrel,
> Seeking the bubble reputation
> Even in the cannon's mouth. And then the justice,
> In fair round belly with good capon lin'd,
> With eyes severe and beard of formal cut,
> Full of wise saws and modern instances;
> And so he plays his part. The sixth age shifts
> Into the lean and slipper'd pantaloon,
> With spectacles on nose and pouch on side,
> His youthful hose, well sav'd, a world too wide
> For his shrunk shank; and his big manly voice,
> Turning again toward childish treble, pipes
> And whistles in his sound. Last scene of all,
> That ends this strange eventful history,
> Is second childishness and mere oblivion;
> Sans teeth, sans eyes, sans taste, sans every thing. [2.7.139–66]

The lines achieve simultaneously a vision of life and a wry, rather than melancholy or despairing, perspective on its mystery. The tears of Jaques's contemplation of the wounded stag, mingled with the merry wonder of Touchstone's motley, become now an equivocal smile. Jaques's attitude, accordingly, is reclaimed from tragedy; and as a mark of this reclamation it sees the vanity of human life in terms of social roles—schoolboy, lover, soldier, justice—rather than in terms of individual agonies.

Jaques's moralizing, however, is here, as in the instance of the sobbing deer, somewhat blunted by a certain misunderstanding of reality. In the earlier instance, he did not consider that the hunters were killing out of necessity and not for sport; now the generalities of his cynical seven ages speech do not relate to the actuality around him. For Adam, who by Jaques's speech should be in "second childishness and mere oblivion . . . sans every thing," is instead—and the point is made by Orlando just before Jaques begins to speak—an "old poor man, / Who after me hath many a weary step / Limp'd in pure love." Adam is not "sans every thing," but full of "pure love." Jaques's speech, in short, does not recognize the facts of human community and mutual concern, and flies in the face of the reality before him:

> ORLANDO. I almost die for food, and let me have it.
> DUKE SENIOR. Sit down and feed, and welcome to our table.
> ORLANDO. Speak you so gently? Pardon me, I pray you;
> I thought that all things had been savage here. . . . [2.7.104–7]

The Duke's answer serves both as a repudiation of Jaques's antisocial cynicism and as a sacramental affirmation of human community:

> True is it that we have seen better days,
> And have with holy bell been knoll'd to church,
> And sat at good men's feasts, and wip'd our eyes
> Of drops that sacred pity hath engend'red;
> And therefore sit you down in gentleness,
> And take upon command what help we have
> That to your wanting may be minist'red. [2.7.120–26]

Then, immediately after Jaques's interruption, the Duke reaffirms the holy sense of mutual concern: he pointedly includes the aged Adam in the communal meal:

> Welcome. Set down your venerable burden.
> And let him feed. [2.7.167–68]

In the midst of gentleness, welcoming, help, and veneration Jaques has revealed himself as deficient in the sympathies shared by "co-mates and brothers," and is therefore finally excluded from the community achieved by comic resolution. He is not only counterbalanced, but humanized, by Touchstone; yet in a sense he is and remains more a fool than does the man in motley.

Although not so profound a creation as Lear's fool, Touchstone is clearly closely related:

> ROSALIND. Well, this is the forest of Arden.
> TOUCHSTONE. Ay, now am I in Arden; the more fool I; when I was at home, I was in a better place; but travellers must be content. [2.4.12–14]

The combination of childlike apprehension and childlike acceptance marks Lear's fool too. Moreover, in this play the fool's apprehension and acceptance upon entering the Forest of Arden are still another way of suggesting that here is a golden world manqué. Like his counterpart in *King Lear*, Touchstone speaks truer than supposedly more intelligent figures: "Thou speak'st wiser than thou art ware of," says Rosalind (2.4.53). So when he anatomizes the "seven causes" of dueling, the old Duke finds it appropriate to say, "He uses his folly like a stalkinghorse, and under the presentation of that he shoots his wit" (5.4.100–101). The attack on the folly and pretense of dueling, however, is not mere random wit; dueling is a social abuse, and by making it ridiculous, at the end of the fifth act (compare *The Alchemist*, 4.2.67–68), Touchstone symbolically makes ridiculous all the verbal duelings and disharmonies that have occupied the inhabitants of the pastoral forest.

These duelings interweave themselves into the encounters of almost all the characters. Orlando, for instance, escapes the deadly duel with Oliver, which is made concrete by his wrestling duel with Charles, only to engage in a duel of wits with Rosalind-Ganymede, and another with Jaques. Indeed, as a recent critic has emphasized, meetings or encounters (of which such duelings are a version) substitute for conventional plot in the play's middle portion and thereby invest the action with a special lightness of tone: ". . . such is the ease and rapidity with which pairs and groups break up, re-form, and succeed one another on the stage that there is a sense of fluid movement. All is done with the utmost lightness and gaiety, but as the lovers move through the forest, part and meet again, or mingle with the other characters in their constantly changing pairs and groups, every view of life seems, sooner or later, to find its opposite."[3]

Such an opposition, playfully cast into dueling's artifice of thrust and riposte, is the encounter between Jaques and Orlando:

> JAQUES. I thank you for your company; but, good faith, I had as lief have been myself alone.
> ORLANDO. And so had I; but yet, for fashion sake, I thank you too for your society.
> JAQUES. God buy you; let's meet as little as we can.
> ORLANDO. I do desire we may be better strangers.
> JAQUES. I pray you, mar no more trees with writing love songs in their barks.
> ORLANDO. I pray you, mar no more of my verses with reading them ill-favouredly.
> JAQUES. Rosalind is your love's name?
> ORLANDO. Yes, just.

JAQUES. I do not like her name.

ORLANDO. There was no thought of pleasing you when she was christen'd. . . .

JAQUES. You have a nimble wit; I think 'twas made of Atalanta's heels. Will you sit down with me? and we two will rail against our mistress the world, and all our misery.

ORLANDO. I will chide no breather in the world but myself, against whom I know most faults.

JAQUES. The worst fault you have is to be in love.

ORLANDO. 'Tis a fault I will not change for your best virtue. I am weary of you.

JAQUES. By my troth, I was seeking for a fool when I found you.

ORLANDO. He is drown'd in the brook; look but in, and you shall see him.

JAQUES. There I shall see mine own figure.

ORLANDO. Which I take to be either a fool or a cipher.

JAQUES. I'll tarry no longer with you; farewell, good Signior Love.

ORLANDO. I am glad of your departure; adieu, good Monsieur Melancholy. [3.2.238–77]

In such a staccato combat, the elegance of which depends on the tension between the content of antagonism and the form of social courtesy, both participants are rebuked for social deviance: Orlando for his lovesickness, Jaques for his misanthropic melancholy; and each, kept within social bounds by the form of courtesy, serves as a comic nullifier of the other's deviance.

Neither, however, is wholly reclaimed. Jaques is never entirely redeemed by the play's action, and Orlando is reclaimed only after complicated and lengthy criticism by Rosalind-Ganymede. Indeed, this comedy, even more than *Twelfth Night*, rejects romantic love as social sickness. In the Forest of Arden romantic love replaces, and thereby almost seems to participate in the antisocial nature of, the darker motif of Cain against Abel that had characterized the action at court.

Orlando indicates his lovesickness by carving his emotion into the bark of forest trees:

O Rosalind! these trees shall be my books
And in their barks my thoughts I'll character; . . .
Run, run, Orlando; carve on every tree
The fair, the chaste, and unexpressive she. [3.2.5–10]

Such a proposal echoes a motif from Virgil's pastorals:

certum est in silvis, inter spelaea ferarum
malle pati tenerisque meos incidere amores
arboribus: crescent illae, crescetis, amores.

it is certain that in the forest, among the caves of the wild beasts, it is
better to suffer and carve my love on the young trees; when they grow,
you will grow, my love.

The lines are from the tenth eclogue, which is where the pain of romantic love
is most specifically recognized. In *As You Like It*, however, it is not the case that
"vincit omnia Amor"; for the comic society rebukes the pain and despair of a
pastoral Gallus-like lover.

A second significance of the love-carving is that it reinforces still further
the sense of Arden as something less than the pastoral ideal. Thomas
Rosenmeyer, in his *The Green Cabinet: Theocritus and the European Pastoral
Lyric*, points out that this "pretty vulgarism"—the "self-defeating attack upon
the surface of trees"—which had its inception in Callimachus rather than in
Theocritus, actually damages rather than honors the sacred environment of
pure pastoral (p. 203). The play makes clear, nonetheless, that the change
from the motif of social sickness as brother-against-brother to the motif
of social sickness as romantic love corresponds to a change from a courtly
to a pastoral environment. It is, accordingly, noteworthy that Orlando's
proposal to carve on the trees is directly followed by a change in the tone
of Arden: it promptly becomes less an English Sherwood Forest and more
a Latinate shepherd's world. As though a signal has been given, Orlando's
proposal is followed by the entrance of Touchstone and of Corin, a shepherd.
They duel:

> CORIN. And how like you this shepherd's life, Master Touchstone?
> TOUCHSTONE. Truly, shepherd, in respect of itself, it is a good life;
> but in respect that it is a shepherd's life, it is nought. In respect that it is
> solitary, I like it very well; but in respect that it is private, it is a very vile
> life. Now in respect it is in the fields, it pleaseth me well; but in respect
> it is not in the court, it is tedious.... Hast any philosophy in thee,
> shepherd?
> CORIN. No more but that I know the more one sickens the worse at
> ease he is; ... that good pasture makes fat sheep; and that a great cause
> of the night is lack of the sun; ...
> TOUCHSTONE. Such a one is a natural philosopher. Wast ever in court,
> shepherd?
> CORIN. No, truly....

TOUCHSTONE. Why, if thou never wast at court, thou never saw'st
good manners. . . . Thou art in a parlous state, shepherd.
     CORIN. Not a whit, Touchstone. Those that are good manners at the
court are as ridiculous in the country as the behaviour of the country is
most mockable at court. [3.2.11–43]

Such extended badinage both confirms the equivocal nature of the pastoral realm
in *As You Like It*, and establishes that realm as in fact pastoral. The shepherd's
world is somewhat criticized as against the court; the court is somewhat criticized
as against the shepherd's world.

     In the shepherd's world, Orlando's love is attacked from many quarters. It
is, first of all, divested of its claim to uniqueness by being ironically echoed
in the pastoral lovesickness of Silvius for Phebe. It is lowered in its claim
to dignity by being distortedly reflected in the bumpkin love of Touchstone
for Audrey. And it is shown as a diminution, rather than a heightening, of
awareness by the fact that Orlando does not know that Ganymede, to whom
he laments the absence of Rosalind, is actually that Rosalind whom he so
extravagantly loves. His emotion, furthermore, is made to appear moist and
ludicrous by the dry criticism of Rosalind. "Then in mine own person I die,"
sighs Orlando. Rosalind replies:

> No, faith, die by attorney. The poor world is almost six thousand
> years old, and in all this time there was not any man died in his own
> person, videlicet, in a love-cause. Troilus had his brains dash'd out with
> a Grecian club; yet he did what he could to die before, and he is one
> of the patterns of love. Leander, he would have liv'd many a fair year,
> though Hero had turn'd nun, if it had not been for a hot midsummer
> night; for, good youth, he went but forth to wash him in the Hellespont,
> and, being taken with the cramp, was drown'd; and the foolish
> chroniclers of that age found it was—Hero of Sestos. But these are all
> lies: men have died from time to time, and worms have eaten them, but
> not for love. [4.1.82–95]

The last justly famous sentence establishes the absolute norm of comedy's rebuke
to romantic love. And the invocation of Hero and Leander directs attention to
Marlowe's poem. Indeed, Marlowe's antisocial life, as well as the unacceptability
of romantic love's exclusiveness, are focused by reference to Marlowe's death and
by direct quotation of a line from *Hero and Leander*: "Dead shepherd, now I find
thy saw of might, / 'Who ever lov'd that lov'd not at first sight?'" (3.5.80–81; *Hero
and Leander*, 1.176). The question is asked, however, by the pastoral Phebe as she
embarks upon a course of patent folly: blind love for Ganymede, who, in reality
a woman, represents a social impossibility for the shepherdess.

Phebe's folly is underscored by her "love at first sight" infatuation; her pastoral lover, Silvius, is equally foolish, for love makes him less than a man:

Sweet Phebe, do not scorn me; do not, Phebe.
Say that you love me not; but say not so
In bitterness. [3.5.1–3]

Both Phebe and Silvius are accordingly dry-beaten with Rosalind's scoff, which is the curative of such extravagant and socially unsettling emotion. To Phebe she says:

I see no more in you than in the ordinary
Of nature's sale-work. 'Od's my little life,
I think she means to tangle my eyes too!
No, faith, proud mistress, hope not after it;
'Tis not your inky brows, your black silk hair,
Your bugle eyeballs, nor your cheek of cream,
That can entame my spirits to your worship. [3.5.42–48]

Having demolished Phebe's pretensions to uniqueness, she then turns her scorn on Silvius:

You foolish shepherd, wherefore do you follow her,
Like foggy south, puffing with wind and rain?
You are a thousand times a properer man
Than she a woman. 'Tis such fools as you
That makes the world full of ill-favour'd children. [3.5.49–53]

Even more explicit, and much more prolonged, are the rebukes administered to Orlando. His romantic extravagance is repeatedly denigrated by being referred to in the language of sickness, and his dramatically pastoral emotion is withered by Rosalind's scorn:

There is a man haunts the forest that abuses our young plants with carving "Rosalind" on their barks; hangs odes upon hawthorns and elegies on brambles; all, forsooth, deifying the name of Rosalind. If I could meet that fancy-monger, I would give him some good counsel, for he seems to have the quotidian of love upon him.

ORLANDO. I am he that is so love-shak'd; I pray you tell me your remedy.

ROSALIND. There is none of my uncle's marks upon you; he taught me how to know a man in love; in which cage of rushes I am sure you are not prisoner.

ORLANDO. What were his marks?

ROSALIND. A lean cheek, which you have not; a blue eye and sunken, which you have not; an unquestionable spirit, which you have not; a beard neglected, which you have not. . . . Then your hose should be ungarter'd, your bonnet unbanded, your sleeve unbutton'd, your shoe untied, and every thing about you demonstrating a careless desolation. . . .

ORLANDO. Fair youth, I would I could make thee believe I love. . . .

ROSALIND. But are you so much in love as your rhymes speak?

ORLANDO. Neither rhyme nor reason can express how much.

ROSALIND. Love is merely a madness. . . .

ORLANDO. I would not be cured, youth.

ROSALIND. I would cure you, if you would but call me Rosalind, and come every day to my cote and woo me. [3.2.334–92]

The artifice of Rosalind pretending to be Ganymede, and Ganymede pretending to be Rosalind again, grants the audience an insight immensely superior to that of Orlando, while equating his exaggerated love with his ignorance; and it also satisfies dramatically the idea that love is a mistaking of reality. Once love comes under the control supplied by Rosalind's criticism, however, the play begins to frolic in the dance-like patterns of *Love's Labour's Lost*. The Cain-against-Abel situation of the two dukes, like that of Orlando and Oliver, had from the first involved the play in doublings; and these, together with the doubling of Rosalind by Celia, and the Ganymede disguise by the Aliena disguise, become, as the action of the play lightens, the symmetrical doublings and repetitions of comedy's artifice. Indeed, perhaps no single place in Shakespeare's comedy achieves a more perfect coordination of symmetry, repetition, and comic inevitability than the merry-go-round of the love doctor's final social disposition of the disease of romantic love. Rosalind says to Orlando:

Therefore, put you in your best array, bid yours friends; for if you will be married tomorrow, you shall; and to Rosalind, if you will.

At this point Silvius and Phebe enter:

PHEBE. Youth, you have done me much ungentleness. . . .

ROSALIND. I care not if I have. . . .

You are there follow'd by a faithful shepherd;

Look upon him, love him; he worships you.

PHEBE. Good shepherd, tell this youth what 'tis to love.

SILVIUS. It is to be all made of sighs and tears;

And so am I for Phebe.

    PHEBE. And I for Ganymede.

    ORLANDO. And I for Rosalind.

    ROSALIND. And I for no woman.

    SILVIUS. It is to be all made of faith and service;

And so am I for Phebe.

    PHEBE. And I for Ganymede.

    ORLANDO. And I for Rosalind.

    ROSALIND. And I for no woman.

    SILVIUS. It is to be all made of fantasy.

All made of passion, and all made of wishes;

All adoration, duty, and observance,

All humbleness, all patience, and impatience,

All purity, all trial, all obedience;

And so am I for Phebe.

    PHEBE. And so am I for Ganymede.

    ORLANDO. And so am I for Rosalind.

    ROSALIND. And so am I for no woman.

    PHEBE. If this be so, why blame you me to love you?

    SILVIUS. If this be so, why blame you me to love you?

    ORLANDO. If this be so, why blame you me to love you? . . .

    ROSALIND. Pray you, no more of this; 'tis like the howling of Irish wolves against the moon. [*To Silvius*] I will help you, if I can. [*To Phebe*] I would love you, if I could.—To-morrow meet me all together. [*To Phebe*] I will marry you if ever I marry woman, and I'll be married to-morrow. [*To Orlando*] I will satisfy you if ever I satisfied man, and you shall be married to-morrow. [*To Silvius*] I will content you if what pleases you contents you, and you shall be married to-morrow. [5.2.66–109]

And thus the play dances to its final resolution. Hymen announces that "Then is there mirth in heaven, / When earthly things made even / Atone together" (5.4.102–4), and his beautiful song pours comic benignity lavishly over the concluding action:

Wedding is great Juno's crown

    O blessed bond of board and bed!

'Tis Hymen peoples every town;

    High wedlock then be honoured.

Honour, high honour, and renown,

To Hymen, god of every town! [5.4.135–40]

The song provides one of literature's most elevated and explicit salutations to the aim and justification of comedy. Under its assurance, the old Duke commands his society to

> fall into our rustic revelry.
> Play, music; and you brides and bridegrooms all,
> With measure heap'd in joy, to th' measures fall. [5.4.171–73]

And yet even this comic happiness cannot totally sweeten the trace of the bitter root in *As You Like It*. Both the usurping Duke and the melancholy Jaques are ejected from, rather than reconciled to, the new society. As Jaques de Boys—the new Jaques—says:

> Duke Frederick, hearing how that every day
> Men of great worth resorted to this forest,
> Address'd a mighty power; which were on foot,
> In his own conduct, purposely to take
> His brother here, and put him to the sword;
> And to the skirts of this wild wood he came,
> Where, meeting with an old religious man,
> After some question with him, was converted
> Both from his enterprise and from the world;
> His crown bequeathing to his banish'd brother,
> And all their lands restor'd to them again
> That were with him exil'd. [5.4.148–59]

And Jaques, the malcontent, is, like Molière's Alceste, equally irredeemable by the comic therapy:

> Jaques. Sir, by your patience. If I heard you rightly,
> The Duke hath put on a religious life
> And thrown into neglect the pompous court.
> Jaques de boys. He hath.
> Jaques. To him will I. Out of these convertites
> There is much matter to be heard and learn'd.
> . . . So to your pleasures;
> I am for other than for dancing measures. [5.4.174–87]

Jaques, indeed, though necessary to the process of comic catharsis in the play, has always exerted counter-pressure against the pastoral ideal. When Amiens sings the lovely song that declares Arden's version of pastoral carefreeness, Jaques immediately seeks to cloud its limpidity:

AMIENS. Under the greenwood tree
Who loves to lie with me,
And turn his merry note
Unto the sweet bird's throat,
Come hither, come hither, come hither.
    Here shall he see
    No enemy
    But winter and rough weather.
JAQUES. More, more, I prithee more.
AMIENS. It will make you melancholy, Monsieur Jaques.
JAQUES. I thank it. More, I prithee, more. I can suck melancholy out
of a song, as a weasel sucks eggs. [2.5.1–13]

And then Jaques produces his own song, which, in its cynicism, superimposes
itself like a blotter on that of Amiens:

    If it do come to pass
    That any man turn ass,
    Leaving his wealth and ease
    A stubborn will to please,
Ducdame, ducdame, ducdame;
    Here shall he see
    Gross fools as he,
    An if he will come to me.
AMIENS. What's that "ducdame"?
JAQUES. 'Tis a Greek invocation, to call fools into a circle. [2.5.46–56]

If the coming together of individuals into social happiness is for Jaques a calling
of "fools into a circle," it is clear that his own deviation is as impervious to comic
reclamation as that of the wicked younger duke.

    Thus Duke Frederick and Jaques are "for other than for dancing measures,"
and by that fact they show that certain persisting threads of action and tone in
this play are alien to the comic vision. By leaving Frederick and Jaques out of
the social resolution, *As You Like It* intensifies the strain on comic limits that
the villainous Don John had exerted in *Much Ado About Nothing*. That play,
like this one, concludes equivocally. Benedick recites the comic benediction:
"Come, come, we are friends. Let's have a dance ere we are married" (*Much Ado*,
5.4.113–14); but Don John is a loose end:

MESSENGER. My lord, your brother John is ta'en in flight,
And brought with armed men back to Messina.

BENEDICK. Think not on him till to-morrow. I'll devise thee brave
punishments for him. Strike up, pipers. [*Much Ado*, 5.4.120–24]

In *As You Like It*, Hymen's song provides a more radiant measure of comic
well-being than any statements at the end of *Much Ado*, but even so the
complications have moved nearer to tragedy, and Hymen cannot eradicate
all the signs of strain. And after *As You Like It*, Shakespeare not only forgoes
pastoral therapy for a while, but his comic vessels, leaving behind the clear
waters sailed by *Twelfth Night* and *The Merry Wives of Windsor*, begin
increasingly to labor in heavy seas of bitterness. The idea of the joyous society
tends henceforth to be more difficult to achieve or maintain. In *The Winter's
Tale*, great cracks run through the artifice of happiness, and are caulked only
with difficulty. Not until *The Tempest* does Shakespeare's art, having traversed
the bitter complications of the middle and late comedies, find quiet harbor
in a renewed paradisal hope. There at last, in the enchanted island's golden
world, the storm of cynicism and tragic disharmony, with a final rage, blows
itself out.

NOTES

1. For a comprehensive discussion of the tradition of human lament for the
death of animals, see D.C. Allen, "Marvell's 'Nymph,'" *ELH*, 23 (1956): 93–111;
see especially note 19, pp. 100–101, for the deer as "the symbol of Christ," as
"good Christian," as "repentant man." For the ancient association of a deer with
"metaphors of love" see pp. 102–3. See further Herrlinger, *Totenklage um Tiere in
der antiken Dichtung* (Stuttgart, 1929).

2. See further Claus Uhlig, "Der weinende Hirsch: *As You Like It*, II.i.21–66,
und der historische Kontext," in *Deutsche Shakespeare-Gesellschaft West; Jahrbuch
1968*, pp. 141–68. Uhlig places the "emblematic" passage of Jaques's "weeping
and commenting / Upon the sobbing deer" (2.1.65–66) in a tradition of "hunt
criticism" extending from Roman antiquity to the late eighteenth century, with
special attention to John of Salisbury's *Policraticus*, More's *Utopia*, and, as direct
progenitor of Shakespeare's passage, Sidney's *Arcadia*. By his "lament over the
tyrannical cruelty of the hunt," Jaques reveals himself as not only a "malcontent"
but a "humanist" as well. But Jaques "does not stop to think that the banished
men pursue the hunt out of bitter necessity, which is permitted in both the
Policraticus and the *Utopia*." By this lack of realism, therefore, Jaques's high moral
earnestness is kept within the bounds of comedy and out of the realm of tragic
criticism.

3. Harold Jenkins, "As You Like It," *Shakespeare Survey* 8 (Cambridge,
1968), p. 50.

1981—Louis Adrian Montrose. "'The Place of a Brother' in 'As You Like It': Social Process and Comic Form," from *Shakespeare Quarterly*

Louis Adrian Montrose is a professor of English and American literature at the University of California, San Diego. He is the author of *"Curious-Knotted Garden": The Form, Themes, and Contexts of Shakespeare's* Love's Labour's Lost," as well as articles and monographs on Shakespeare, Elizabethan pastorals, and other topics.

I

As You Like It creates and resolves conflict by mixing what the characters call Fortune and Nature—the circumstances in which they find themselves, as opposed to the resources of playfulness and boldness, moral virtue and witty deception, with which they master adversity and fulfill their desires.

The romantic action is centered on the meeting, courtship, and successful pairing of Rosalind and Orlando. This action is complicated, as Leo Salingar reminds us, by "a cardinal social assumption . . . (which would have been obvious to . . . Shakespeare's first audiences)—that Rosalind is a princess, while Orlando is no more than a gentleman. But for the misfortune of her father's exile, they might not have met in sympathy as at first; but for the second misfortune of her own exile, as well as his, they could not have met in apparent equality in the Forest."[1] The personal situations of Rosalind and Orlando affect, and are affected by, their relationship to each other. Rosalind's union with Orlando entails the weakening of her ties to her natural father and to a cousin who has been closer to her than a sister; Orlando's union with Rosalind entails the strengthening of his ties to his elder brother and to a lord who becomes his patron. Orlando's atonements with other men—a natural brother, a social father—precede his atonement with Rosalind. They confirm that the disadvantaged young country gentleman is worthy of the princess, by "nature" and by "fortune." The atonement of earthly things celebrated in Hymen's wedding song incorporates man and woman within a process that reunites man with man. This process is my subject.

As the play begins, Orlando and Adam are discussing the terms of a paternal will; the first scene quickly explodes into fraternal resentment and envy, hatred and violence. By the end of the second scene, the impoverished youngest son of Sir Rowland de Boys finds himself victimized by "a tyrant Duke" and "a tyrant brother" (I.iii.278).[2] The compact early scenes expose hostilities on the manor and in the court that threaten to destroy both the family and the state. Although modern productions have shown that these scenes can be powerful and effective in the theatre, modern criticism has repeatedly downplayed their seriousness and significance. They are often treated merely as Shakespeare's mechanism for propelling his characters—and us—into the forest as quickly and efficiently as possible. Thus Harold Jenkins, in his influential essay on the play, writes of "the inconsequential nature of the action" and of "Shakespeare's haste to get ahead"; for him, the plot's interest consists in Shakespeare's ability to get "most of it over in the first act."[3] If we *reverse* Jenkins' perspective, we will do justice to Shakespeare's dramaturgy and make better sense of the play. What happens to Orlando at home is not Shakespeare's contrivance to get him into the forest; what happens to Orlando in the forest is Shakespeare's contrivance to remedy what has happened to him at home. The form of *As You Like It* becomes comic in the process of resolving the conflicts that are generated within it; events unfold and relationships are transformed in accordance with a precise comic teleology.

II

Jaques sententiously observes that the world is a stage; the men and women, merely players; and one man's time, a sequence of acts in which he plays many parts. Shakespeare's plays reveal many traces of the older drama's intimate connection to the annual agrarian and ecclesiastical cycles. But more pervasive than these are the connections between Shakespearean comic and tragic forms and the human life cycle—the sequence of acts performed in several ages by Jaques' social player. Action in Shakespearean drama usually originates in combinations of a few basic kinds of human conflict: conflict among members of different families, generations, sexes, and social classes. Shakespeare tends to focus dramatic action precisely *between* the social "acts," between the sequential "ages," in the fictional lives of his characters. Many of the plays turn upon points of transition in the life cycle—birth, puberty, marriage, death—where discontinuities arise and where adjustments are necessary to basic interrelationships in the family and in society. Such dramatic actions are analogous to rites of passage. Transition rites symbolically impose markers upon the life cycle and safely conduct people from one stage of life to the next; they give a social shape, order, and sanction to personal existence.[4]

In *As You Like It*, the initial conflict arises from the circumstances of inheritance by primogeniture. The differential relationship between the first born and his younger brothers is profoundly augmented at their father's death: the eldest son assumes a paternal relationship to his siblings; and the potential for sibling conflict increases when the relationship between brother and brother becomes identified with the relationship between father and son. The transition of the father from life to death both fosters and obstructs the transition of his sons from childhood to manhood. In *As You Like It*, the process of comedy accomplishes successful passages between ages in the life cycle and ranks in the social hierarchy. By the end of the play, Orlando has been brought from an impoverished and powerless adolescence to the threshold of manhood and marriage, wealth and title.

A social anthropologist defines inheritance practices as "the way by which property is transmitted between the living and the dead, and especially between generations."

> Inheritance is not only the means by which the reproduction of the social system is carried out . . . it is also the way in which interpersonal relationships are structured. . . .
>
> The linking of patterns of inheritance with patterns of domestic organization is a matter not simply of numbers and formations but of attitudes and emotions. The manner of splitting property is a manner of splitting people; it creates (or in some cases reflects) a particular constellation of ties and cleavages between husband and wife, parents and children, sibling and sibling, as well as between wider kin.[5]

As Goody himself concedes, the politics of the family are most powerfully anatomized, not by historians or social scientists, but by playwrights. Parents and children in Shakespeare's plays are recurrently giving or withholding, receiving or returning, property and love. Material and spiritual motives, self-interest and self-sacrifice, are inextricably intertwined in Shakespearean drama as in life.

Lear's tragedy, for example, begins in his division of his kingdom among his daughters and their husbands. He makes a bequest of his property to his heirs before his death, so "that future strife / May be prevented now" (I.i.44–45). Gloucester's tragedy begins in the act of adultery that begets an "unpossessing bastard" (II.i.67). Edmund rails against "the plague of custom . . . the curiosity of nations" (I.ii.3–4); he sees himself as victimized by rules of legitimacy and primogeniture. *As You Like It* begins with Orlando remembering the poor bequest from a dead father and the unnaturalness of an elder brother; he is victimized by what he bitterly refers to as "the courtesy of nations" (I.i.45–46). Rosalind dejectedly remembers "a banished father" (I.ii.4) and the consequent loss of her own preeminent social place. Celia responds to her cousin with naive girlhood loyalty: "You know my father hath no child but I, nor none is like to have; and truly when he dies, thou shalt be his heir; for what he hath taken away from thy father perforce, I will render thee again in affection" (I.ii.14–19). The comic action of *As You Like It* works to atone elder and younger brothers, father and child, man and woman, lord and subject, master and servant. Within his play, Rosalind's magician-uncle recreates situations that are recurrent sources of ambiguity, anxiety, and conflict in the society of his audience; he explores and exacerbates them, and he resolves them by brilliant acts of theatrical prestidigitation.

The tense situation which begins *As You Like It* was a familiar and controversial fact of Elizabethan social life. Lawrence Stone emphasizes that "the prime factor affecting all families which owned property was . . . primogeniture"; that "the principle and practice of primogeniture . . . went far to determine the behaviour and character of both parents and children, and to govern the relationship between siblings."[6] In the sixteenth and seventeenth centuries, primogeniture was more widely and rigorously practiced in England—by the gentry and lesser landowners, as well as by the aristocracy— than anywhere else in Europe. The consequent hardships, frequent abuses, and inherent inequities of primogeniture generated a "literature of protest by and for younger sons" that has been characterized as "plentiful," "vehement" in tone, and "unanimous" in its sympathies.[7]

Jaques was not the only satirist to "rail against all the first-born of Egypt" (II. v.57–58). John Earle included the character of a "younger Brother" in his *Micro-Cosmographie* (1628):

His father ha's done with him, as *Pharaoh* to the children of Israel, that
would have them make brick, and give them no straw, so he taskes
him to bee a Gentleman, and leaves him nothing to maintaine it. The
pride of his house has undone him, which the elder Knighthood must
sustaine, and his beggery that Knighthood. His birth and bringing up
will not suffer him to descend to the meanes to get wealth: but hee
stands at the mercy of the world, and which is worse of his brother. He
is something better then the Servingmen; yet they more saucy with him,
then hee bold with the master, who beholds him with a countenance
of sterne awe, and checks him oftner then his Liveries. . . . Nature hath
furnisht him with a little more wit upon compassion; for it is like to be
his best revenew. . . . Hee is commonly discontented, and desperate, and
the forme of his exclamation is, that Churle my brother.[8]

As a class, the gentry experienced a relative rise in wealth and status during this period. But the rise was achieved by inheriting eldest sons at the expense of their younger brothers. As Earle and other contemporaries clearly recognized, the gentry's drive to aggrandize and perpetuate their estates led them to a ruthless application of primogeniture; this left them without the means adequately to provide for their other offspring. The psychological and socio-economic consequences of primogeniture for younger sons (and for daughters) seem to have been considerable: downward social mobility and relative impoverishment, inability to marry or late marriage, and fewer children.

In 1600, about the time *As You Like It* was first performed, Thomas Wilson wrote a valuable analysis of England's social structure. His description of gentlemen reveals a very personal involvement:

Those which wee call Esquires are gentlemen whose ancestors are or have bin Knights, or else they are the heyres and eldest of their houses and of some competent quantity of revenue fitt to be called to office and authority in their Country. . . . These are the elder brothers.

I cannot speak of the number of yonger brothers, albeit I be one of the number myselfe, but for their estate there is no man hath better cause to knowe it, nor less cause to praise it; their state is of all stations for gentlemen most miserable. . . . [A father] may demise as much as he thinkes good to his younger children, but such a fever hectick hath custome brought in and inured amongst fathers, and such fond desire they have to leave a great shewe of the stock of their house, though the branches be withered, that they will not doe it, but my elder brother forsooth must be my master. He must have all, and all the rest that which the catt left on the malt heape, perhaps some smale annuytye during his life or what please our elder brother's worship to bestowe upon us if wee please him.[9]

The foregoing texts characterize quite precisely the situation of Orlando and his relationship to Oliver at the beginning of *As You Like It*. They suggest that Shakespeare's audience may have responded with some intensity to Orlando's indictment of "the courtesy of nations."

In his constitutional treatise, *De Republica Anglorum* (written ca. 1562; printed 1583), Sir Thomas Smith observes that "whosoever studies the laws of the realm, who studies at the universities, who professes liberal sciences and to be short, who can live idly and without manual labour, and will bear the port, charge and countenance of a gentleman . . . shall be taken for a gentleman."[10] The expected social fate of a gentleborn Elizabethan younger son was to lose the ease founded upon landed wealth that was the very hallmark of gentility. Joan Thirsk suggests that, although there were places to be had for those who were industrious and determined to make the best of their misfortune,

the habit of working for a living was not ingrained in younger sons of this class, and no amount of argument could convince them of the justice of treating them so differently from their elder brothers. The contrast was too sharp between the life of an elder son, whose fortune was made for him by his father, and who had nothing to do but maintain, and perhaps augment it, and that of the younger sons who faced a life of hard and continuous effort, starting almost from nothing. Many persistently refused to accept their lot, and hung around at home, idle, bored, and increasingly resentful.[11]

At the beginning of *As You Like It*, Orlando accuses Oliver of enforcing his idleness and denying him the means to preserve the gentility which is his birthright: "My brother Jaques he keeps at school, and report speaks goldenly of his profit; for my part, he keeps me rustically at home, or, to speak more properly, stays me here at home unkept; for call you that keeping for a gentleman of my birth, that differs not from the stalling of an ox? . . . [He] mines my gentility with my education" (I.i.5–10, 20–21). Orlando is "not taught to make anything" (l. 30); and his natural virtue is marred "with idleness" (ll. 33–34). When Adam urges him to leave the family estate, Orlando imagines his only prospects to be beggary and highway robbery (II.iii.29–34). He finally agrees to go off with Adam, spending the old laborer's "youthful wages" in order to gain "some settled low content" (II.iii.67–68).

Shakespeare's opening strategy is to plunge his characters and his audience into the controversy about a structural principle of Elizabethan personal, family, and social life. He is not merely using something topical to get his comedy off to a lively start: the expression and resolution of sibling conflict and its social implications are integral to the play's form and function. The process of comedy works against the seemingly inevitable prospect of social degradation suggested at the play's beginning, and against its literary idealization in conventions of humble pastoral retirement. In the course of *As You Like It*, Orlando's gentility is preserved and his material well-being is enhanced. Shakespeare uses the machinery of pastoral romance to remedy the lack of fit between deserving and having, between Nature and Fortune. Without actually violating the primary Elizabethan social frontier separating the gentle from the base, the play achieves an illusion of social leveling and of unions across class boundaries. Thus, people of every rank in Shakespeare's socially heterogeneous audience might construe the action as they liked it. Primogeniture is rarely mentioned in modern commentaries on *As You Like It*, despite its obvious prominence in the text and in the action.[12] Shakespeare's treatment of primogeniture may very well have been a vital—perhaps even the dominant—source of engagement for many in his Elizabethan audience. The public theatre brought together people from all the status and occupational groups to be found in Shakespeare's London (except, of course, for the poorest laborers and the indigent). Alfred Harbage points out that the two groups "mentioned again and again in contemporary allusions to the theatres" are "the students of the Inns of Court and the apprentices of London."[13] In addition to these youthful groups, significant numbers of soldiers, professionals, merchants, shopkeepers, artisans, and household servants were also regular playgoers. The careers most available to the younger sons of gentlemen were in the professions—most notably the law, but also medicine and teaching—as well as in trade, the army, and the church.[14] Thus, Shakespeare's audience, must have included a high proportion of gentleborn younger sons—adults, as well as the youths who were students and apprentices. Among these gentleborn younger sons, and among the baseborn youths who were themselves socially subordinate apprentices and servants, it is likely that Orlando's desperate situation was the focus of personal projections and a catalyst of powerful feelings. "During the sixteenth century," Thirsk concludes, "to describe anyone as '*a younger son*' was a short-hand way of summing up a host of grievances. . . . *Younger son* meant an angry young man, bearing more than his share of injustice and resentment, deprived of means by his father and elder brother, often hanging around his elder brother's house as a servant, completely dependent on his grace and favour."[15] Youths, younger sons, and all Elizabethan playgoers who felt that Fortune's benefits had been "mightily misplaced" (II.i.33–34) could identify with Shakespeare's Orlando.

III

It is precisely in the details of inheritance that Shakespeare makes one of the most significant departures from his source. Sir John of Bordeaux is on his deathbed at the beginning of Lodge's *Rosalynde*; he divides his land and chattels among his three sons:

> Unto thee *Saladyne* the eldest, and therefore the chiefest piller of
> my house, wherein should be ingraven as well the excellence of thy
> fathers qualities, as the essentiall forme of his proportion, to thee I
> give foureteene ploughlands, with all my Mannor houses and richest
> plate. Next unto *Fernadyne* I bequeath twelve ploughlands. But unto
> *Rosader* the youngest I give my Horse, my Armour and my Launce, with
> sixteene ploughlands: for if inward thoughts be discovered by outward
> shadowes, *Rosader* will exceed you all in bountie and honour.[16]

The partible inheritance devised by Lodge's Sir John was an idiosyncratic variation on practices widespread in Elizabethan society among those outside the gentry.[17] Saladyne, the eldest born, inherits his father's authority. Rosader receives more land and love—he is his father's joy, although his last and least. Saladyne, who becomes Rosader's guardian, is deeply resentful and decides not to honor their father's will: "What man thy Father is dead, and hee can neither helpe thy fortunes, nor measure thy actions: therefore, burie his words with his carkasse, and bee wise for thy selfe" (p. 391).

Lodge's text, like Thomas Wilson's, reminds us that primogeniture was not a binding law but rather a flexible social custom in which the propertied sought to perpetuate themselves by preserving their estates intact through successive generations. Shakespeare alters the terms of the paternal will in Lodge's story so as to alienate Orlando from the status of a landed gentleman. The effect is to intensify the differences between the eldest son and his siblings, and to identify the sibling conflict with the major division in the Elizabethan social fabric: that between the landed and the unlanded, the gentle and the base. (Within half a century after Shakespeare wrote *As You Like It*, radical pamphleteers were using "elder brother" and "younger brother" as synonyms for the propertied,

enfranchised social classes and the unpropertied, unenfranchised social classes.)
Primogeniture complicates not only sibling and socio-economic relationships
but also relationships between generations: between a father and the eldest son
impatient for his inheritance; between a father and the younger sons resentful
against the "fever hectic" that custom has inured among fathers.

Shakespeare's plays are thickly populated by subjects, sons, and younger
brothers who are ambivalently bound to their lords, genitors, and elder
siblings—and by young women moving ambivalently between the lordships of
father and husband. If this dramatic proliferation of patriarchs suggests that
Shakespeare had a neurotic obsession, then it was one with a social context.
To see father-figures everywhere in Shakespeare's plays is not a psychoanalytic
anachronism, for Shakespeare's own contemporaries seem to have seen father-
figures everywhere. The period from the mid-sixteenth to the mid-seventeenth
century in England has been characterized by Lawrence Stone as "the patriarchal
stage in the evolution of the nuclear family."[18] Writing of the early seventeenth-
century family as "a political symbol and a social institution," Gordon J. Schochet
documents that

> virtually all social relationships—not merely those between fathers and
> children and magistrates and subjects—were regarded as patriarchal or
> familial in essence. The family was looked upon as the basis of the entire
> social order. . . .
>
> So long as a person occupied an inferior status within a household—
> as a child, servant, apprentice, or even as a wife—and was subordinated
> to the head, his social identity was altogether vicarious. . . .
>
> Before a man achieved social status—if he ever did—he would
> have spent a great many years in various positions of patriarchal
> subordination.[19]

This social context shaped Shakespeare's preoccupation with fathers; and it gave
him the scope within which to reshape it into drama, satisfying his own needs
and those of his paying audience. His plays explore the difficulty or impossibility
of establishing or authenticating a self in a rigorously hierarchical and patriarchal
society, a society in which full social identity tends to be limited to propertied
adult males who are the heads of households.

Shakespeare's Sir Rowland de Boys is dead before the play begins. But
the father endures in the power exerted by his memory and his will upon the
men in the play—his sons, Adam, the dukes—and upon their attitudes toward
each other. The play's very first words insinuate that Orlando's filial feeling is
ambivalent "As I remember, Adam, it was upon this fashion bequeathed me
by will but poor a thousand crowns, and, as thou sayst, charged my brother on
his blessing to breed me well; and there begins my sadness" (I.i.1–4). Orlando's

diction is curiously indirect; he conspicuously avoids naming his father. Absent from Shakespeare's play is any expression of the special, compensatory paternal affection shown to Lodge's Rosader. There is an implied resentment against an unnamed father, who has left his son a paltry inheritance and committed him to an indefinite and socially degrading dependence upon his own brother. Ironically, Orlando's first explicit acknowledgment of his filial bond is in a declaration of personal *independence*, a repudiation of his bondage to his eldest brother: "The spirit of my father, which I think is within me, begins to mutiny against this servitude" (I.i.21–23). Orlando's assertions of filial piety are actually self-assertions, directed against his father's eldest son. As Sir Rowland's inheritor, Oliver perpetuates Orlando's subordination within the patriarchal order; he usurps Orlando's selfhood.

In a private family and household, the eldest son succeeds the father as patriarch. In a royal or aristocratic family, the eldest son also succeeds to the father's title and political authority. Thus, when he has been crowned as King Henry V, Hal tells his uneasy siblings, "I'll be your father and your brother too. / Let me but bear your love, I'll bear your cares" (*2 Henry IV*, V.ii.57–58). Like Henry, Oliver is simultaneously a father and a brother to his own natural sibling; he is at once Orlando's master and his peer. Primogeniture conflates the generations in the person of the elder brother and blocks the generational passage of the younger brother. What might be described dispassionately as a contradiction in social categories is incarnated in the play, as in English social life, in family conflicts and identity crises.[20]

Orlando gives bitter expression to his personal experience of this social contradiction: "The courtesy of nations allows you my better in that you are the firstborn, but that same tradition takes not away my blood, were there twenty brothers betwixt us. I have as much of my father in me as you, albeit I confess that your coming before me is nearer his reverence" (I.i.45–51). Here Orlando asserts that all brothers are equally their father's sons. Oliver might claim a special paternal relationship because he is the first born; but Orlando's own claim actually to incorporate their father renders insubstantial any argument based on age or birth order. Thus, Orlando can indict his brother and repudiate his authority: "You have trained me like a peasant, obscuring and hiding from me all gentlemanlike qualities. The spirit of my father grows strong in me, and I will no longer endure it" (I.i.68–71). Because the patriarchal family is the basic political unit of a patriarchal society, Orlando's protests suggest that primogeniture involves contradictions in the categories of social status as well as those of kinship. Orlando is subordinated to his sibling as a son to his father; and he is subordinated to a fellow gentleman as a peasant would be subordinated to his lord.

Orlando incorporates not only his father's likeness and name ("Rowland") but also his potent "spirit"—his personal genius, his manliness, and his moral virtue.

To Adam, Orlando is "gentle, strong, and valiant" (II.iii.6). He is his father's gracious and virtuous reincarnation: "O you memory of old Sir Rowland!" (II. iii.3–4). Adam challenges the eldest son's legal claim to be his father's heir by asserting that Oliver is morally undeserving, that he is spiritually illegitimate:

> Your brother, no, no brother, yet the son—
> Yet not the son, I will not call him son—
> Of him I was about to call his father. (II.iii.19–21)

Orlando's claim to his spiritual inheritance leads immediately to physical coercion: Oliver calls him "boy" and strikes him. Orlando responds to this humiliating form of parental chastisement not with deference but with rebellion: he puts his hands to Oliver's throat. Orlando's assertion of a self which "remembers" their father is a threat to Oliver's patriarchal authority, a threat to his own social identity: "Begin you to grow upon me?" (I.i.85). The brothers' natural bond, in short, is contaminated by their ambiguous social relationship.

Because fraternity is confused with filiation—because the generations have, in effect, been collapsed together—the conflict of elder and younger brothers also projects an oedipal struggle between father and son. In the second scene, the private violence between the brothers is displaced into the public wrestling match. Oliver tells Charles, the Duke's wrestler, "I had as lief thou didst break [Orlando's] neck as his finger" (I.i.144–45). Sinewy Charles, the "general challenger" (I.ii.159), has already broken the bodies of "three proper young men" (l. 111) before Orlando comes in to try "the strength of [his] youth" (l. 161). In a sensational piece of stage business, Orlando and Charles enact a living emblem of the generational struggle. When Orlando throws Charles, youth is supplanting age, the son is supplanting the father. This contest is preceded by a remarkable exchange:

> *Cha.* Come, where is this young gallant that is so desirous to lie with his mother earth?
> *Orl.* Ready sir, but his will hath in it a more modest working.
> (I.ii.188–91)

Charles's challenge gives simultaneous expression to a filial threat of incest and a paternal threat of filicide. In this conspicuously motherless play, the social context of reciprocal father-son hostility is a male struggle for identity and power fought between elders and youths, first-born and younger brothers.[21]

Orlando's witty response to Charles suggests that he regards neither his fears nor his threats. Orlando's "will" is merely to come to man's estate and to preserve the status of a gentleman. At the beginning of *As You Like It*, then, Shakespeare sets himself the problem of resolving—the consequences of a conflict between Orlando's powerful assertion of identity—his spiritual claim to be a true inheritor—and the social fact that he is a subordinated and disadvantaged younger son. In the forest, Oliver will be spiritually reborn and confirmed in his original inheritance. Orlando will be socially reborn as heir apparent to the reinstated Duke. Orlando will regain a brother by "blood" and a father by "affinity."

IV

Orlando is not only a younger son but also a youth. And in its language, characterization, and plot, *As You Like It* emphasizes the significance of age categories. Most prominent, of course, is Jaques' disquisition on the seven ages of man. But the play's *dramatis personae* actually fall into the three functional age groups of Elizabethan society: youth, maturity, and old age. Orlando's youth is referred to by himself and by others some two dozen times in the first two scenes: he is young; a boy; a youth; the youngest son; a younger brother; a young fellow; a young gallant; a young man; a young gentleman. Social historians have discredited the notion that adolescence went unexperienced or unacknowledged in early modern England. Lawrence Stone, for example, emphasizes that in Shakespeare's time there was "a strong contemporary consciousness of adolescence (then called 'youth'), as a distinct stage of life between sexual maturity at about fifteen and marriage at about twenty-six."[22] Shakespeare's persistent epithets identify Orlando as a member of the group about which contemporary moralists and guardians of the social order were most obsessively concerned. The Statute of Artificers (1563) summarizes the official attitude: "Until a man grow unto the age of twenty-four years he . . . is wild, without judgment and not of sufficient experience to govern himself."[23] The youthful members of an Elizabethan household—children, servants, and apprentices—were all supposed to be kept under strict patriarchal control. Stone points out that "it was precisely because its junior members were under close supervision that the state had a very strong interest in encouraging and strengthening the household. . . . It helped to keep in check potentially the most unruly element in any society, the floating mass of young unmarried males."[24] Orlando is physically mature and powerful, but socially infantilized and weak.

That Shakespeare should focus so many of his plays on a sympathetic consideration of the problems of youth is not surprising when we consider that perhaps half the population was under twenty, and that the youthfulness of Shakespeare's society was reflected in the composition of his audience.[25] In his richly documented study, Keith Thomas demonstrates that

> So far as the young were concerned, the sixteenth and seventeenth
> centuries are conspicuous for a sustained drive to subordinate persons
> in their teens and early twenties and to delay their equal participation

in the adult world. This drive is reflected in the wider dissemination of apprenticeship; in the involvement of many more children in formal education; and in a variety of measures to prolong the period of legal and social infancy.[26]

Elizabethan adolescence seems to have been characterized by a high degree of geographical mobility: youths were sent off to school, to search for work as living-in servants, or to be apprenticed in a regional town or in London. Alan Macfarlane has suggested that, "at the level of family life," this widespread and peculiarly English custom of farming out adolescent children was "a mechanism for separating the generations at a time when there might otherwise have been considerable difficulty." "The changes in patterns of authority as the children approached adulthood would . . . be diminished." He speculates further that, at the collective level, "the whole process was a form of age ritual, a way of demarcating off age-boundaries by movement through space."[27]

The family was a source of social stability, but most families were short-lived and unstable. Youth was geographically mobile, but most youths were given no opportunity to enjoy their liberty. In schools and in households, the masters of scholars, servants, and apprentices were to be their surrogate fathers. Thomas stresses that, "though many children left home early and child labour was thought indispensable, there was total hostility to the early achievement of economic independence."[28] The material basis of that hostility was alarm about the increasing pressure of population on very limited and unreliable resources. One of its most significant results was delayed marriage: "Combined with strict prohibition on alternative forms of sexual activity, late marriage was the most obvious way in which youth was prolonged. For marriage was the surest test of adult status and on it hinged crucial differences in wages, dress, and economic independence."[29] Most Elizabethan youths and maidens were in their mid or late twenties by the time they entered Hymen's bands.[30] When Touchstone quips that "the forehead of a married man [is] more honourable than the bare brow of a bachelor" (III.iii.53–55), he is giving a sarcastic twist to a fundamental mark of status. And when, late in his pseudo-mock-courtship of Ganymede, Orlando remarks ruefully that he "can live no longer by thinking" (V.ii.50), he is venting the constrained libido of Elizabethan youth. One of the critical facts about the Elizabethan life cycle—one not noted in Jaques' speech—was that a large and varied group of codes, customs, and institutions regulated "a separation between physiological puberty and social puberty."[31] "Youth," then, was the Elizabethan age category separating the end of childhood from the beginning of adulthood. It was a social threshold whose transitional nature was manifested in shifts of residence, activity, sexual feeling, and patriarchal authority.

The dialectic between Elizabethan dramatic form and social process is especially conspicuous in the triadic romance pattern of exile and return that underlies *As You Like It*. Here the characters' experience is a fictional analogue of both the theatrical and the social experiences of its audience. "The circle of this forest" (V.iv.34) is equivalent to Shakespeare's Wooden O. When they enter the special space-time of the theatre, the playgoers have voluntarily and temporarily withdrawn from "this working-day world" (I.iii.12) and put on "a holiday humour" (IV.i.65–66). When they have been wooed to an atonement by the comedy, the Epilogue conducts them back across the threshold between the world of the theatre and the theatre of the world. The dramatic form of the characters' experience corresponds, then, not only to the theatrical experience of the play's audience but also to the social process of youth in the world that playwright, players, and playgoers share. In a playworld of romance, Orlando and Rosalind experience separation from childhood, journeying, posing and disguising, altered and confused relationships to parental figures, sexual ambiguity, and tension. The fiction provides projections for the past or ongoing youthful experiences of most of the people in Shakespeare's Elizabethan audience. The forest sojourn conducts Orlando and Rosalind from an initial situation of oppression and frustration to the threshold of interdependent new identities. In one sense, then, the whole process of romantic pastoral comedy— the movement into and out of Arden—is what Macfarlane calls "a form of age ritual, a way of demarcating off age-boundaries by movement through space." The characters' fictive experience is congruent with the ambiguous and therefore dangerous period of the Elizabethan life cycle that is betwixt and between physical puberty and social puberty.

V

Not only relationships between offspring and their genitors, or between youths and their elders, but any relationship between subordinate and superior males might take on an oedipal character in a patriarchal society. Orlando is perceived as a troublemaker by Oliver and Frederick; his conflicts are with the men who hold power in his world, with its insecure and ineffectual villains. "The old Duke is banished by his younger brother the new Duke" (I.i.99–100). Old Adam has served Orlando's family "from seventeen years, till now almost fourscore" (II.iii.71), but under Oliver he must endure "unregarded age in corners thrown" (l. 42). It is precisely the elders abused by Frederick and Oliver who ally themselves to Orlando's oppressed youth.[32] Adam gives to Orlando the life savings that were to have been the "foster-nurse" (II.iii.40) of his old age; he makes his "young master" (l. 2) his heir. The idealized relationship of Orlando and his old servant compensates for the loss or corruption of Orlando's affective ties to men of his own kin and class. But Adam's paternity is only a phase in the reconstitution of Orlando's social identity. In the process of revealing his lineage to the old Duke, Orlando exchanges the father-surrogate who was his own father's servant for the father-surrogate who was his own father's lord.

If that you were the good Sir Rowland's son,
As you have whisper'd faithfully you were,
And as mine eye doth his effigies witness
Most truly limn'd and living in your face,
Be truly welcome hither. I am the duke
That lov'd your father. (II.vii.194–99)

The living son replaces his dead father in the affections of their lord. The Duke, who has no natural son, assumes the role of Orlando's patron, his social father: "Give me your hand / And let me all your fortunes understand" (ll. 202–3). Orlando's previous paternal benefactor has been supplanted: Adam neither speaks nor is mentioned again.

The reunion of the de Boys brothers is blessed by "the old Duke"; the circumstance which makes that reunion possible is Oliver's expulsion by "the new Duke." In Lodge's *Rosalynde*, the two kings are not kin. Shakespeare's departure from his immediate source unifies and intensifies the conflicts in the family and the polity. The old Duke who adopts Orlando in the forest has been disinherited by his own younger brother in the court; Frederick has forcibly made himself his brother's heir. In the course of the play, fratricide is attempted, averted, and repudiated in each sibling relationship. Tensions in the nuclear family and in the body politic are miraculously assuaged within the forest. The Duke addresses his first words to his "co-mates and brothers in exile" (II.i.1). The courtly decorum of hierarchy and deference may be relaxed in the forest, but it has not been abrogated; the Duke's "brothers in exile" remain courtiers and servants attendant upon his grace. An atmosphere of charitable community has been created among those who have temporarily lost or abandoned their normal social context; the sources of conflict inherent in the social order are by no means genuinely dissolved in the forest, but rather are translated into a quiet and sweet style. In the forest, the old usurped Duke is a co-mate and brother to his loyal subjects and a benevolent father to Orlando. The comedy establishes *brotherhood* as an ideal of social as well as sibling male relationships; at the same time, it reaffirms a positive, nurturing image of *fatherhood*. And because family and society are a synecdoche, the comedy can also work to mediate the ideological contradiction between spiritual fraternity and political patriarchy, between social communion and social hierarchy.[33]

Like Richard of Gloucester, Claudius, Edmund, and Antonio, Frederick is a discontented younger brother whom Shakespeare makes the malevolent agent of his plot. Frederick generates action in *As You Like It* by banishing successively his elder brother, his niece, and his subject. Like his fellow villains, Frederick is the effective agent of a dramatic resolution which he himself does not intend; the tyrant's perverted will subserves the comic dramatist's providential irony.

Frederick enforces the fraternal bond between Orlando and Oliver by holding
Oliver responsible for Orlando on peril of his inheritance, forcing Oliver out to
apprehend his brother. By placing Oliver in a social limbo akin to that suffered
by Orlando, Frederick unwittingly creates the circumstances that lead to the
brothers' reunion:

> *Duke F.* Thy lands and all things that thou dost call thine,
> Worth seizure, do we seize into our hands,
> Till thou canst quit thee by thy brother's mouth
> Of what we think against thee.
>   *Oli.* O that your Highness knew my heart in this!
> I never lov'd my brother in my life.
>   *Duke F.* More villain thou. (III.i.9–15)

Oliver has abused the letter and the spirit of Sir Rowland's will: "It was . . .
charged my brother on his blessing to breed me well" (I.i.3–4). Frederick is
Oliver's nemesis.

In the exchange I have just quoted, Frederick's attitude toward Oliver is
one of *moral* as well as political superiority. His judgment of Oliver's villainy
is sufficiently ironic to give us pause. Is the usurper in Frederick projecting
onto Oliver his guilt for his own unbrotherliness? Or is the younger brother
in him identifying with Orlando's domestic situation? In seizing Oliver's lands
and all things that he calls his until Oliver's (younger) brother can absolve
him, Frederick parodies his own earlier usurpation of his own elder brother.
Frederick's initial seizure takes place before the play begins; its circumstances
are never disclosed. We do better to observe Frederick's dramatic function
than to search for his unconscious motives. Frederick actualizes the destructive
consequences of younger brothers' deprivation and discontent, in the family
and in society at large. The first scenes demonstrate that such a threat exists
within Orlando himself. The threat is neutralized as soon as Orlando enters
the good old Duke's comforting forest home; there his needs are immediately
and bountifully gratified:

> *Duke Sen.* What would you have? Your gentleness shall force,
> More than your force move us to gentleness.
>   *Orl.* I almost die for food, and let me have it.
> *Duke Sen.* Sit down and feed, and welcome to our table.
>   *Orl.* Speak you so gently? Pardon me, I pray you.
> I thought that all things had been savage here,
> . . . .
> Let gentleness my strong enforcement be;
> In the which hope, I blush, and hide my sword. (II.vii.102–7, 118–19)

What is latent and potential within Orlando is displaced onto Frederick and realized in his violence and insecurity, his usurpation and tyranny.

Frederick sustains the role of villain until he too comes to Arden:

> Duke Frederick hearing how that every day
> Men of great worth resorted to this forest,
> Address'd a mighty power, which were on foot
> In his own conduct, purposely to take
> His brother here, and put him to the sword.
> And to the skirts of this wild wood he came,
> Where, meeting with an old religious man,
> After some question with him, was converted
> Both from his enterprise and from the world,
> His crown bequeathing to his banish'd brother
> And all their lands restor'd to them again
> That were with him exil'd. (V.iv.153–64)

Like Orlando, Frederick finds a loving father in the forest. And his conversion is the efficient cause of Orlando's elevation. In the denouement of Lodge's *Rosalynde*, the reunited brothers, Rosader and Saladyne, join the forces of the exiled King Gerismond; the army of the usurping King Torismond is defeated, and he is killed in the action. With striking formal and thematic economy, Shakespeare realizes his change of plot as a change *within* a character; he gets rid of Frederick not by killing him off but by morally transforming him. Frederick gives all his worldly goods to his natural brother and goes off to claim his spiritual inheritance from a heavenly father.

VI

The reunion of the de Boys brothers is narrated retrospectively by a reborn Oliver, in the alien style of an allegorical dream romance:

> . . . pacing through the forest,
> Chewing the food of sweet and bitter fancy,
> Lo what befell! He threw his eye aside,
> And mark what object did present itself.
> Under an old oak, whose boughs were moss'd with age
> And high top bald with dry antiquity,
> A wretched ragged man, o'ergrown with hair,
> Lay sleeping on his back. (IV.iii.100–107)

These images of infirm age and impotence, of regression to wildness and ruin through neglect, form a richly suggestive emblem. Expounded in the context of the present argument, the emblem represents the precarious condition into which fratricidal feeling provoked by primogeniture has brought these brothers and their house: "Such a fever hectic hath custome brought in and inured among fathers, and such fond desire they have to leave a great shewe of the *stock* of their house, though the *branches* be *withered*, that . . . my elder brother forsooth must be my master."[34] Orlando, whose "having in beard is a younger brother's revenue" (III.ii.367–68), confronts a hairy man asleep amidst icons of age and antiquity. The description suggests that, in confronting "his brother, his elder brother" (IV.iii.120), young Orlando is confronting a personification of his patriline and of the patriarchal order itself. The brothers find each other under an *arbor consanguinitatis*, at the de Boys "family tree."[35]

Agnes Latham suggests that the snake and the lioness which menace Oliver are metaphors for his own animosities: as the snake "slides away, Oliver's envy melts, and his wrath goes with the lion."[36] The text suggests that it is Orlando who undergoes such an allegorical purgation. When it sees Orlando, the snake slips under the bush where the lioness couches.

> *Oli.* This seen, Orlando did approach the man,
> And found it was his brother, his elder brother.
> . . . .
> *Ros.* But to Orlando. Did he leave him there,
> Food to the suck'd and hungry lioness?
> *Oli.* Twice did he turn his back, and purpos'd so.
> But kindness, nobler ever than revenge,
> And nature, stronger than his just occasion,
> Made him give battle to the lioness,
> Who quickly fell before him; in which hurtling
> From miserable slumber I awak'd. (IV.iii.119–20, 125–32)

In killing the lioness which threatens to kill Oliver, Orlando kills the impediment to atonement within himself. Oliver's narrative implies a causal relationship between Orlando's act of self-mastery and purgation and Oliver's own "awakening." When the brothers have been "kindly bath'd" (IV.iii.140) in mutual tears, Oliver's "conversion" (l. 136) and his atonement with Orlando are consecrated by the Duke who loved their father. In the play's first words, Orlando remembered that Oliver had been charged, on his blessing, to breed him well. The Duke's bequest and injunction reformulate Sir Rowland's last will and testament:

> he led me to the gentle Duke,
> Who gave me fresh array and entertainment
> Committing me unto my brother's love. (IV.iii.142–44)

What has taken place offstage is a conversion of the crucial event that precipitated the fraternal conflict, the event "remembered" in the very first words of the play.

At this point in the atonement, paternity and fraternity are reaffirmed as spiritual bonds rather than as bonds of blood and property. Brotherhood can now come to mean friendship freed from the material conflicts of kinship. Some remarks by Julian Pitt-Rivers illuminate the point:

> Kinship's nature ... is not free of jural considerations. Rights and duties are distributed differentially to kinsmen because kinship is a system, not a network of dyadic ties like friendship. Status within it is ascribed by birth. ... Rules of succession and inheritance are required to order that which cannot be left to the manifestations of brotherly love. ... A revealing assertion echoes through the literature on ritual kinship: 'Blood-brothers are like brothers,' it is said, then comes, 'in fact they are closer than real brothers.' The implication is troubling, for it would appear that true fraternity is found only between those who are not real brothers. Amity does not everywhere enjoin the same open-ended generosity, least of all between kinsmen, who quarrel only too often, in contrast to ritual kinsmen, who are bound by sacred duty not to do so.[37]

Before he goes to Arden, Orlando feels he has no alternative but to subject himself "to the malice / Of a diverted blood and bloody brother" (II.iii.36–37). Shakespeare's task is to bring the relationship of Orlando and Oliver under the auspices of Hymen:

> Then is there mirth in heaven,
> When earthly things made even
> Atone together. (V.iv.107–9)

In Touchstone's terms (V.iv.101–2), hostile siblings are brought to shake hands and swear their brotherhood by the virtue of comedy's If. The spiritual principle of "brotherly love" is reconciled to the jural principle of primogeniture; "real brothers" are made "blood brothers"—as the napkin borne by Oliver so graphically testifies.[38]

Some commentators have seen the outlines of a Christian allegory of redemption in the play. They point to the presence of a character named Adam; the Duke's disquisition on "the penalty of Adam"; the iconography of the serpent, the tree, and the *vetus homo*; the heroic virtue of Orlando; the comic rite of atonement.[39] Perhaps we do better to think of Shakespeare as creating resonances between the situations in his play and the religious archetypes at the foundations of his culture; as invoking what Rosalie Colie, writing of *King Lear*, calls "Biblical echo." What echoes deeply through the scenes I have discussed is the fourth chapter of Genesis, the story of Cain and Abel and what another of

Shakespeare's fratricides calls "the primal eldest curse . . . / A brother's murther" (*Hamlet*, III.iii.37–38). Adam's two sons made offerings to the Lord: "and the Lord had respect unto Habel, and to his offering,"

> But unto Kain and to his offring he had no regarde: wherefore Kain was exceding wroth, & his countenance fel downe.
>
> Then the Lord said unto Kain, Why art thou wroth? and why is thy countenance cast downe?
>
> If thou do wel, shalt thou not be accepted? and if thou doest not well, sinne lieth at the dore: also unto thee his desire *shal be subject*, and thou shalt rule over him.
>
> Then Kain spake to Habel his brother. And when they were in the field, Kain rose up against Habel his brother, and slewe him.
>
> Then the Lord said unto Kain, Where is Habel thy brother? Who answered, I canot tel. Am I my brothers keper?
>
> Againe he said, What hast thou done? the voyce of thy brothers blood cryeth unto me from the grounde.
>
> Now therefore thou art cursed from the earth, which hath opened her mouth to receive thy brothers blood from thine hand.[40]

The Geneva Bible glosses the italicized phrase in the seventh verse as a reference to the foundations of primogeniture: "The dignitie of ye first borne is given to Kain over Habel."

The wrath of Cain echoes in Oliver's fratricidal musings at the end of the first scene: "I hope I shall see an end of him; for my soul—yet I know not why—hates nothing more than he. Yet he's gentle, never schooled and yet learned, full of noble device, of all sorts enchantingly beloved, and indeed so much in the heart of the world, and especially of my own people, that I am altogether misprised. But it shall not be so long" (I.1.162–69). Oliver feels humanly rather than divinely misprized; and it is his tyrannical secular lord to whom he declares that he is not his brother's keeper. Orlando sheds his own blood for his elder brother, which becomes the sign of Oliver's conversion rather than the mark of his fratricidal guilt. Oliver finds acceptance in the old Duke, who commits him to his brother's love. Shakespeare is creating a resonance between his romantic fiction and Biblical history, between the dramatic process of assuaging family conflict in the atonements of comedy and the exegetical process of redeeming the primal fratricide of Genesis in the spiritual fraternity of the Gospel:

> For brethren, ye have bene called unto libertie: onely use not your libertie as an occasion unto the flesh, but by love serve one another.
>
> For all the Law is fulfilled in one worde, which is this, Thou shalt love thy neighbour as thy self.

If ye byte & devoure one another, take hede lest ye be consumed one of another.

Then I say, walke in the Spirit, and ye shal not fulfil the lustes of the flesh.[41] (Galatians v. 13–16)

The rivalry or conflict between elder and younger brothers is a prominent motif in the fictions of cultures throughout the world. Its typical plot has been described as "the disadvantaged younger sibling or orphan child besting an unjust elder and gaining great fortune through the timely intercession of a benevolent supernatural being."[42] Cultural fictions of the triumphs of younger siblings offer psychological compensation for the social fact of the deprivation of younger siblings. Such fictions are symbolic mediations of discrepancies between the social categories of status and the claims of individual merit, in which the defeat and supplanting of the elder sibling by the younger reconciles ability with status: "The younger outwits, displaces, and becomes the elder; the senior position comes to be associated with superior ability."[43]

The folk-tale scenario of sibling rivalry is clear in the fourteenth-century tale of *Gamelyn*, to which Lodge's Rosader plot and Shakespeare's Orlando plot are indebted.[44] The disinherited Gamelyn and his outlaw cohorts sentence Gamelyn's eldest brother to death by hanging. Their topsy-turvy actions are sanctioned and absorbed by the social order: the King pardons Gamelyn, restores his inheritance, and makes him Chief Justice. In *As You Like It*, Shakespeare's characters emphasize the discrepancy between "the gifts of the world" and "the lineaments of Nature" (I.ii.40–41), between social place and personal merit. The comedy's task is to "mock the good hussif Fortune from her wheel, that her gifts may henceforth be bestowed equally" (I.ii.30–32). Shakespeare transcends *Gamelyn* and its folktale paradigm in a wholehearted concern not merely to eliminate social contradictions, but also to redeem and reconcile human beings.[45] Oliver is not defeated, eliminated, supplanted; he is converted, reintegrated, confirmed. In the subplot of *King Lear*, the unbrotherly struggle for mastery and possession is resolved by fratricide; the comic resolution of As You *Like It* depends instead upon an expansion of opportunities for mastery and possession.

VII

In Lodge's *Rosalynde*, the crude heroic theme of *Gamelyn* is already fused with the elegant love theme of Renaissance pastorals. In constructing a romantic comedy of familial and sexual tension resolved in brotherhood and marriage, Shakespeare gives new complexity and cohesiveness to his narrative source. The struggle of elder and younger brothers is not simply duplicated; it is inverted. In the younger generation, the elder brother abuses the younger; in the older generation, the younger abuses the elder. The range of experience and affect is thereby enlarged, and the protest against primogeniture is firmly balanced by its reaffirmation. Myth, Scripture, and Shakespearean drama record "the bond crack'd betwixt son and father" (*King Lear*, I.ii.113–14). Hostilities between elder and younger brothers and between fathers and sons are homologous: "Yea, and the brother shal deliver the brother to death, and the father the sonne, and the children shal rise against their parents, and shal cause them to dye" (Mark xiii.14). Because in *As You Like It* the doubling and inversion of fraternal conflict links generations, the relationship of brother and brother can be linked to the relationship of father and son. In the process of atonement, the two families and two generations of men are doubly and symmetrically bound: the younger brother weds the daughter of the elder brother, and the elder brother weds the daughter of the younger brother. They create the figure of *chiasmus*. Whatever vicarious benefit *As You Like It* brings to younger brothers and to youths, it is not achieved by perverting or destroying the bonds between siblings and between generations, but by transforming and renewing them—*through marriage*.

In Arden, Orlando divides his time between courting Rosalind (who is played by Ganymede, who is played by Rosalind) and courting the old Duke who is Rosalind's father. Celia teases Rosalind about the sincerity of Orlando's passion, the truth of his feigning, by reminding her of his divided loyalties: "He attends here in the forest on the Duke your father" (III.iv.29–30). Rosalind, who clearly resents that she must share Orlando's attentions with her father, responds: "I met the Duke yesterday and had much question with him. He asked me of what parentage I was: I told him of as good as he, so he laughed and let me go. But what talk we of fathers, when there is such a man as Orlando?" (III. iv.31–35). Celia has already transferred her loyalties from her father to Rosalind; Rosalind is transferring hers from her father and from Celia to Orlando. But she withholds her identity from her lover in order to test and to taunt him. In the forest, while Orlando guilelessly improves his place in the patriarchal order, Rosalind wittily asserts her independence of it. Rosalind avoids her father's recognition and establishes her own household within the forest; Orlando desires the Duke's recognition and gladly serves him in his forest-court.

It is only after he has secured a place within the old Duke's benign all-male community that Orlando begins to play the lover and the poet: "Run, run Orlando, carve on every tree/The fair, the chaste, and unexpressive she" (III.ii.9–10):

> *But upon the fairest boughs,*
> *Or at every sentence end,*
> *Will I Rosalinda write,*
> *Teaching all that read to know*
> *The quintessence of every sprite*
> *Heaven would in little show.*
> *Therefore Heaven Nature charg'd*

That one body should be fill'd
With all graces wide-enlarg'd.
Nature presently distill'd
Helen's cheek, but not her heart,
Cleopatra's majesty,
Atalanta's better part,
Sad Lucretia's modesty.
Thus Rosalind of many parts
By heavenly synod was devis'd,
Of many faces, eyes, and hearts,
To have the touches dearest priz'd.
Heaven would that she these gifts should have,
And I to live and die her slave. (ll. 132–51)

The Petrarchan lover "writes" his mistress or "carves" her in the image of his own desire, incorporating virtuous feminine stereotypes and scrupulously excluding what is sexually threatening. The lover masters his mistress by inscribing her within his own discourse; he worships a deity of his own making and under his control. When Rosalind-Ganymede confronts this "fancy-monger" (III.ii.354–55) who "haunts the forest . . . deifying the name of Rosalind" (ll. 350, 353–54), she puts a question to him: "But are you so much in love as your rhymes speak?" (l. 386). Rosalind and Touchstone interrogate and undermine self-deceiving amorous rhetoric with bawdy wordplay and relentless insistence upon the power and inconstancy of physical desire. All the love-talk in the play revolves around the issue of mastery in the shifting social relationship between the sexes: in courtship, maidens suspect the faithfulness of their suitors; in wedlock, husbands suspect the faithfulness of their wives. The poems of feigning lovers and the horns of cuckolded husbands are the complementary preoccupations of Arden's country copulatives.

Consider the crucially-placed brief scene (IV.ii) which is barely more than a song inserted between the betrothal scene of Orlando and Rosalind-Ganymede and the scene in which Oliver comes to Rosalind bearing the bloody napkin. In IV.i, Rosalind mocks her tardy lover with talk of an emblematic snail: "He brings his destiny with him. . . . Horns—which such as you fain to be beholding to your wives for" (ll. 54–55, 57–58). Touchstone has already resigned himself to the snail's destiny with his own misogynistic logic: "As horns are odious, they are necessary. It is said, many a man knows no end of his goods. Right. Many a man has good horns and knows no end of them. Well, that is the dowry of his wife, 'tis none of his own getting" (III.iii.45–49). Now, in IV.ii, Jaques transforms Rosalind's jibes into ironic male self-mockery: "He that killed the deer" is to have the horns set on his head "for a branch of victory" (ll. 1, 5). Jaques calls for a song—"'Tis no matter how it be in tune, so it makes noise enough" (ll. 8–9). The rowdy horn song is a kind of *charivari* or "rough music," traditionally the form of ridicule to which cuckolds and others who offended the community's moral standards were subjected.[46] This *charivari*, however, is also a song of consolation and good fellowship, for not only the present "victor" but all his companions "shall bear this burden" (ll. 12–13).

> *Take thou no scorn to wear the horn,*
> *It was a crest ere thou wast born.*
> *Thy father's father wore it,*
> *And thy father bore it.*
> *The horn, the horn, the lusty horn,*
> *Is not a thing to laugh to scorn.* (ll. 14–19)

The play's concern with patriarchal lineage and the hallmarks of gentility is here transformed into an heraldic celebration of the horn—instrument of male potency and male degradation—which marks all men as kinsmen. Thus, although cuckoldry implies the uncertainty of paternity, the song celebrates the paradox that it is precisely the common destiny they share with the snail that binds men together—father to son, brother to brother. Through the metaphor of hunting (with its wordplays on "deer" and "horns") and the medium of song, the threat that the power of insubordinate women poses to the authority of men is transformed into an occasion for affirming and celebrating patriarchy and fraternity.

After the mock-marriage (IV.i) in which they have indeed plighted their troth, Rosalind-Ganymede exuberantly teases Orlando about the shrewishness and promiscuity he can expect from his wife. Naively romantic Orlando abruptly leaves his threatening Rosalind in order "to attend the Duke at dinner" (IV.i.170). On his way from his cruel mistress to his kind patron, Orlando encounters his own brother. It is hardly insignificant that Shakespeare changes the details of the fraternal recognition scene to include an aspect of sexual differentiation wholly absent from Lodge's romance. He adds the snake which wreathes itself around Oliver's neck; and he makes it into an insidious female, "who with her head, nimble in threats, approach'd / The opening of his mouth" (IV.iii.109–10). Furthermore, he changes Lodge's lion into a lioness whose nurturing and aggressive aspects are strongly and ambivalently stressed: "a lioness, with udders all drawn dry" (l. 114); "the suck'd and hungry lioness" (l. 126). Orlando has retreated in the face of Rosalind's verbal aggressiveness. He has wandered through the forest, "chewing the food of sweet and bitter fancy" (l. 101), to seek the paternal figure who has nurtured him. Instead, he has found Oliver in a dangerously passive condition, threatened by a double source of oral aggression.

Oliver's fantastic narrative suggests a transformation of the sexual conflict initiated by Rosalind when she teases Orlando in IV.i. Rosalind and the lioness are coyly linked in the exchange between the lovers at their next meeting:

> *Ros.* O my dear Orlando, how it grieves me to see thee wear thy heart in a scarf!
> *Orl.* It is my arm.
> *Ros.* I thought thy heart had been wounded with the claws of a lion.
> *Orl.* Wounded it is, but with the eyes of a lady. (V.ii.19–23)

The chain which Rosalind bestows upon Orlando at their first meeting ("Wear this for me" [I.ii.236]) is the mark by which Celia identifies him in the forest ("And a chain, that you once wore, about his neck" [III.ii.178]). The "green and gilded snake" (IV.iii.108) encircling Oliver's neck is a demonic parody of the emblematic stage property worn by his brother throughout the play. The gynephobic response to Rosalind is split into the erotic serpent and the maternal lioness, while Orlando is split into his victimized brother and his heroic self. Orlando's mastery of the lioness ("Who quickly fell before him" [IV.iii.131]) is, then, a symbolic mastery of Rosalind's challenge to Orlando. But it is also a triumph of fraternal "kindness" (l. 128) over the fratricidal impulse. Relationships between elder and younger brothers and between fathers and sons are purified by what the text suggests is a kind of matricide, a triumph of men over female powers. Thus the killing of the lioness may also symbolize a repudiation of the consanguinity of Orlando and Oliver. If this powerful female—the carnal source of siblings—is destroyed, both fraternity and paternity can be reconceived as male relationships unmediated by woman, relationships of the spirit rather than of the flesh. Orlando's heroic act, distanced and framed in an allegorical narrative, condenses aspects of both the romantic plot and the sibling plot. And these plots are themselves the complementary aspects of a single social and dramatic process.

Before Orlando is formally married to Rosalind at the end of the play, he has reaffirmed his fraternal and filial bonds in communion with other men. Orlando's rescue of Oliver from the she-snake and the lioness frees the brothers' capacity to give and to receive love. Now Oliver can "fall in love" with Celia; and now Orlando "can live no longer by thinking" (V.ii.50) about Rosalind. Oliver asks his younger brother's consent to marry, and resigns to him his birthright: "My father's house and all the revenue that was old Sir Rowland's will I estate upon you, and here live and die a shepherd" (ll. 10–12).[47] Orlando agrees with understandable alacrity: "You have my consent. Let your wedding be to-morrow" (ll. 13–14). Marriage, the social institution at the heart of comedy, serves to ease or eliminate fraternal strife. And fraternity, in turn, serves as a defense against the threat men feel from women.

Rosalind-as-Ganymede and Ganymede-as-Rosalind—the woman out of place—exerts an informal organizing and controlling power over affairs in the forest. But this power lapses when she relinquishes her male disguise and formally acknowledges her normal status as daughter and wife: "I'll have no father, if you be not he. / I'll have no husband, if you be not he" (V.iv.121–22). In a ritual gesture of surrender, she assumes the passive role of mediatrix between the Duke and Orlando:

[*To the Duke.*] To you I give myself, for I am yours.
[*To Orl.*] To you I give myself, for I am yours. (V.iv.115–16)

The Duke's paternal bond to Orlando is not established through the natural fertility of a mother but through the supernatural virginity of a daughter: "Good Duke receive thy daughter, / Hymen from heaven brought her" (V.iv.110–11). The play is quite persistent in creating strategies for subordinating the flesh to the spirit, and female powers to male controls. Hymen's marriage rite gives social sanction to the lovers' mutual desire. But the atonement of man and woman also implies the social subordination of wife to husband. Rosalind's exhilarating mastery of herself and others has been a compensatory "holiday humor," a temporary, inversionary rite of misrule, whose context is a transfer of authority, property, and title from the Duke to his prospective male heir. From the perspective of the present argument, the romantic love plot serves more than its own ends: it is also the means by which other actions are transformed and resolved. In his unions with the Duke and with Rosalind, Orlando's social elevation is confirmed. Such a perspective does not deny the comedy its festive magnanimity; it merely reaffirms that Shakespearean drama registers the form and pressure of Elizabethan experience. If *As You Like It* is a vehicle for Rosalind's exuberance, it is also a structure for her containment.[48]

Jaques de Boys, "the second son of old Sir Rowland" (V.iv.151), enters suddenly at the end of the play. This Shakespearean whimsy fits logically into the play's comic process. As the narrator of Frederick's strange eventful history, Jaques brings the miraculous news that resolves the conflict between his own brothers as well as the conflict between the brother-dukes. As Rosalind mediates the affinity of father and son, so Jaques—a brother, rather than a mother—mediates the kinship of eldest and youngest brothers; he is, in effect, the incarnate middle term between Oliver and Orlando. The Duke welcomes him:

Thou offer'st fairly to thy brothers' wedding;
To one his lands withheld, and to the other
A land itself at large, a potent dukedom. (V.iv.166–68)

Jaques' gift celebrates the wedding of his brothers to their wives and to each other. Solutions to the play's initial conflicts are worked out between brother and brother, father and son—among men. Primogeniture is reaffirmed in public and private domains: the Duke, newly restored to his own authority and possessions, now restores the de Boys patrimony to Oliver. The aspirations and deserts of the youngest brother are rewarded when the Duke acknowledges Orlando as his own heir, the successor to property, power, and title that far exceed Oliver's birthright. The eldest brother regains the authority due him by primogeniture at the same time that the youngest brother is freed from subordination to his sibling and validated in his claim to the perquisites of gentility.

With his patrimony restored and his marriage effected, Oliver legitimately assumes the place of a patriarch and emerges into full social adulthood; he is now worthy to be the son and heir of Sir Rowland de Boys. Orlando, on the other hand, has proved himself worthy to become son and heir to the Duke. Thomas Wilson, another Elizabethan younger brother, made the bitter misfortune of primogeniture the spur to personal achievement: "This I must confess doth us good someways, for it makes us industrious to apply ourselves to letters or to armes, whereby many time we become my master elder brothers' masters, or at least their betters in honour and reputacion."[49] Unlike Thomas Wilson, Shakespeare's Orlando is spectacularly successful, and his success is won more by spontaneous virtue than by industry. But like Wilson's, Orlando's accomplishments are those of a gentleman and a courtier. Unlike most Elizabethan younger sons, Orlando is not forced to descend to commerce or to labor to make his way in the world. He succeeds by applying himself to the otiose courtship of his mistress and his prince. Although the perfection of his social identity is deferred during the Duke's lifetime, Orlando's new filial subordination is eminently beneficent. It grants him by affinity what he has been denied by kinship: the social advancement and sexual fulfillment of which youths and younger sons were so frequently deprived. The de Boys brothers atone together when the eldest replaces a father and the youngest recovers a father.

VIII

Social and dramatic decorum require that, "to work a comedy kindly, grave old men should instruct, young men should show the imperfections of youth."[50] London's city fathers, however, were forever accusing the theatres and the plays of corrupting rather than instructing youth: "We verely think plays and theatres to be the chief cause . . . of . . . disorder & lewd demeanours which appear of late in young people of all degrees."[51] Shakespeare's play neither preaches to youths nor incites them to riot. In the world of its Elizabethan audience, the form of Orlando's experience may indeed have functioned as a collective compensation, a projection for the wish-fulfillment fantasies of younger brothers, youths, and all who felt themselves deprived by their fathers or their fortunes. But Orlando's mastery of adversity could also provide support and encouragement to the ambitious individuals who identified with his plight. The play may have fostered strength and perseverance as much as it facilitated pacification and escape. For the large number of youths in Shakespeare's audience—firstborn and younger siblings, gentle and base—the performance may have been analogous to a rite of passage, helping to ease their dangerous and prolonged journey from subordination to identity, their difficult transition from the child's part to the adult's.

My subject has been the complex interrelationship of brothers, fathers, and sons in *As You Like It*. But I have suggested that the play's concern with relationships among men is only artificially separable from its concern with relationships between men and women. The androgynous Rosalind—boy actor and princess—addresses Shakespeare's heterosexual audience in an epilogue: "My way is to conjure you, and I'll begin with the women. I charge you, O women, for the love you bear to men, to like as much of this play as please you. And I charge you, O men, for the love you bear to women—as I perceive by your simpering none of you hates them—that between you and the women the play may please" (V.iv.208–14). Through the subtle and flexible strategies of drama— in puns, jokes, games, disguises, songs, poems, fantasies—*As You Like It* expresses, contains, and discharges a measure of the strife between the men and the women. Shakespeare's comedy manipulates the differential social relationships between the sexes, between brothers, between father and son, master and servant, lord and subject. It is by the conjurer's art that Shakespeare manages to reconcile the social imperatives of hierarchy and difference with the festive urges toward leveling and atonement. The intense and ambivalent personal bonds upon which the play is focused—bonds between brothers and between lovers—affect each other reciprocally and become the means of each other's resolution. And as the actions within the play are dialectically related to each other, so the world of Shakespeare's characters is dialectically related to the world of his audience. *As You Like It* is both a theatrical *reflection* of social conflict and a theatrical *source* of social conciliation.

NOTES

A much abbreviated version of this study was presented at the 1979 meeting of the Philological Association of the Pacific Coast (UCLA, 10 November 1979). My work on *As You Like It* has been stimulated and improved by the interest and criticism of Page du Bois, Phyllis Gorfain, and Ronald Martinez.

1. Leo Salingar, *Shakespeare and the Traditions of Comedy* (Cambridge: Cambridge Univ. Press, 1974), pp. 297–98. On the *topos*, see John Shaw, "Fortune and Nature in *As You Like It*," *Shakespeare Quarterly*, 6 (1955), 45–50; *A New Variorum Edition of Shakespeare: "As You Like It*," ed. Richard Knowles, with Evelyn Joseph Mattern (New York: MLA, 1977), pp. 533–37.

2. *As You Like It* is quoted from the new Arden edition, ed. Agnes Latham (London: Methuen, 1975); all other plays are quoted from *The Riverside Shakespeare*, gen. ed. G. Blakemore Evans (Boston: Houghton Mifflin, 1974).

3. Harold Jenkins, "*As You like It*," *Shakespeare Survey*, 8 (1955), 40–51; quotation from p. 41. There is an exception to this predominant view in Thomas McFarland, *Shakespeare's Pastoral Comedy* (Chapel Hill: Univ. of North Carolina Press, 1972), pp. 98–103.

4. The paradigm for transition rites—the triadic movement from separation through marginality to reincorporation—was formulated in Arnold Van Gennep's classic, *The Rites of Passage* (1909), trans. M.B. Vizedom and G.L. Caffee (Chicago: Univ. of Chicago Press, 1960). Among more recent discussions, see *Essays on the Ritual of Social Relations*, ed. Max Gluckman (Manchester: Manchester Univ. Press, 1962); Victor Turner, *Dramas, Fields, and Metaphors* (Ithaca: Cornell Univ. Press, 1974); and Edmund Leach, *Culture and Communication* (Cambridge: Cambridge Univ. Press, 1976). For further discussion of analogies to transition rites in Shakespearean drama and Elizabethan theatre, see Louis Adrian Montrose, "The Purpose of Playing: Reflections on a Shakespearean Anthropology," *Helios*, NS, 7 (Winter 1980), 51–74.

5. Jack Goody, "Introduction," in *Family and Inheritance: Rural Society in Western Europe, 1200–1800*, ed. Jack Goody, Joan Thirsk, and E.P. Thompson (Cambridge: Cambridge Univ. Press, 1976), pp. 1, 3.

6. Lawrence Stone, *The Family, Sex and Marriage in England 1500–1800* (New York: Harper & Row, 1977), pp. 87–88.

7. Joan Thirsk, "Younger Sons in the Seventeenth Century," *History* (London), 54 (1969), 358–77; quotation from p. 359. Thirsk cites *As You Like It*, I.i, as part of that literature.

8. Ed. Edward Arber (1869; rpt., New York: AMS Press, 1966), pp. 29–30. I have modernized obsolete typographical conventions in quotations from this and other Renaissance texts.

9. Thomas Wilson, *The State of England Anno Dom. 1600*, ed. F.J. Fisher, Camden Miscellany, 16 (London: Camden Society, 1936), pp. 1–43; quotation from pp. 23–24.

10. Rpt. in *Social Change and Revolution in England 1540–1640*, ed. Lawrence Stone (New York: Barnes & Noble, 1965), p. 120.

11. Thirsk, "Younger Sons," p. 368.

12. An exception is John W. Draper, "Orlando, the Younger Brother," *Philological Quarterly*, 13 (1934), 72–77.

13. See Alfred Harbage, *Shakespeare's Audience* (New York: Columbia Univ. Press, 1941), pp. 53–91; quotation from p. 80.

14. See Thirsk, "Younger Sons," pp. 363, 366–68.

15. Thirsk, "Younger Sons," p. 360.

16. *New Variorum* ed. of *AYL*, p. 382; future page references will be to this text of *Rosalynde*, which follows the First Quarto (1590). On the relationship of *AYL* to *Rosalynde*, see *Narrative and Dramatic Sources* of *Shakespeare*, ed. Geoffrey Bullough (London: Routledge & Kegan Paul, 1958), II, 143–57; Marco Mincoff, "What Shakespeare Did to *Rosalynde*," *Shakespeare Jahrbuch*, 96 (1960), 78–89; *New Variorum* ed. of *As You Like It*, pp. 475–83.

17. See Joan Thirsk, "The European Debate on Customs of Inheritance, 1500–1700," in *Family and Inheritance*, pp. 177–91: "The inheritance customs of

classes below the gentry did not give rise to controversy: practices were as varied as the circumstances of families. Primogeniture in the original sense of advancing the eldest son, but nevertheless providing for the others, was common, perhaps the commonest custom among yeoman and below, but it did not exercise a tyranny. Among the nobility primogeniture was most common. . . . In general it did not cause excessive hardship to younger sons because the nobility had the means to provide adequately for all" (p. 186).

18. Stone, *Family, Sex and Marriage*, p. 218. *Contra* Stone, there is evidence to suggest that the nuclear family was in fact the pervasive and traditional pattern in English society outside the aristocracy; that the English family at this period was profoundly patriarchal remains, however, undisputed. The assumptions and conclusions of Stone's massive study have not found complete acceptance among his colleagues. See the important review essays on Stone's book by Christopher Hill, in *The Economic History Review*, 2nd. Ser., 31 (1978), 450–63; by Alan Macfarlane, in *History and Theory*, 18 (1979), 103–26; and by Richard T. Vann, in *The Journal of Family History*, 4 (1979), 308–14.

19. *Patriarchalism in Political Thought* (New York: Basic Books, 1975), pp. 65–66.

20. Orlando's predicament may be compared to Hamlet's: for each of these young Elizabethan heroes, the process of becoming himself involves a process of "remembering" the father for whom he is named. But the generational passage of each is blocked by a "usurper" of his spiritual inheritance, who mediates ambiguously between the father and the son: Oliver is a brother-father to Orlando; Claudius, himself the old King's younger brother, is an uncle-father to Hamlet.

21. Thus, I am not suggesting that the text and action of *As You Like It* displace a core fantasy about mother-son incest. My perspective is socio-anthropological rather than psychoanalytic: allusions to incest amplify the confusion between older and younger generations, kin and non-kin; they exemplify the tension inherent in the power relations between male generations in a patriarchal society. Perhaps one reason for Shakespeare's fascination with kingship as a dramatic subject is that it provides a paradigm for patriarchy and succession. Prince Hal's destiny is to replace his father as King Henry; his father's death is the legal condition for the creation of his own identity. A major aspect of comic form in the *Henry IV* plays is Hal's process of projecting and mastering his patricidal impulse until he comes into his kingdom legitimately.

22. Stone, *Family, Sex and Marriage*, p. 108.

23. Quoted in Keith Thomas, "Age and Authority in Early Modern England," *Proceedings of the British Academy*, 62 (1976), 205–48; quotation from p. 217.

24. Stone, *Family, Sex and Marriage*, p. 27.

25. See Stone, *Family, Sex and Marriage*, p. 72; Thomas, "Age and Authority," p. 212; Harbage, *Shakespeare's Audience*, p. 79.

26. Thomas, "Age and Authority," p. 214.

27. Alan Macfarlane, *The Family Life of Ralph Josselin, A Seventeenth-Century Clergyman: An Essay in Historical Anthropology* (Cambridge: Cambridge Univ. Press, 1970), Appendix B: "Children and servants: the problem of adolescence," pp. 205, 210.

28. Thomas, "Age and Authority," p. 216.

29. Stone, *Family, Sex and Marriage*, p. 226.

30. See Peter Laslett, *The World We Have Lost*, 2nd ed. (New York: Charles Scribner's Sons, 1973), pp. 85–86; Stone, *Family, Sex and Marriage*, pp. 46–54; Thomas, "Age and Authority," pp. 225–27.

31. Thomas, "Age and Authority," p. 225.

32. In his learned and suggestive study, Thomas shows that youths were regarded with suspicion and were subordinated, while the very old—unless they had wealth—were regarded with scorn and were ignored. (*King Lear* records the consequences of an old man's self-divestment.) Thomas notes that the trend to exclude the young and the aged from "full humanity" was "already implicit in the plea made to an Elizabethan archdeacon's court to disregard the evidence of two witnesses. One was a youth of eighteen, the other was a man of eighty. Both, it was urged, lacked discretion. The one was too young; the other too old" (p. 248).

33. On pastoral form and social order in *As You Like It*, see Charles W. Hieatt, "The Quality of Pastoral in *As You Like It*," *Genre*, 7 (1974), 164–82; Harold Toliver, *Pastoral Forms and Attitudes* (Berkeley: Univ. of California Press, 1971), pp. 100–114; Judy Z. Kronenfeld, "Social Rank and the Pastoral Ideals of *As You Like It*," *SQ*, 29 (1978), 333–48. For an interesting discussion of the interplay between patriarchal and fraternal models of social relations in the sixteenth century, see Mary Ann Clawson, "Early Modern Fraternalism and the Patriarchal Family," *Feminist Studies*, 6 (1980), 368–91.

34. Wilson, *State of England, 1600*, p. 24; italics mine.

35. Orlando and Oliver are sons of Sir Rowland de Boys, whose surname is a play on "woods" and "boys." The tree is an heraldic emblem for Orlando, as well as for Oliver: in Arden, Celia tells Rosalind that she "found him under a tree like a dropped acorn . . . . There lay he stretched along like a wounded knight" (III.ii.230–31, 236–37); we find him carving Rosalind's name "on every tree" (1 .9). If my interpretation of the emblematic reunion scene seems fanciful, the fancy is decidedly Elizabethan. Unprecedented social mobility created an obsessive concern with marks of status: "One of the most striking features of the age was a pride of ancestry which now reached new heights of fantasy and elaboration. . . . Genuine genealogy was cultivated by the older gentry to reassure themselves of their innate superiority over the upstarts; bogus genealogy was cultivated by the new gentry in an effort to clothe their social nakedness" (Lawrence Stone, *The Crisis of the Aristocracy 1558–1641* [Oxford: Clarendon Press, 1965], p. 23). In the passage on primogeniture I have quoted in my text, Thomas Wilson's arboreal metaphors have a naturalness in their context that suggests that such metaphors were an integral part of Elizabethan thought patterns. Stone notes that in the sixteenth century the lengthy genealogies of the "upper landed classes, the country gentry and nobility," tended "to pay only cursory attention to collateral branches, and are mainly concerned with tracing the male line backward in time. Similarly, the growing complexity of coats of arms recorded alliances in the male line of the heir by primogeniture of the nuclear family, not kin connections. . . . The family mausoleums of the period contain the remains of the male heirs of the nuclear family and their wives from generation to generation, but only rarely adult younger children or kin relatives. The rule of primogeniture is clearly reflected in the disposal of the bodies after death" (*Family, Sex and Marriage*, p. 135). Orlando is in danger of becoming merely a withered branch of the old "de Boys" stock.

36. Latham, Arden ed. of *As You Like It*, p. xliii.

37. See Julian Pitt-Rivers, "The Kith and the Kin," in *The Character of Kinship*, ed. Jack Goody (Cambridge Univ. Press, 1973), pp. 89–105; quotation from p. 101.

38. The histories of brotherhood and sisterhood follow opposite directions in the play. We are introduced to Rosalind and Celia as first cousins "whose loves / Are dearer than the natural bond of sisters" (I.ii.265–66); since childhood, they have been "coupled and inseparable" (I.iii.72). In the course of the play, they are uncoupled and separated from each other and from their girlhoods by the intervention of sexual desire and the new emotional and social demands of marriage. All four female characters in the play are maidens on the threshold of wedlock. The inverse relationship between brotherhood and sisterhood within the play and the conspicuous absence of matronly characters are reflections of the male and patriarchal bias of Elizabethan family and social structures.

39. See Richard Knowles, "Myth and Type in *As You Like It*," *ELH*, 33 (1966), 1–22; Rene E. Fortin, "'Tongues in Trees': Symbolic Patterns in *As You Like It*," *Texas Studies in Literature and Language*, 14 (1973), 569–82.

40. Genesis iv. 4–11, in *The Geneva Bible* (1560), facsimile ed. (Madison: Univ. of Wisconsin Press, 1969). Italics in the original. All further references to the Bible from this source.

41. "The flesh lusteth against the Spirit" (Galatians v.17) is glossed in the Geneva Bible: "That is, the natural man striveth against ye Spirit of regeneration." The spiritually regenerate Oliver marries the aptly named Celia; the socially regenerate Orlando marries a Rosalind brought "from heaven" (V.iv.111) by Hymen.

42. Michael Jackson, "Ambivalence and the Last-Born: Birth-order position in convention and myth," *Man*, NS, 13 (1978), 341–61; quotation from p. 350. This anthropological essay, based on comparative ethnography of the Kuranko (Sierra Leone) and Maori (New Zealand), has clarified my thinking about the society of Arden.

43. Jackson, "Ambivalence and the Last-Born," p. 354.

44. *New Variorum* ed. of *As You Like It*, pp. 483–87, provides a synopsis of the plot of *Gamelyn* and a digest of opinions about its direct influence on *As You Like It*.

45. Compare Lodge's address to the reader at the end of *Rosalynde*: "Heere Gentlemen may you see . . . that vertue is not measured by birth but by action; that younger brethren though inferiour in yeares, yet may be superiour to honours; that concord is the sweetest conclusion, and amitie betwixt brothers more forceable than fortune" (pp. 474–75).

46. On *charivari* and cuckoldry, see the masterful 1976 Neale Lecture in English History by Keith Thomas, "The Place of Laughter in Tudor and Stuart England," published in *The Times Literary Supplement*, 21 January 1977, pp. 77–81. Students of Shakespearean comedy would do well to bear in mind Thomas' point that "laughter has a social dimension. Jokes are a pointer to joking situations, areas of structural ambiguity in society itself, and their subject-matter can be a revealing guide to past tensions and anxieties." From this perspective, "Tudor humour about shrewish and insatiable wives or lascivious widows was a means of confronting the anomalies of insubordinate female behaviour which constantly threatened the actual working of what was supposed to be a male-dominated marital system. Hence the . . . obsession with cuckoldry" (p. 77).

47. Of course, Oliver's gallant gesture of social and economic deference to his youngest brother (a spontaneous reversal of the primogeniture rule into the ultimo-geniture rule) cannot be made good until there is a profound change in the society from which they have fled. Oliver's lands and revenues are no longer his to give to Orlando; it is because of Orlando that Frederick has confiscated them.

48. Several generations of critics—most of them men, and quite infatuated with Rosalind themselves—have stressed the exuberance and ignored the containment. Much the same may be said of some recent feminist critics (see, for example, Juliet Dusinberre, *Shakespeare and the Nature of Women* [London: Macmillan, 1975]), although they approach the character in another spirit. The "feminism" of Shakespearean comedy seems to me more ambivalent in tone and more ironic in form than such critics have wanted to believe. *Contra* Dusinberre, Linda T. Fitz emphasizes that "the English Renaissance institutionalized, where it did not invent, the restrictive marriage-oriented attitude toward women that feminists have been struggling against ever since. . . . The insistent demand for the right—nay, obligation—of women to be happily married arose as much in reaction against women's intractable pursuit of independence as it did in reaction against Catholic ascetic philosophy" ("'What Says the Married Woman?' Marriage Theory and Feminism in the English Renaissance," *Mosaic*, 13, no. 2 [Winter 1980], 1–22; quotations from pp. 11, 18). A provocative Renaissance context for Shakespeare's Rosalind is to be found in the essay, "Women on Top," in Natalie Zemon Davis, *Society and Culture in Early Modern France* (Stanford: Stanford Univ. Press, 1975), pp. 124–51.

49. Wilson, *State of England, 1600*, p. 24.

50. George Whetstone, Epistle Dedicatory to *Promos and Cassandra* (1578), quoted in Madeleine Doran, *Endeavors of Art* (Madison: Univ. of Wisconsin Press, 1954), p. 220.

51. From a document (1595) in the "Dramatic Records of the City of London," quoted in Harbage, *Shakespeare's Audience*, p. 104.

1988—Harold Bloom.
"Introduction," from *As You Like It*

Harold Bloom is a professor at Yale University. He has edited dozens of anthologies of literature and literary criticism and is the author of more than 30 books, including *The Western Canon* and *Shakespeare: The Invention of the Human*.

As You Like It is Rosalind's play as *Hamlet* is Hamlet's. That so many critics have linked her to Hamlet's more benign aspects is the highest of compliments, as though they sensed that in wit, intellect, and vision of herself she truly is Hamlet's equal. Orlando is a pleasant young man, but audiences never quite can be persuaded that he merits Rosalind's love, and their resistance has its wisdom.

Among Shakespearean representations of women, we can place Rosalind in the company only of the Portia of act 5 of *The Merchant of Venice*, while reserving the tragic Sublime for Cleopatra. All of us, men and women, like Rosalind best. She alone joins Hamlet and Falstaff as absolute in wit, and of the three she alone knows balance and proportion in living and is capable of achieving harmony.

That harmony extends even to her presence in *As You Like It*, since she is too strong for the play. Touchstone and Jaques are poor wits compared to her, and Touchstone truly is more rancid even than Jaques. Neither is capable of this wise splendor, typical of Rosalind's glory:

> ROSALIND: No, faith, die by attorney. The poor world is almost six
> thousand years old, and in all this time there was not any man died in
> his own person, videlicet, in a love-cause. Troilus had his brains dash'd
> out with a Grecian club, yet he did what he could to die before, and
> he is one of the patterns of love. Leander, he would have liv'd many
> a fair year though Hero had turn'd nun, if it had not been for a hot
> midsummer night; for, good youth, he went but forth to wash him in
> the Hellespont, and being taken with the cramp was drown'd; and the
> foolish chroniclers of that age found it was—Hero of Sestos. But these
> are all lies: men have died from time to time, and worms have eaten
> them, but not for love.

It seems a miracle that so much wit should be fused with such benignity. Rosalind's good humor extends even to this poor world, so aged, and to the amorous heroes she charmingly deromanticizes: the wretched Troilus who is deprived even of his honorable end at the point of the great Achilles's lance, and Marlowe's Leander, done in by a cramp on a hot midsummer night. Cressida and Hero are absolved: "men have died from time to time, and worms have eaten them, but not for love." Heroic passion is dismissed, not because Rosalind does not love romance, but because she knows it must be a sentimental rather than a naive mode. In the background to *As You Like It* is the uneasy presence of Christopher Marlowe, stabbed to death six years before in a supposed dispute over "a great reckoning in a little room," and oddly commemorated in a famous exchange between Touchstone and Audrey:

> TOUCHSTONE: When a man's verses cannot be understood, nor a
> man's good wit seconded with the forward child, understanding,
> it strikes a man more dead than a great reckoning in a little
> room. Truly, I would the gods had made thee poetical.
> AUDREY: I do not know what "poetical" is. Is it honest in deed and
> word? Is it a true thing?

TOUCHSTONE: No, truly; for the truest poetry is the most feigning,
and lovers are given to poetry; and what they swear in
poetry may be said as lovers they do feign.

Touchstone is sardonic enough to fit into Marlowe's cosmos, even as Jaques at moments seems a parody of Ben Jonson's moralizings, yet Rosalind is surely the least Marlovian being in Elizabethan drama. That may be why Marlowe hovers in *As You Like It*, not only in the allusions to his death but in an actual quotation from *Hero and Leander*, when the deluded shepherdess Phebe declares her passion for the disguised Rosalind:

Dead shepherd, now I find thy saw of might,
Who ever lov'd that lov'd not at first sight?

Marlowe, the dead shepherd, defines *As You Like It* by negation. Rosalind's spirit cleanses us of false melancholies, rancid reductions, corrupting idealisms, and universalized resentments. An actress capable of the role of Rosalind will expose both Jaques and Touchstone as sensibilities inadequate to the play's vision. Jaques is an eloquent rhetorician, in Ben Jonson's scalding vein, but Arden is not Jonson's realm; while Touchstone must be the least likeable of Shakespeare's clowns. I suspect that the dramatic point of both Jaques and Touchstone is how unoriginal they are in contrast to Rosalind's verve and splendor, or simply her extraordinary originality. She is the preamble to Hamlet's newness, to the Shakespearean inauguration of an unprecedented kind of representation of personality.

Richard III, Iago, and Edmund win their dark if finally self-destructive triumphs because they have quicker minds and more power over language than anyone else in their worlds. Rosalind and Hamlet more audaciously manifest the power of mind over the universe of sense than anyone they could ever encounter, but their quickness of thought and language is dedicated to a different kind of contest, akin to Falstaff's grosser agon with time and the state. It is not her will but her joy and energy that Rosalind seeks to express, and Hamlet's tragedy is that he cannot seek the same. Richard III, Iago, and Edmund superbly deceive, but Rosalind and Hamlet expose pretensions and deceptions merely by being as and what they are, superior of windows, more numerous of doors. We could save Othello and Lear from catastrophe by envisioning Iago and Edmund trying to function if Rosalind or Hamlet were introduced into their plays. Shakespeare, for reasons I cannot fathom, chose not to give us such true clashes of mighty opposites. His most intelligent villains are never brought together on one stage with his most intelligent heroes and heroines. The possible exception is in the confrontation between Shylock and Portia in *The Merchant of Venice*, but the manipulated clash of Jew against

Christian there gives Shylock no chance. Even Shakespeare's capacities would have been extended if he had tried to show Richard III attempting to gull Falstaff, Iago vainly practising upon Hamlet, or Edmund exercising his subtle rhetoric upon the formidably subtle Rosalind. Poor Jaques is hopeless against her; when he avers "why, 'tis good to be sad and say nothing," she replies: "why, then, 'tis good to be a post," and she sweeps away his boasts of melancholy experience. And what we remember best of Touchstone is Rosalind's judgment that, like a medlar, he will be rotten ere he is ripe.

Perhaps Rosalind's finest remark, amid so much splendor, is her reply when Celia chides her for interrupting. There are many ways to interpret: "Do you not know I am a woman? When I think, I must speak. Sweet, say on." We can praise Rosalind for spontaneity, for sincerity, for wisdom, and those can be our interpretations; or we can be charmed by her slyness, which turns a male complaint against women into another sign of their superiority in expressionistic intensity. Rosalind is simply superior in everything whatsoever.

1992—Harold Bloom.
"Introduction," from *Rosalind*

Harold Bloom is Sterling Professor of the Humanities at Yale University. He has edited many anthologies of literature and literary criticism and is the author of more than 30 books, including *The Western Canon* and *Shakespeare: The Invention of the Human*.

Many of us have had a particular reading experience, one that is rather difficult to describe or categorize, in which we pass from a protracted immersion in Shakespeare's plays to a perusal of some other author, old or new. Even if that author is one of Shakespeare's few peers, say Chaucer or Cervantes or Tolstoy, we are still highly conscious that the transition away from reading Shakespeare involves a difference both in degree and in kind. The difference is a falling away in what seems the persuasiveness in representing what we want to call reality, particularly the reality of a self with which we can identify. We have a sense that Shakespeare portrays human inwardness not only far better than anyone else, but in a way that partakes of the inwardness, indeed augments the inwardness. My language is of course impressionistic; it lacks the concern for materiality, race, gender, social history, and all those other indubitable verities of what I am asked to believe is a New Historicism, without which no current studies of Shakespeare can be politically correct. But then Shakespeare, rather sublimely, is not politically correct, and is anything but an historicist. You can go hunting for what is vital in John Marston or George Chapman, armed with your Foucaultian bow and Marxist arrow, but you will return from the forest of Arden with nothing to show for your enlightened zeal.

Be old-fashioned with me, as archaic as Dr. Johnson and William Hazlitt, and start again with Shakespeare's characters, abysses of inwardness. How exactly do they differ from literary characters before them, and why do the most intense of them continue to surpass all characters since? Shakespeare's greatest originality, as I have ventured before, is that his characters overhear themselves, ponder what they themselves have said, and on that basis frequently resolve to change and subsequently do change. In the Hebrew Bible, characters change, but not because they have overheard and pondered their own asides or soliloquies. The J Writer's principal character, Yahweh himself, changes profoundly at Sinai, and behaves very badly indeed in the Wilderness, but his changes are not Shakespearean, as a close comparison with his literary descendant, King Lear, will demonstrate. Lear learns humility by learning his own violent nature, because he is struck by his own utterances. Yahweh is not capable of overhearing himself, and so learns nothing, and remains therefore always violent, always unpredictable.

A preference among Shakespearean protagonists, where there is so bewildering a plenitude, almost always will have a subjective element, and yet it is a commonplace to affirm the superior, indeed the heroic wit of three figures to particular: Rosalind, Falstaff, Hamlet. Of these, Rosalind's wit is the most balanced, the most proportionate to the pragmatics of everyday existence, and clearly the most capable of harmony, of what Yeats liked to call Unity of Being. Like Falstaff in the two parts of *Henry IV*, and like *Hamlet*, Rosalind is larger than her play, and restores our sense of the overwhelming reality of literary character. In ways almost too subtle for critical description to encompass, Rosalind could be judged as Shakespeare's supreme representation of a possible human personality. Her clearest rival is Hamlet, but he is too strong for any context, and reaches so far beyond us that we cannot always apprehend him. Rosalind, a miracle of wit, is closer to us and requires no mediation between ourselves and her role.

C.L. Barber catches one of the several senses in which Rosalind touches the limits of Shakespearean representation:

> The dramatist tends to show us one thing at a time, and to realize that
> one thing, in its moment, to the full; his characters go to extremes,
> comical as well as serious: and no character, not even a Rosalind, is in
> a position to see all around the play and so be completely poised, for if
> this were so the play would cease to be dramatic.

Let us repeat Barber's point, but in the other direction: more than any other Shakespearean character, more even than Falstaff or Hamlet, Rosalind is almost completely poised, nearly able to see all around the play. What Barber names as a poise that transcends perspectivizing, I would rather term heroic wit, a stance that comprehends both skepticism and a vitalistic exuberance. Falstaff darkens because his educational and paternal love is rejected; in losing his pupil, he loses himself, having invested too much of his wit in Hal. Hamlet darkens because he is Hamlet, and is too supremely intelligent for any context or any action available to him. Rosalind, best balanced of all Shakespearean figures, does not darken though, like Falstaff and Hamlet, immense wit compels her to change, however subtly, each time she speaks. Her difference from Falstaff and from Hamlet, otherwise her peers, lies in the nature of her will. Like them, she has a will to power over the interpretation of her own play, and like them she is a dramatist, forever devising fresh scenes and skits. But Rosalind never seeks to express her will, as Hamlet and Falstaff do, in different but complementary ways. Her quest is to express her energy and joy, her sense of more life. Falstaff has a contest to win, against both time and the interests of the state. Agonistically, Falstaff's energy and joy are superbly activated, yet his will necessarily is contaminated by his two great antagonists. Hamlet's mighty opposite is hardly the wretched Claudius, but is himself, since another of the Prince of Denmark's great originalities is that he inaugurates the great trope that Freud appropriated, the civil war in the psyche in which each of us is her own worst enemy. In our hearts there is a kind of fighting that will not let us sleep, but such is not the heart of Rosalind.

The touchstones for Rosalind's spirit are Jaques and Touchstone himself, both of them fundamentally rancid beings, though Shakespeare scholars see Jaques for what he is, while they are weirdly charmed by Touchstone. I exempt only Harold Goddard, Shakespeare's best critic since Hazlitt, for Goddard sees Touchstone precisely as Rosalind sees this vicious wit, a Fool who will be rotten ere he is ripe. Here is Touchstone's vision of human reality:

And so, from hour to hour we ripe and ripe,
And then from hour to hour we rot and rot.

Historicists, whether Old or New, tend to be reductionists: they all are would-be Touchstones. The late Helen Gardner, Old Historicist, was enchanted by Touchstone: "In everything that Touchstone says and does gusto, high spirits and a zest for life ring out. Essentially comic, he can adapt himself to any situation in which he may find himself. Never at a loss, he is life's master." Gardner goes on to tell us that Jaques is Touchstone's opposite: "He is the cynic, the person who prefers the pleasures of superiority, cold-eyed and cold-hearted."

Rosalind has even less esteem for Touchstone than she does for Jaques, but then Rosalind is anything but an historicist, let alone a politically correct master of sexual politics. Like the nurse in Romeo and Juliet, Touchstone is popular with our modern groundlings, and like the nurse Touchstone has vicious elements in his nature. Rosalind, heroically free of the Death Drive, repudiates every intimation of sadism with her astonishing wit, perhaps the only wit in all Western literature that has affection at its core. Speaking as Ganymede playing Rosalind, Rosalind playfully denies her lover Orlando, who resorts to grand hyperbole, and is answered by the only prose in Shakespeare that is equal to Falstaff's, a prose that here mocks Christopher Marlowe, who is so strange a presence-by-absence throughout As You Like It:

> *Rosalind:* Well, in her person, I say I will not have you.
> *Orlando:* Then, in mine own person, I die.
> *Rosalind:* No, faith, die by attorney. The poor world is almost six
> thousand years old, and in all this time there was not any man died in
> his own person, videlicet, in a love cause. Troilus had his brains dashed
> out with a Grecian club; yet he did what he could to die before, and
> he is one of the patterns of love, Leander, he would have lived many
> a fair year though Hero have turned nun, if it had not been for a hot
> midsummer night; for, good youth, he went but forth to wash him in
> the Hellespont, and being taken with the cramp, was drowned; and the
> foolish chroniclers of that age found it was "Hero of Sestos." But these
> are all lies. Men have died from time to time, and worms have eaten
> them, but not for love.

How many of us, suffering the agonies of passion, requited or rejected, have been aided by Rosalind's amiable wisdom: "Men have died from time to time, and worms have eaten them, but not for love." That competes with several of Falstaff's for the eminence of being the best sentence in the language. Rosalind, as much in love as anyone else in Shakespeare, or in what we call reality, teaches Orlando, herself, and her audience the limits of love. Would that we could die by proxy, but even then, the cause would not be love. Troilus, paradigm of the true lover, is obliterated by Rosalind's double jest: his dignified death by the spear of Achilles is transformed into having "his brains dashed out with a Grecian club," and the metaphysical agonies he will undergo a year or two later in *Troilus and Cressida* are reduced to masochism, "yet he did what he could to die before." Rosalind, least Marlovian of all stage protagonists whatsoever, joins in the general mockery of poor Marlowe that rather strangely runs all through As You Like It as an undersong. Touchstone, directly before defining the truest poetry as the most feigning, and love as another feigning, throws away Shakespeare's astonishing epitaph for his truest precursor: "When a man's verses cannot be understood, nor a man's good wit seconded with the forward child, understanding, it strikes a man more dead than a great reckoning in a little room." The "great reckoning in a little room" was the disputed tavern bill that supposedly caused Ingram Frizer to strike Marlowe dead, with a dagger-thrust through the poet's eye. Phebe the shepherdess, smitten with love for Rosalind disguised as Ganymede, is employed for a mockery of the most famous line in Marlowe's *Hero and Leander*:

Dead shepherd, now I find thy saw of might,
"Who ever loved that loved not at first sight."

Marlowe, permanently esteemed as the poet of the lyric, "The Passionate Shepherd to His Love," is not only the dead shepherd of *As You Like It*, but he is the spirit of the negation that the play repudiates in rejecting the viciousness of Touchstone and the rancidity of Jaques. Marlowe (and Chapman) are the last of the "foolish chroniclers" who gave the verdict that the cause of Leander's cramp and subsequent drowning was Hero of Sestos. Rosalind's amiable skepticism is the cure for Marlowe's Ovidian eroticizing of human failings and accidents into the Death Drive. Just as *Twelfth Night* is a comedy in part directed against Ben Jonson, with Malvolio a displaced Jonsonian moralist, so *As You Like It* stages an implicit polemic against Marlovian hyperboles of desire. There is something of Rosalind in Emily Dickinson, and Dickinson can give us the apt phrase for Rosalind: "adequate desire." The mystery of Rosalind's character centers upon the astonishing poise with which Shakespeare has endowed her. How do we describe an intellect that has faith both in itself and in language? Hamlet, who has faith in neither, is incommensurate with us, and so requires the mediation of Horatio's love. No one mediates Rosalind for us, except perhaps Touchstone and Jaques, who accomplish that by negation.

All that Rosalind asks for her will is that it not be violated or usurped; she has no will to power over others. She is the ancestor of that grand tradition of fictive heroines of the Protestant Will that includes Jane Austen's Elizabeth Bennet and Emma Woodhouse. The tradition, which goes from Richardson's Clarissa Harlowe through Austen and George Eliot and George Meredith, has its American, representatives in Hawthorne and James, and reverberates still in the heroines of Forster and Woolf, and in the Brangwen sisters of Lawrence. Like Rosalind, these figures concentrate upon the giving and receiving of esteem, a very different dialectical exchange from the Marlovian agon of rhetoric, in which the will to power over other souls is always at the center. Rosalind's wit is heroic because it struggles against every invidious quality that could debase or compromise it.

Shakespeare chose never to bring his grandest negations and his most heroic wits onto the same stage. One's imagination plays with the possible confrontations: duels of intellect between Iago and Falstaff, or Edmund and Hamlet But one cannot imagine Rosalind in the cosmos of the great Shakespearean villains, and not just because her context is the Forest of Arden. Her freedom is that of a wholly normative personality: mature, without malice, needing to turn aggressivity neither against herself nor against others. We rejoice in her because no other figure in Western literature, not even in Shakespeare, is at once so accomplished in wit, and so little interested in the power that great wit can bring if properly exercised. No one else, in Shakespeare or any other author, is so free of resentment while yet retaining all of the natural human endowments of curiosity, vitality, and desire. We intensely welcome her company, because no other fictive presence is at once so naturalistically refreshing, or less insistent upon appropriating for herself.

AS YOU LIKE IT
IN THE TWENTY-FIRST CENTURY

❧

The twenty-first century has brought fresh critical approaches to *As You Like It*. One critic, E.A.J. Honigmann, has looked at the play in comparison to other romantic comedies that Shakespeare wrote around the same time period—*The Merchant of Venice*, *Much Ado About Nothing*, and *Twelfth Night*. *As You Like It* actually exemplifies two types of pastoral, according to Honigmann. One is the traditional pastoral of shepherds and shepherdesses; the other is a more sophisticated pastoral. In his view, in *As You Like It* the real shepherds and shepherdesses, Silvius and Phebe, make the fake ones, Rosalind and Celia, appear real. Honigmann explained how, aside from pastoral, the play uses satire, romance, and folk tale. He wrote that audiences enjoy the play for its innocence and simplicity but that the play offers much more. In a highly sophisticated manner, it presents an alternative world thoroughly different from that in Shakespeare's other romantic comedies.

2002—E.A.J. Honigmann. "The Charm of *As You Like It*," from *Shakespeare: Seven Tragedies Revisited: The Dramatist's Manipulation of Response*

E.A.J. Honigmann taught English literature at the Shakespeare Institute at the University of Birmingham. He is the author or editor of numerous titles, many of which are about Shakespeare, including *The Stability of Shakespeare's Text* and *Shakespearian Tragedy and the Mixed Response*.

Like the members of a family, every one of Shakespeare's plays has a character of its own, and also a family resemblance to his other plays. Language, prosody, conventions, attitudes to authority, the length of plays, scenes, speeches—these and many other components tell us 'This is one of Shakespeare's plays. No one else could have written it.' Plays in the same genre can be particularly close. If we want to identify the distinctive character of a play it helps to compare it with its immediate siblings—for example, to consider *As You Like It* in relation to other

223

romantic comedies, in particular the great comedies written within a few years of it. *The Merchant of Venice*, *Much Ado* and *Twelfth Night* have much in common with *As You Like It*, like four sisters: to understand the special charm of one, as any producer of the play or literary critic must try to do, we may begin by placing it beside the others and asking why it differs, in so many finely nuanced ways, from its nearest relatives.

Because Shakespeare wrote for actors whose strengths and weaknesses he knew well, many of the parts were designed for specialists who reappear in one play after another. When Robert Armin, a qualified goldsmith, joined the Lord Chamberlain's Men, probably in 1598 or 1599, Shakespeare created Touchstone to exploit his gifts as a performer of witty, cynical fools (see also *Twelfth Night*, *All's Well* and *King Lear*). A playwright himself and the author of a book about famous fools, Armin seems to have been a wry, thoughtful man, and it is widely thought that Shakespeare stopped the play to pay tribute to this no doubt congenial colleague at *Twelfth Night* III. 1. 57ff.

> This fellow is wise enough to play the fool;
> And to do that well craves a kind of wit.
> He must observe their mood on whom he jests,
> The quality of persons, and the time;
> And like the haggard, check at every feather
> That comes before his eye. This is a practice
> As full of labour as a wise man's art;
> For folly that he wisely shows is fit;
> But wise men, folly-fall'n, quite taint their wit.

We do not know the names of the actors who played other parts in *As You Like It*, yet we may assume that Shakespeare was no less aware of their gifts and created the parts to suit them. So I guess that one actor played Orlando and Orsino, another Jaques and Malvolio, a third Oliver and Sebastian, and that the company's leading boy-actors would take Rosalind, Celia and Audrey and also Viola, Olivia and Maria.[1] If we then ask ourselves how and why these paired roles differ, we may discover that their differences are related to the larger differences of their plays. For instance, Armin could sing. In *As You Like It* Touchstone sings only two short snatches of nonsense (or does he recite them?), but Shakespeare may allude to Armin's musical know-how when Touchstone dismisses 'It was a lover and his lass' as 'the note was very untuneable' and 'God mend your voices' (V. 3. 32ff.). Perhaps as a newcomer in the company Armin did not yet care to sing in public. In *Twelfth Night*, two or so years later, Feste sings 'O mistress mine', usually in a lugubrious voice, 'Come away, come away, death' and the far from happy 'When that I was and a little tiny boy', songs, it seems, that suited Armin's style.

Furthermore, Touchstone has tender feelings, if that is the correct word, as do the other 'copulatives' in *As You Like It*. Celia says 'He'll go along o'er the wide world with me; / Leave me alone to woo him' (I. 3. 128). At any rate he seems to be susceptible to feminine charms: he recalls Jane Smile and 'the wooing of a peascod instead of her' and he is drawn to Audrey. Even if we are uneasy about his feelings it is true that he does not hide them—unlike Feste, a Fool more cut off from other people, more introspective, more inclined to exploit and torment others.[2] Similarly Olivia rejects Orsino's love and Malvolio's, 'Cesario' rejects Olivia's, Toby does not care for Maria's, whereas in *As You Like It* everyone freely accepts love and life (even Phebe relents and accepts Silvius). Again, Malvolio at the end of *Twelfth Night* swears revenge and sometimes does so in tears, Jaques merely retires to enjoy a new kind of melancholy in the company of the converted Duke Frederick; Rosalind can talk to Celia about her love, Viola (like Feste) confides in no one. In short, Shakespeare kept in mind the special talents of his actors and at the same time adapted each role to the special needs of the play.

The more we think about it the more different *As You Like It* and *Twelfth Night* appear to be, despite their superficial resemblances. Though we classify both as romantic comedies, Illyria is not the Forest of Arden, nor is the Forest of Arden in the least like 'a wood near Athens', one of the locations of *A Midsummer Night's Dream*. In *As You Like It* the pastoralism of Acts II to V defines both action and atmosphere (not so in *Much Ado* or *Twelfth Night*) and yet there are really two kinds of pastoral in the play. Corin, Silvius and Phebe, two shepherds and a shepherdess, belong to the conventions of classical pastoral, of Theocritus and Virgil, where shepherds tend their flocks, pipe ditties and praise cruel mistresses; Rosalind and Celia belong to a more sophisticated world where princes and princesses dress up as shepherds and shepherdesses, a tradition that flourished in sixteenth-century Italy and Spain, and in England culminated in Sir Philip Sidney's *Arcadia* (1590). That is, *As You Like It* combined what we may call primary and secondary pastoral, with the curious effect that Silvius and Phebe make Rosalind, Celia and their lovers seem more 'real', though both groups are equally the products of a purely literary tradition.

A second classical tradition also influenced *As You Like It*—classical satire. When we compare the play with its source, Thomas Lodge's prose romance *Rosalynde* (1590), we find that Shakespeare followed Lodge quite closely yet added a number of characters who reinforce the play's satirical sub-text: Touchstone and Audrey, Jaques, Le Beau. Shakespeare, however, did not choose mainstream satire—the tradition of Juvenal and Martial, often bordering on invective—but a variant, the gentle and often playful satire associated with Horace. This must have been particularly striking when *As You Like It* was first produced because 'lashing' satire had become so fashionable (in the works of poets such as Hall, Marston, Middleton and many others, and prose-writers such as Nashe) that the official censor, the Archbishop of Canterbury, banned all verse satire on 1 June 1599, the year to which the play is usually assigned. While Shakespeare was certainly capable of writing like Juvenal, as we see in *Troilus and Cressida* and *Timon of Athens*, playful satire—like playful humour—seems to have come more naturally to him. It had the added advantage in *As You Like It* that it tones in with the twinkling mockery of men and love that we identify with Rosalind and to a lesser extent with Touchstone.

In Rosalind, therefore, the traditions of pastoral and satire converge. What else is distinctive about her? The sexes also converge in her. Dressed as 'Ganymede'—as in Lodge's *Rosalynde*—she enjoys performing a 'pretty youth', never more so than when she pretends that she wants to help Orlando get over the lunacy of love (we know that that is the last thing she wants). At this point a boy-actor plays Rosalind who plays Ganymede who plays Rosalind, while at the same time Celia and Touchstone know her to be the 'real' Rosalind. The confusion far exceeds that of *The Merchant of Venice* IV.1, where Portia and Nerissa appear as a lawyer and his clerk, or of *Twelfth Night*, where no one suspects Viola's disguise. And whereas the disguised Portia and Viola perform their masculine roles to perfection (except when Viola, terrified, has to fight a duel with Sir Andrew), Rosalind-as-Ganymede flaunts her double sexuality and relishes it. (The mythological Ganymede, cup-bearer of Zeus, inspired homosexual love in his master, and Orlando's attraction to Ganymede and more explicitly Phebe's, glancingly touches on such emotions, about which the 'lashing' satirists of the late 1590s were particularly frenzied in their denunciations.)

Rosalind pushes her 'boyishness' to the very limits of the permissible, as Celia laughingly complains. 'You have simply misus'd our sex in your love-prate.' Disguised as Ganymede she can tease Orlando ('I had as lief be woo'd of a snail'), joke about horns, cry 'Come, woo me, woo me; for now I am in a holiday humour, and like enough to consent'—speeches that would be quite improper if Orlando knew who she was, which adds to her enjoyment, and to ours. And we, of course, get extra-dramatic pleasure from the performance of a gifted boy-actor who at one and the same time manages to look and sound like a boy *and* a girl.

Much more than in the other romantic comedies, Shakespeare extracts delightful fun from disguise, inventing one situation after another that becomes a verbal hide-and-seek. Orlando says 'my Rosalind is virtuous', she replies 'And I am your Rosalind'—holding her breath, half-hoping that he will *see*.

> *Orlando.* Fair youth, I would I could make thee believe I love.
> *Rosalind.* Me believe it! You may as soon make her that you love believe it . . . (III. 2. 356)

In *Rosalynde* 'Celia' proposes the mock-marriage:

> And thereupon (quoth *Aliena*) Ile play the priest; from this day forth
> *Ganimede* shall call thee husband, and thou shalt call *Ganimede* wife, and
> so weele have a marriage. Content (quoth *Rosader*[3]) and laught. Content
> (quoth *Ganimede*) and changed as redde as a rose.

Shakespeare makes Rosalind propose the marriage ('Come, sister, you shall
be the priest, and marry us'), and puts the words of the official marriage
ceremony in Celia's mouth ('You must begin "Will you, Orlando"—'): using
these very words he brings the conventions of disguise hard up against 'reality'.
So, too, when Orlando observes that Rosalind's speech is not right for the
role she plays ('Your accent is something finer than you could purchase in
so removed a dwelling', III. 2. 318: compare p. 197, where Henry V forgets
the role he has assumed) and perhaps he should start in surprise when
he first sets eyes on 'Ganymede'. As he tells the Duke, 'My lord, the first
time that I ever saw him / Methought he was a brother to your daughter'
(v. 4. 28). In some productions Orlando touches or slaps Ganymede's chest,
another surprise.

I think it a mistake, though, to let Orlando know, or even seriously suspect,
that Ganymede is Rosalind. The fun of the play depends on our not knowing
what he knows (so, too, with Oliver). When Rosalind sees the bloody napkin
and swoons (IV. 3. 155) the girl-boy's performance trembles on the edge
of discovery.

> *Rosalind*. I would I were at home.
> *Celia*. We'll lead you thither.
> I pray you, will you take him by the arm?
> *Oliver*. Be of good cheer, youth. You a man! You lack a man's heart.
> *Rosalind*. I do so, I confess it. Ah, sirrah, a body would think this was
> well counterfeited.

The swoon is pure Shakespeare, as is the repetition of counterfeit.

> I pray you tell your brother how well I counterfeited. Heigh-ho!
> *Oliver*. This was not counterfeit . . .
> *Rosalind*. Counterfeit, I assure you.
> *Oliver*. Well then, take a good heart and counterfeit to be a man.
> *Rosalind*. So I do; but, i'faith, I should have been a woman by right . . .
> I pray you, commend my counterfeiting.

Can we doubt that this was meant to prompt a burst of applause for a brilliant
boy-actor?

Shakespeare's attitude to disguise is typical of all the conventions used in *As You Like It*. Instead of concealing them, he wants the audience to notice and savour them. The very first speech resembles the opening of many pre-Shakespearian plays, in which a character introduces himself and explains the situation. ('As I remember, Adam, it was upon this fashion bequeathed me by will . . .'.) 'Primitive technique', critics are tempted to say—except that the language of *As You Like It* would sound more 'modern' in Elizabethan ears than

I Pompey am, Pompey surnam'd the Great,
That oft in field, with targe and shield, did make my foe to sweat
   (*Love's Labour's Lost*, V. 2. 543)

or

This man is Pyramus, if you would know;
This beauteous lady Thisby is certain . . .
   (*A Midsummer Night's Dream*, V. 1. 128)

Orlando's first speech, however, with its measured sentences, has its own artifice —just enough to cushion what might be thought a clumsy exposition against the derisive hoots that greet the primitive technique in *A Midsummer Night's Dream* and *Love's Labour's Lost* from the stage-audience. Shakespeare balances one artifice against another, for mutual support or contrast, a characteristic Shakespearian 'mingle'.[4]

We must accept, then, that self-displaying artifice is an important technique in *As You Like It*. The conventions of romance are paraded, but we are not asked to believe in them: they are more visible than in *The Merchant of Venice*, *Much Ado* or *Twelfth Night*, and the dramatist entertains us by juggling with them—as Peele had done in a more 'folksy' way in *The Old Wive's Tale*. Shakespeare resumes his seemingly 'primitive' or clumsy exposition several times over.

There's no news at the court, sir, but the old news; that is, the old Duke is banished by his younger brother the new Duke . . .

If my uncle, thy banished father, had banished thy uncle, the Duke my father . . .

Repeating such blatant information-giving, Shakespeare intimates that the play will not be concerned with 'realism'.

So, too, at the other end of the play, when we hear that Duke Frederick, having marched an army to the outskirts of the Forest of Arden, intending to capture the exiled Duke and put him to the sword,

> meeting with an old religious man,
> After some question with him, was converted
> Both from his enterprise and from the world;
> His crown bequeathing to his banish'd brother . . .

In *Rosalynde* 'Duke Frederick' and his army are defeated in battle and he is killed; some critics shake their heads and explain that Shakespeare, wanting a 'happy ending' for his romance, huddled up the close of *As You Like It* too cavalierly and improbably. True: but we have to add that the improbability was intended, a perfect conclusion for this improbable play. Sudden conversions, like love at first sight and disguise and transparent information-giving, are amongst the most familiar conventions of romance: critics who are unhappy about Duke Frederick's conversion should be consistent and condemn the whole play.

In addition to pastoral, satire and romance, *As You Like It* also reminds us of folk-tale and its not very different conventions. Shakespeare found in Lodge's *Rosalynde* a father with three sons, the youngest being the father's favourite: he built on this motif by changing Lodge's 'lustie Francklin' and his two sons (who come to wrestle with the Duke's champion) into 'an old man and his three sons' (I. 2. 198), and again by changing Lodge's 'hungrie Lion' into 'A lioness, with udders all drawn dry' (IV. 3. 113) and adding a 'green and gilded snake' (IV. 3. 107), so that the sleeping Oliver is at the mercy of three enemies (the lioness, the snake and Orlando). I have no doubt that Shakespeare very willingly followed Lodge in Act V, introducing Jaques de Boys ('I am the second son of old Sir Rowland'), when any messenger would have served just as well, for this allowed him to remind the audience of his father-and-three-sons beginning. Then, inventing Duke Frederick's strange conversion, Shakespeare invites us to laugh at the collapse of his house of cards—and who could wish for a more appropriate ending?

As You Like It differs from Shakespeare's other comedies in making a virtue of improbability, and this helps to give it its special charm. Cause and effect are reduced to the absolute minimum hence Duke Frederick's unexpected banishment of Rosalind ('Mistress, dispatch you with your safest haste') and equally sudden fury with Oliver—

> *Oliver.* I never lov'd my brother in my life.
> *Duke Frederick.* More villain thou. (III. 1. 14)

where Shakespeare positively winks at us, expecting us to smile at Duke Frederick's own fraternal villainy. Hence, too, all the chance encounters in the forest, Orlando's discovery of his sleeping brother and Hymen's unexplained intervention (is it someone else performing Hymen? or could it be the 'real'

Hymen, a supernatural visitation like that of Diana in *Pericles* V. 1. 238 or of Jupiter in *Cymbeline* V. 4. 93?).

In *As You Like It* Shakespeare unbends, as never before. He decided to entertain the Globe's audiences with a play as they liked it and he consciously wrote down to their level, adapting Lodge's popular romance and accentuating its improbability. This is Shakespeare at his most playful, and he found the ideal 'objective correlative' for his mood in Rosalind, by far his most playful heroine. Central to his conception of her, the idea that she, as Ganymede, challenges Orlando to 'woo me, woo me' (IV. 1. 61ff.), again comes straight from Lodge, though transformed by Shakespeare's wit and delicacy. Already in their first scene, Rosalind responds to Celia's repeated promptings to 'be merry' with the promise 'From henceforth I will, coz, and devise sports. Let me see; what think you of falling in love?'—here speaking against the grain, as it were, merely to please Celia. But when she is in the mood for love her playfulness, like Shakespeare's own, cannot be tethered.

The signs of Shakespeare's playfulness abound. Even more than elsewhere he asks us to see the play as an entertainment, and not to confuse it with life. Quite apart from barely disguised romance conventions, he introduces 'show stopper' speeches—the weeping stag (II. 1. 29ff.), 'A fool, a fool' (II. 7. 12ff.), 'All the world's a stage' (II. 7. 139), Touchstone's 'horn' speech (III. 3. 42), the art of quarrelling (V. 4. 65)—during which the play pauses, other actors on-stage more or less freeze, and the speaker does a solo, equivalent to an aria in opera or a juggling turn in a pantomime. When the play then resumes we become doubly conscious of it as a play. And these longer speeches are supported by shorter ones that are less obviously excrescences—'Time travels in divers paces with divers persons'—and also by songs and poems that stop the show and give the actor *and the dramatist* the opportunity to preen himself and go through his paces. The same effect is achieved by lists such as 'A lean cheek, which you have not; a blue eye and sunken, which you have not; an unquestionable spirit, which you have not; a beard neglected, which you have not . . .' (III. 2. 346), or 'your brother and my sister no sooner met but they look'd; no sooner look'd but they lov'd; no sooner lov'd but they sigh'd; no sooner sigh'd but they ask'd one another the reason; no sooner knew the reason . . .' (V. 2. 30ff.). In these different ways Shakespeare seems to say 'Don't watch the story, watch the *words!*' Repeatedly he stops the story, time stands still and we enjoy these diversions for their own sake—noticing that they are not wholly divorced from the story, they still retain a flimsy connection with it. The deliberate flimsiness, I suggest, reveals Shakespeare's playful attitude to the comedy and to its audience.

The near-autonomy of the 'show stopper' speeches depends on other converging factors. In 'All the world's a stage', allusions to the world of the theatre encourage the audience's self-awareness (that is, as distinct from awareness of the story); Shakespeare steps further away from the story by describing not the world of romance but life as seen from a contemporary, satirical angle—

> the infant
> Mewling and puking in the nurse's arms;
> Then the whining school-boy with his satchel . . .

And, as others have observed, Jaques' account of life's last scene, 'second childishness and mere oblivion; / Sans teeth, sans eyes . . .' flies in the face of the story, for as he speaks Orlando enters carrying Adam, his 'venerable burden'; and 'Blow, blow, thou winter wind', again, dwelling on 'man's ingratitude' and 'friend rememb'red not', seems to contradict the 'story', Adam's gratitude to his old master and Orlando's to Adam. And why 'a lie *seven* times removed' (v. 4. 65)? An extra-dramatic echo of the '*seven* ages of Man'? Raising such questions Shakespeare gives the 'solo' speeches a semi-independence of their own, partly detaching them from the fabric of the play: for a while each one is more important than the story, and together they almost challenge the supremacy of the story. So Shakespeare not only takes a playful view of romance, he is equally playful in slotting in other forms of entertainment. His own semi-visible presence in the play, moving the story along or stopping it with 'solo' speeches, songs, poems, dialogue that leads nowhere, a wrestling match, other fights and so on, holds the loose baggy monster together.

Except, of course, that *As You Like It* is not a loose baggy monster. Quite the contrary: it has the delicacy of an intricate dance, of some of Mozart's most radiant music. If we may compare its heroine with one of her descendants, Elizabeth Bennet of *Pride and Prejudice*, we shall see more clearly how the flimsiness of the world of *As You Like It* contributes to the success of the whole. 'I must confess that I think her as delightful a creature as ever appeared in print', Jane Austen said of Elizabeth, and I can imagine Shakespeare thinking of Rosalind along similar lines. Though the two heroines have much in common— wit, mockery, irreverence—they exist in different worlds. The later one solidly English, with all the fine shadings of period and class distinctions, while *As You Like It* seems to be set in both France and England, in the living present and the literary past, and class distinctions dissolve in the brotherhood of Arden. Jane Austen located Elizabeth in a recognisable world and observed the rules of probability, Shakespeare created a never-never land and asks us to rejoice in its improbabilities.

At the very centre of his implausible romance Shakespeare placed his most brilliant heroine who, like Hamlet a year or so later, seems to many to partake of her creator's own genius. The play's title reflects its author's playfulness (it may have started life as *Rosalind, or As You Like It*: compare *Twelfth Night, or What You Will*), yet beneath the playfulness we should also be conscious of artistic seriousness, equal to that of *Henry V, Julius Caesar* and *Hamlet. As You Like It* is the work of a great dramatist at the height of his powers: as an artistic achievement I rank it in the same class as the plays I have just named, though in a different genre.

A masterpiece cannot be created by accident. What prompted Shakespeare to write his most playful and improbable romantic comedy? To appreciate the originality of *As You Like It* we have to examine the literary scene in 1598–99, and the effect of two individuals in particular. In September 1598 or a little later Francis Meres published a survey of 'modern' English literature, a treatise called *Palladis Tamia* that first identified Shakespeare as a major dramatist. It is easy to forget that until 1598 Shakespeare was admired as the poet of *Venus and Adonis* (1593) and *The Rape of Lucrece* (1594), and was almost unknown as a dramatist— for before 1598 not one of his plays had been published with his name, and it may well be that many of those who applauded his plays in the theatre did not know the name of their author. Meres named twelve of Shakespeare's most popular plays—including *A Midsummer Night's Dream, The Merchant of Venice, Richard III, Romeo and Juliet* but not *As You Like It*, which is taken to indicate that *As You Like It* had not yet been performed—and announced that 'as Plautus and Seneca are accounted the best for comedy and tragedy among the Latins: so Shakespeare among the English is the most excellent in both kinds.' Shakespeare's name now began to appear prominently on the title-pages of his plays, and even of plays that were not his, proving that he had arrived as a powerful presence in the English theatre.

Meres also named a younger man, 'Beniamin Iohnson', as one of 'our best for tragedy'. Jonson had written plays from July 1597 and perhaps earlier, and enjoyed his first real success with *Every Man in his Humour* in September 1598, the very month when *Palladis Tamia* was entered in the Stationers' Register. According to a story first told by Rowe (1709), Jonson's play was about to be turned down by the Lord Chamberlain's Men when Shakespeare 'luckily cast his eye upon it', liked it and recommended it to his colleagues. Shakespeare himself acted a part in it and his company also produced *Every Man Out of his Humour* in 1599 or early 1600.[5] Jonson, therefore, eight years junior to Shakespeare, had reason to be grateful to him, yet did not hesitate to speak contemptuously of romantic comedy (of which Shakespeare was the leading practitioner). This was the literary situation when *As You Like It* came to be written, between late 1598 and early 1600, and almost certainly in 1599.

Shakespeare's relationship with Jonson in and around 1599 was complicated by other frictions—so many that I deal with them in a special annexe to this chapter and merely summarise the more important ones here. Let me begin with two uncontroversial points about Jonson. (1) From at latest 1597, Jonson became notorious as an overbearing and fearless quarreller. His character, which seems to have changed very little in his adult years, was described by a

friend as 'a great lover and praiser of himself, a contemner and scorner of others
. . . passionately kind and angry.'[6] (2) From at latest 1598, Jonson saw himself
as a champion of neo-classical writing and criticism. It is equally certain (3)
that Jonson and Shakespeare were on opposite sides in the so-called 'War of
the Theatres' (1599–1601), and (4) that Jonson remained an outspoken critic of
Shakespeare for many years. More controversially, I believe (5) that there are
strong reasons for thinking Jonson the 'rival poet' whose learning and proud,
overbearing nature made the poet of the *Sonnets* lament his own ignorance
(78. 6). The *Sonnets*, or at least some of them, were already referred to by Meres
in 1598.

Probably at the very time when Shakespeare wrote *As You Like It*, Jonson
ridiculed the improbable 'cross-wooing' of romantic comedy ('as of a duke to be
in love with a countess, and that countess to be in love with the duke's son, and
the son to love the lady's waiting maid') and declared his faith in neo-classical
principles.

> I would fain hear one of these autumn-judgements define once, *Quid sit
> Comoedia?* If he cannot, let him content himself with Cicero's definition
> . . . who would have a comedy to be *imitatio vitae, speculum consuetudinis,
> imago veritatis* [an imitation of life, a mirror of custom, an image of
> truth].[7]

Now it may be that Jonson's unkind thoughts about romantic comedy were
not aired in *Every Man Out of his Humour* until after the first performance of
As You Like It. Even if it were so, Jonson was never backward in announcing his
own opinions. We know that he told many important people to their face that
their literary efforts or their views were rubbish: in 1613, while in France, Jonson
informed Cardinal Perron that his translations of Virgil 'were naught', and he
said of himself that 'he would not flatter though he saw death'.[8] Given Jonson's
character, and knowing that he regarded 'truth to life' as all-important in drama,
can we doubt that he spoke his mind to the Lord Chamberlain's Men, with
whom he must have been in close contact—spoke frankly, and probably with
brutal directness, about romantic comedy?

I can imagine one ripe or 'autumn judgement', eight years older than Jonson,
contenting himself with the riposte that romantic comedy is 'how they like it'.
One of the most interesting personal traits in the *Sonnets* is Shakespeare's habit
of refusing to argue when argument seemed pointless or degrading: on certain
issues he refused to engage with the Young Man and the Rival Poet (I am aware
that it has become fashionable to deny any autobiographical dimension in the
Sonnets. But fashions do change.) So, challenged by Jonson to define 'what is
a comedy', Shakespeare, I like to think, permitted Jonson to suppose that 'he
cannot', and instead answered him with his most fanciful send-up of truth to
life, namely *As You Like It*.

Nevertheless Shakespeare's comedy exhibits another kind of truth—emotional truth. If one compares Rosalind's experience of love with Juliet's or Viola's or Beatrice's, it is immediately clear that Rosalind's differs from the others; each love is individualised, like each heroine's character. The shock of falling in love may be equally breathtaking, but the response to this shock differs as only Shakespeare could imagine such psychic events. The panic and flutter of Rosalind's love, her twisting and turning, like a bird desperate to escape, and at the same time her willing surrender to this new emotion, her luxuriating in it—her zig-zag thinking and language give us the illusion that we hear her very heartbeats. Her relationship with Celia, their perfect understanding of one another and near-identity of feeling, again generates a 'true' emotion—idealised, to be sure, as everything in the play is idealised, yet 'true' and 'real' within its parameters. How instantly they read each other's minds!

> *Celia.* Trow you who hath done this?
> *Rosalind.* Is it a man?
> *Celia.* And a chain, that you once wore, about his neck. Change you colour?

Possibly also in reaction to Jonson's self-consciously careful plotting, Shakespeare again strikes out in a different direction in making *As You Like It* an almost plotless play. The newly acclaimed dramatist seems to improvise effortlessly—like Beethoven, like many composers—though of course years of practice have made him the master of his medium, dramatic dialogue. He may have been indebted for the idea to Lodge, who refers several times to the 'prattle' (or 'prattle prattle' or 'sweet prattle') of Rosalynde and 'Celia'. By the standards of 1590 Lodge's own dialogue deserves some praise, though still fettered to the artifice that persisted after *Euphues* (for example in the prose romances of Robert Greene), as a typical extract will show.

> You may see (quoth *Ganimede*) what mad cattell you women be,
> whose hearts sometimes are made of Adamant that will touch with
> no impression; and sometime of waxe that is fit for everie forme: they
> delight to be courted, and then they glorie to seeme coy; and when they
> are most desired then they freese with disdaine . . .[9]

There are occasional flashes of 'natural' speech ('what mad cattell you women be') usually embedded in stylised sentences. What appealed to Shakespeare, I think, was the opportunity to develop prattle to a higher level, an art-form as entertaining as his best comic prose. He, therefore, transformed Rosalynde into a heroine who not only makes speeches but excels in quick-fire repartee (as apparently Shakespeare himself did) and in every kind of verbal wriggle and wiggle. 'Do you not know I am a woman? When I think, I must speak. Sweet, say on' (III. 2. 234). If we compare her wit with Beatrice's, the wonderful thing about Rosalind's is that it very rarely seeks to hurt, it remains (like *As You Like It* itself) sweet-tempered and delightful.

On the other hand, if we compare Rosalind's prattle with Celia's, it may strike us as curious that Shakespeare seems to make little effort to distinguish them. Their moods, rather than the brilliance of their wit, make Rosalind the more interesting, for Rosalind's wit coexists with her melancholy and then (from I. 2. 135) with her love-longing. Sometimes Celia dazzles us even more than her cousin.

> *Rosalind.* Never talk to me; I will weep.
> *Celia.* Do, prithee; but yet have the grace to consider that tears do not become a man.
> *Rosalind.* But have I not cause to weep?
> *Celia.* As good cause as one would desire; therefore weep.
> *Rosalind.* His very hair is of the dissembling colour.
> *Celia.* Something browner than Judas's. Marry, his kisses are Judas's own children.
> *Rosalind.* I'faith, his hair is of a good colour ... And his kissing is as full of sanctity as the touch of holy bread.
> *Celia.* He hath bought a pair of cast lips of Diana. (III. 4. 1ff.)

This exchange and many others in the play might be classified as a 'wit-combat', in the manner of John Lyly's comedies, except that the combat element almost disappears, and neither speaker seeks to triumph over the other. (Celia here seems to get the better of it, though only because Rosalind is out of spirits.) At its purest, as in the lines just quoted, I prefer to think of such a sequence as a duet, with both speakers emotionally in harmony. Elsewhere, as in the dialogues of Rosalind and Touchstone, Orlando and Jaques (II. 7. 88ff.), Corin and Touchstone, the duet becomes a little more like a duel, yet always good-tempered, really a mock-duel, with both participants dancing the same dance.

> *Jaques.* God buy you; let's meet as little as we can.
> *Orlando.* I do desire we may be better strangers.
>
> *Jaques.* I'll tarry no longer with you; farewell, good Signior Love.
> *Orlando.* I am glad of your departure; adieu, good Monsieur Melancholy. (III. 2. 240ff.)

Rosalind and Celia's prattle, therefore, is supported by not very different sequences in which we are gripped by the verbal inventiveness of the dramatist, rather than any pretence of moving forward the story, and this helps to make

As You Like It a very special play. Shakespeare stakes a claim for his own kind of wit, which can carry a whole comedy with only the minimum of story. Here let us remember that the cult of wit had dominated the literary scene for some twenty years, from the time of Lyly's *Euphues, or the anatomy of wit* (1578), and that it had spread into adjacent fields (witness Ling's *Politeuphuia, or wit's commonwealth*, 1597, or Allott's *Wit's Theatre of the little world*, 1599), then along comes Ben Jonson with his 'Humour' plays and the wit of their neo-classical echoes. So what could Shakespeare do, the Shakespeare whose preeminence in drama had suddenly been trumpeted abroad in late 1598?

Shakespeare had already proved himself a master of conversation in *Love's Labour's Lost*, in the Falstaff scenes of *Henry IV* and in *Much Ado*. In these earlier plays, however, the conversation is largely plot-driven, whereas in *As You Like It* it sometimes seems to float free, or very nearly so, and to be an end in itself. This almost aimless dialogue, contrasting as it does with Jonson's chiselled language, combines with the flimsiness and improbability and love-longing and enchanting fancifulness of *As You Like It* to make this play Shakespeare's answer to the question *Quid sit comoedia?*—a put-down for that 'pestilent fellow' Ben Jonson. It was not intended as a straightforward romance, such as Lodge's *Rosalynde*: at one and the same time Shakespeare made *As You Like It* a romance and a burlesque of romance. (Compare *Don Quixote*, a picaresque novel which is also a send-up of the picaresque novel.) In short, Shakespeare's romantic comedy is much more than mere romance: it mingles genres and different kinds of artifice with 'truth' and 'realism' and thus outsoars Jonson's pedestrian and blinkered opposition to clowns and 'cross-wooing'. Or, to vary the metaphor, in the words of a contemporary, Thomas Fuller, who conveys the temperamental antagonism of the two dramatists quite perfectly—

> Many were the wit-combats betwixt him and Ben Jonson, which two I behold like a Spanish great galleon and an English man-of-war; Master Jonson, like the former, was built far higher in learning . . . Shakespeare, with the English man-of-war, lesser in bulk but lighter in sailing, could turn with all tides, tack about and take advantage of all winds, by the quickness of his wit and invention.[10]

* * *

While Jonson evidently despised romantic comedy on account of its remoteness from everyday life and the fatuousness of its story, Shakespeare deliberately chose an improbable story and made something magical out of it. How was it done? Just as music transforms story in an opera, the language of *As You Like It* acts as the music of the play. Not that every dramatist could achieve this result: when Shakespeare undertook a dramatisation of Lodge's *Rosalynde*, however, he must have known roughly how he would go about it.

The sheer exuberance of the language of *As You Like It* dazzles—its unexpected changes of direction, its inexhaustible range of allusion. Rosalind's oaths and adjurations are a good example. 'Speak sad brow and true maid' (III. 2. 200), ''Ods my little life' (III. 5. 43), 'By my troth, and in good earnest, and so God mend me, and by all pretty oaths that are not dangerous . . .' (IV. 1. 168): Shakespeare coins phrases that vividly express Rosalind's personality and excitement at that particular moment. She speaks as a melancholy princess, then as one who forces herself to be merry, then pityingly of the old man and his sons, then smitten by Orlando—and these quicksilver changes of mood and language continue throughout the play. The boy-actor performs a princess who dresses up as a swaggering youth ('A gallant curtle-axe upon my thigh'), re-enters almost in tears (II. 4. 1), speaks 'like a saucy lackey' (III. 2. 278), then in an accent that seems wrong to Orlando (III. 2. 318), then haughtily reprimands Phebe (III. 5. 35), scolds Orlando (IV. 1. 36), adopts a 'more coming-on disposition' (IV. 1. 99), and so on. All these changes of mood are brought about by language that appears to be in character and at the same time mocks itself and the world at large. And yet, despite her disguises and ever-changing moods—or is it because of them?—Shakespeare makes her more life-like and intimately known to us than Portia or Beatrice or Viola. Her prattle is not just babbling 'girl-talk': it veils, and also displays, an incisive intelligence. The romance heroine has her feet firmly on the ground.

> *Rosalind.* Now tell me how long you would have her, after you have possess'd her.
> *Orlando.* For ever and a day.
> *Rosalind.* Say 'a day' without the 'ever'.

She knows, of course, what it means to 'have' and to 'possess' a woman.

Caroline Spurgeon noticed the 'unusual number of what may be called "topical" similes' in the play,

> similes, that is, which refer to things familiar to the Elizabethan audience, but not to us, or indeed in many cases to any but the people of that day. Such are Rosalind's threat that she will weep for nothing 'like Diana in the fountain', by which she may mean the fountain set up in Cheapside in 1596, described by Stowe . . . or Silvius' description of the common executioner asking pardon from his victim before chopping off his head (III. 5. 3); or Orlando's retort to Jaques' taunting query as to whether he has not culled his 'pretty answers' out of the posies on rings, 'Not so; but I answer you right painted cloth, from whence you have studied your questions . . .'[11]

Not only topical similes but the everyday life brought before us by the play's words and phrases contrast with the unreality of romance—creating, almost, a sense of double vision. 'As dry as the remainder biscuit / After a voyage' 'plain as way to parish church', 'dinners, and suppers, and sleeping hours, excepted', 'all like one another as halfpence are', 'without candle may go dark to bed', 'shut that, and 'twill out at the key-hole; stop that, 'twill fly with the smoke out at the chimney': the familiar objects and routines of everyday life distance the play's romance and at the same time authenticate it. A similar effect is achieved by sudden changes of register, as when the language of make-believe is punctured by a simple statement, a genuine emotion. 'I would not be cured, youth' (III. 2. 389); 'Besides, I like you not' (III. 5. 73); 'I would I were at home' (IV. 3. 160).

The play's preoccupation with time and timelessness also contributes to our sense of a 'real' world somehow underpinning an 'unreal' one. I am thinking not only of major speeches such as

> And then he drew a dial from his poke,
> And, looking on it with lack-lustre eye,
> Says very wisely 'It is ten o'clock . . .'

and the Seven Ages of Man and 'Time travels in divers paces with divers persons' but also of allusions to the seasons and days of the week ('Blow, blow, thou winter wind', 'Then love me, Rosalind.—Yes, faith, will I, Fridays and Saturdays, and all', 'men are April when they woo, December when they wed'). The most deliberately jolting jugglery with time comes when Rosalind first meets Orlando in the forest, decides 'I will speak to him' and addresses him.

> Do you hear, forester?
> *Orlando.* Very well; what would you?

Overcome by the momentousness of their encounter, her quick mind seizes up ('I pray you, what—what—what is't o'clock?'), and he has to put her right. 'You should ask me what time o'day; there's no clock in the forest.' Here Shakespeare stages a multiple collision—two kinds of awareness, two emotions, two 'realities'. On another occasion—

> *Orlando.* My fair Rosalind, I come within an hour of my promise.
> *Rosalind.* Break an hour's promise in love! He that will divide a
> minute into a thousand parts, and break but a part of the thousand part
> of a minute in the affairs of love . . .

'real' time, 'psychological' time and 'theatre' time collide, different clocks ticking away at different speeds, and again Shakespeare asks us to observe a clash of conventions—for what is time if not a convention?

Related to the mingle of 'time' and 'timelessness' in *As You Like It* there is also a mix of pace, jumping from dead slow to whirlwind in an instant.

> *Rosalind.* Well, Time is the old justice that examines all such offenders, and let time try. Adieu. [*Exit Orlando.*] . . . O coz, coz, coz, my pretty little coz, that thou didst know how many fathom deep I am in love!

We are meant to be aware, of course, that beneath Rosalind's polite prattle with Orlando there throbs intense emotion, more intense than any attempted by Shakespeare since *Romeo and Juliet*. The comic prose of 1599 can lift us to the same heights as Shakespeare's most admired lyrical masterpiece.

With the help of good acting, a modern audience cannot miss these subsurface complexities. We today, however, may overlook other tonal innovations in *As You Like It*, for example, its mingle of romance and sexual explicitness. Shakespeare had permitted this in earlier comedies, yet Rosalind's unsqueamish imagination changes the rules, venturing a little beyond maiden modesty in her first scene with Orlando ('Sir, you have wrestled well, and overthrown / More than your enemies'), and later informing him that Oliver and Celia have 'made a pair of stairs to marriage, which they will climb incontinent, or else be incontinent before marriage.' How many other heroines of romance are told 'So you may put a man in your belly' (III. 2. 190)? without, it seems, noticing? Rosalind's quick mind has darted on, she has no time to say 'Come, come, you talk greasily; your lips grow foul' (*Love's Labour's Lost* IV. 2.130). So, too, at IV. 1. 179, though here the editors' quick minds have darted on as well.

> You have simply misus'd our sex in your love-prate. We must have your doublet and hose pluck'd over your head, and show the world what the bird hath done to her own nest.

A woman's nest could be pubic hair.[12] She means 'show the world that you are female, i.e. you have fouled (= slandered) your own nest (= the female sex)'. The interesting thing, again, is that Rosalind does not object to Celia's immodest jesting, perhaps even laughs at it—she takes sex for granted. Others in the play speak of sex matter-of-factly ('man hath his desires . . . wedlock would be nibbling') because Shakespeare has extended the boundaries of romance, partly by endowing Rosalind (like Hamlet) with his own capaciousness of mind.

Audiences enjoy the innocence and simplicity of *As You Like It*, and they are right to do so. We all like to revert to childhood attitudes. Nevertheless we must not allow ourselves to be misled by the apparent thinness of the play. Shakespeare has 'thickened' Lodge's romance by threading through it mockery of romance conventions, satire, sudden spurts of genuine emotion, 'modern' words and allusions, a scale of self-awareness that descends from Rosalind and Touchstone at one extreme (and how different they are) to Audrey and William at the other. Above all, by his verbal and dramaturgic inventiveness, a licence granted by the very thinness of the plot. Despite appearances, therefore, *As You Like It* is a highly sophisticated romance, even more so than Sidney's *Arcadia*. If it combines primary and secondary pastoral, as I have suggested, it also combines primary and secondary romance. It mingles time and timelessness, the classical and 'modern' world, England and France, physical and emotional wrestling, and in every possible way creates an alternative world where 'truth to life' is simply irrelevant. In this world we see the story with a child's eyes *and* with an adult's: we enjoy a teasing sense of double vision (cf. p. 228), a mingle of ingredients utterly different from any found in the other romantic comedies.

NOTES

1. Boy actors had much shorter careers in leading parts than adults: I believe that Rosalind and Viola were, therefore, played by different boys (see my edition of *Othello*, the Arden Shakespeare, 1997, pp. 347-9).

2. See my edition of *Twelfth Night*, the Macmillan Shakespeare (1971), pp. 10–13.

3. I quote Lodge's *Rosalynde* from Bullough's *Narrative and Dramatic Sources*, vol. 2 (1958). In *Rosalynde* Orlando and Celia are called Rosader and Alinda (Aliena in the Forest of Arden); when I refer to 'Celia' (in inverted commas) I mean Celia in Lodge's romance, that is Alinda.

4. For Shakespeare's tendency to 'mingle' compare 'Shakespeare's Mingled Yarn and *Measure for Measure*' in *Proceedings of the British Academy*, vol. 67 (1982), reprinted in *British Academy Shakespeare Lectures 1980–89*, ed. Honigmann (Oxford, 1993).

5. See *Ben Jonson*, ed. C.H. Herford, Percy and Evelyn Simpson (Oxford, 11 vols, 1925–52, I, 20.

6. See *Ben Jonson*, I, 151.

7. *Ben Jonson*, III, 515.

8. *Ben Jonson*, I, 134, 141.

9. Bullough, II, 181. Shakespeare liked this passage: cf. *As You Like It* III. 2. 380, 'boys and women are for the most part *cattle of this colour*'.

10. See Chambers, *William Shakespeare*, II, 245.

11. Spurgeon, *Shakespeare's Imagery*, p. 277.

12. Cf. *Romeo and Juliet* II. 5. 74; *Richard III* IV. 4. 424; *Much Ado* II. 1. 199.

BIBLIOGRAPHY

Bamber, Linda. *Comic Women, Tragic Men: A Study of Gender and Genre in Shakespeare* (Stanford: Stanford University Press, 1982).

Barnaby, Andrew. "The Political Conscious of Shakespeare's *As You Like It*," from *SEL: Studies in English Literature, 1500-1900* 36, no. 2 (spring 1996), pp. 373–395.

Beckman, Margaret Boemer. "The Figure of Rosalind in *As You Like It*," from *Shakespeare Quarterly* 29 (1978), pp. 44–51.

Bergeron, David Moore. *Shakespeare's Romances and the Royal Family* (Lawrence, Kan.: University Press of Kansas, 1985).

Berry, Edward I. *Shakespeare's Comic Rites* (Cambridge: Cambridge University Press, 1984).

Bloom, Harold, ed. *Rosalind* (New York: Chelsea House, 1991).

———. *William Shakespeare. Comedies and Romances.* (New York: Chelsea House, 1986).

Brown, John Russell, ed. *Shakespeare:* Much Ado About Nothing *and* As You Like It. *A Casebook* (Basingstoke: Macmillan Press, 1979).

Calvo, Clara. "In Defence of Celia: Discourse Analysis and Women's Discourse in *As You Like It*," from *Essays and Studies* 47 (1994), pp. 91-115.

Carroll, William C. *The Metamorphoses of Shakespearean Comedy* (Princeton: Princeton University Press, 1985).

Collins, Michael J., ed. *Shakespeare's Sweet Thunder: Essays on the Early Comedies* (Newark: University of Delaware Press; London; Cranbury, N.J.: Associated University Presses, 1997).

Daley, A. Stuart. "The Dispraise of the Country in *As You Like It*," from *Shakespeare Quarterly* 36 (1985), pp. 300–314.

———. "The Idea of Hunting in *As You Like It*," from *Shakespeare Studies* 21 (1993), pp. 72–95.

———. "Where Are the Woods in *As You Like It*," from *Shakespeare Quarterly* 34 (1983), pp. 172–180.

Draper, R.P. *Shakespeare; The Comedies* (New York: St. Martin's Press, 2000).

Dusinberre, Juliet. "As Who Liked It?" from *Shakespeare Survey: An Annual Survey of Shakespeare Studies and Production* 46 (1993), pp. 9–21.

———. "Touchstone and Kemp in *As You Like It*," from *Shakespeare Newsletter* 52, no. 4 (winter 2002–2003), pp. 93–94, 106, 110, 126.

Fendt, Gene. "Resolution, Catharsis, Culture: *As You Like It*," from *Philosophy and Literature* 19, no. 2 (October 1995), pp. 248–260.

Frye, Northrop. *A Natural Perspective; The Development of Shakespearean Comedy and Romance* (New York: Columbia University Press, 1965).

Gardner, Helen. "*As You Like It*," from *More Talking of Shakespeare*, edited by John W.P. Garret (London: Ayer, 1959), pp. 17–32.

Goldsmith, Robert Hillis. *Wise Fools in Shakespeare* (East Lansing: Michigan State University Press, 1955).

Halio, Jay L. *Twentieth Century Interpretations of* As You Like It (Englewood Cliffs, N.J.: Prentice Hall, 1968).

Halio, Jay L. and Barbara Millard. As You Like It: *An Annotated Bibliography, 1940–1980* (New York: Garland, 1985).

Hassel, R. Chris. *Faith and Folly in Shakespeare's Romantic Comedies* (Athens: University of Georgia Press, 1980).

Haylres, Nancy K. "Sexual Disguise in *As You Like It* and *Twelfth Night*," from *Shakespeare Survey* 32 (1979), pp. 63–72.

Hopkins, Lisa. "Orlando and the Golden World: The Old World and the New in *As You Like It*," from *Early Modern Literary Studies: A Journal of Sixteenth- and Seventeenth-Century English Literature* 8, no. 2 (September 2002), p. 21.

Hyland, Peter. "Shakespeare's Heroines; Disguise in the Romantic Comedies," from *Ariel* 9 (April 1978), pp. 23–39.

Kelly, Thomas. "Shakespeare's Romantic Heroes: Orlando Reconsidered," from *Shakespeare Quarterly* 24 (winter 1973), pp. 22–32.

Kott, Jan. "The Gender of Rosalind," from *New Theatre Quarterly* 7, no. 26 (May 1991), pp. 113–125.

Leach, Robert. "*As You Like It*—A 'Robin Hood' Play," from *English Studies: A Journal of English Language and Literature* 82, no. 5 (October 2001), pp. 393–400.

Leggatt, Alexander, ed. *The Cambridge Companion to Shakespearean Comedy* (Cambridge, U.K.; New York: Cambridge University Press, 2002).

———. *Shakespeare's Comedy of Love* (London: Methuen, 1980).

Levin, Richard A. *Love and Society in Shakespearean Comedy: A Study of Dramatic Form and Content* (Newark: University of Delaware Press; London: Associated University Presses, 1985).

Lewis, Cynthia. "Horns, the Dream-Work, and Female Potency in *As You Like It*," from *South Atlantic Review* 66, no. 4 (fall 2001), pp. 45–69.

Lynch, Stephen J. As You Like It: *A Guide to the Play* (Westport, Conn.; London: Greenwood Press, 2003).

Marshall, Cynthia. "The Doubled Jaques and Constructions of Negation in *As You Like It*," from *Shakespeare Quarterly* 49, no. 4 (winter 1998), pp. 375–392.

Martin, Louis. "As She Liked It: Rosalind as Subject," from *Pennsylvania English* 22, nos. 1–2 (fall–spring 2000), pp. 91–96.

Mills, Perry. *As You Like It.* Cambridge Student Guide (Cambridge: Cambridge University Press, 2002).

Milward, Peter. "Religion in Arden," from *Shakespeare Survey: An Annual Survey of Shakespeare Studies and Production* 54 (2001), pp. 115–21.

Newman, Karen. *Shakespeare's Rhetoric of Comic Character: Dramatic Convention in Classical and Renaissance Comedy* (New York: Methuen, 1985).

Novy, Marianne. *Love's Argument: Gender Relations in Shakespeare* (Chapel Hill: University of North Carolina Press, 1984).

Ornstein, Robert. *Shakespeare's Comedies: From Roman Farce to Romantic Mystery* (Newark, Del.: University of Delaware Press; London; Cranbury, N.J.: Associated University Presses, 1986).

Reynolds, Peter. *Shakespeare;* As You Like It (Harmondsworth: Penguin, 1988).

Ronk, Martha. "Locating the Visual in *As You Like It*," from *Shakespeare Quarterly* 52, no. 2 (summer 2001), pp. 255–276.

Salinger, L.G. *Shakespeare and the Traditions of Comedy* (Cambridge: Cambridge University Press, 1974).

Soule, Lesley Wade. "Actor as Anti-Character: Dionysus, the Devil, and the Boy Rosalind," from *Contributions in Drama and Theatre Studies* 93 (Westport, Conn.: Greenwood, 2000).

Tomarken, Edward, ed. As You Like It *from 1600 to the Present: Critical Essays* (New York: Garland, 1997).

Van Laan, Thomas F. *Role-playing in Shakespeare* (Toronto; Buffalo: University of Toronto Press, 1978).

Ward, John Powell. *As You Like It.* Twayne's New Critical Introductions to Shakespeare (New York: Twayne Publishers, 1992).

Watson, Robert N. "As You Liken It: Simile in the Wilderness," from *Shakespeare Survey: An Annual Survey of Shakespeare Studies and Production* 56 (2003), pp. 79–92.

Williamson, Marilyn L. and Nochimson, Richard L. As You Like It, Much Ado About Nothing, *and* Twelfth Night, or What You Will: *An Annotated Bibliography of Shakespeare Studies, 1673–2001* (Fairview, N.C.: Pegasus, 2003).

Wilson, Richard. "'Like the Old Robin Hood': *As You Like It* and the Enclosure Riots," from *Shakespeare Quarterly* 43, no. 1 (spring 1992), pp. 1–19.

ACKNOWLEDGMENTS

❧

Twentieth Century

G.K. Chesterton, "The Repetition of Rosalind" (1932), from *Chesterton on Shakespeare*, edited by Dorothy Collins (Henley-on-Thames: Darwen Finlayson, 1971), pp. 100–101.

W.H. Auden, *"As You Like It,"* from *Lectures on Shakespeare*, reconstructed and edited by Arthur Kirsch (Princeton: Princeton University Press, 2000), pp. 138–151. © 2000 by The Estate of W.H. Auden; lectures given from 1946 to 1947.

Harold C. Goddard, *"As You Like It."* In *The Meaning of Shakespeare*, pp. 281–293. Chicago: University of Chicago Press, 1951. © 1951 by the University of Chicago.

Harold Jenkins, *"As You Like It,"* from *Shakespeare Survey* 8, ed. by Allardyce Nicoll. Cambridge: Cambridge University Press, 1955. © 1955 by Cambridge University Press. Reprinted with the permission of Cambridge University Press.

Barber, Cesar Lombardi. "The Alliance of Seriousness and Levity in *As You Like It*," from *Shakespeare's Festive Comedy*. © 1959 by Princeton University Press, 1987 renewed PUP. Reprinted by permission of Princeton University Press.

Thomas McFarland, "For Other Than for Dancing Measures: The Complications of *As You Like It*," from *Shakespeare's Pastoral Comedy* (Chapel Hill: University of North Carolina Press, 1972), pp. 98–121. © 1972 by the University of North Carolina Press. Used by permission of the publisher, www.uncpress.unc.edu.

Louis Adrian Montrose, "'The Place of a Brother' in 'As You Like It': Social Process and Comic Form," from *Shakespeare Quarterly* 32, no. 1 (spring 1981): pp. 28–54. © 1981 Louis Montrose.

Harold Bloom, "Introduction," from *As You Like It* (New York: Chelsea House, 1988), pp. 1-4.

Twenty-first Century

E.A.J. Honigmann, "The Charm of *As You Like It*," from *Shakespeare: Seven Tragedies Revisited: The Dramatist's Manipulation of Response* (Hampshire: Palgrave, 2002), pp. 211–230. © 1976, 2002 by E.A.J. Honigmann. Reproduced by permission of Palgrave Macmillan.

Index

❧